THE CAMBRIDGE COMPANION TO
THE GRAPHIC NOVEL

Since the graphic novel rose to prominence half a century ago, it has become one of the fastest growing literary/artistic genres, generating interest from readers globally. The *Cambridge Companion to the Graphic Novel* examines the evolution of comic books into graphic novels and the distinct development of this art form both in America and around the world. This *Companion* also explores the diverse subgenres often associated with it, such as journalism, fiction, historical fiction, autobiography, biography, science fiction, and fantasy. Leading scholars offer insights into graphic novel adaptations of prose works and the adaptation of graphic novels to films; analyses of outstanding graphic novels, like *Maus* and *The Walking Man*; an overview which distinguishes the international graphic novel from its American counterpart; and analyses of how the form works and what it teaches, making this book a key resource for scholars, graduate students, and undergraduate students alike.

STEPHEN E. TABACHNICK is Professor of English Literature at the University of Memphis. He has edited or written eleven books, including three on the graphic novel, and has been teaching university courses on the graphic novel for over twenty years. In 2015, he guest-edited a special issue of the journal *Studies in the Novel* on the graphic novel. He recently won the University of Memphis' award for distinguished research in the Humanities. His original field of specialization is Lawrence of Arabia as a writer, and Tabachnick has written or edited four books on Lawrence, including *Images of Lawrence*, the 1988 centenary volume published by Lawrence's own publisher, Jonathan Cape, in London.

A complete list of books in the series is at the back of this book.

THE CAMBRIDGE
COMPANION TO
THE GRAPHIC NOVEL

EDITED BY
STEPHEN E. TABACHNICK
University of Memphis

CAMBRIDGE
UNIVERSITY PRESS

CAMBRIDGE
UNIVERSITY PRESS

University Printing House, Cambridge CB2 8BS, United Kingdom

One Liberty Plaza, 20th Floor, New York, NY 10006, USA

477 Williamstown Road, Port Melbourne, VIC 3207, Australia

4843/24, 2nd Floor, Ansari Road, Daryaganj, Delhi - 110002, India

79 Anson Road, #06-04/06, Singapore 079906

Cambridge University Press is part of the University of Cambridge.

It furthers the University's mission by disseminating knowledge in the pursuit of education, learning and research at the highest international levels of excellence.

www.cambridge.org
Information on this title: www.cambridge.org/9781107108790
DOI: 10.1017/9781316258316

© Cambridge University Press 2017

First published 2017

Printed in the United States of America by Sheridan Books, Inc.

A catalogue record for this publication is available from the British Library

ISBN 978-1-107-10879-0 Hardback
ISBN 978-1-107-51971-8 Paperback

CONTENTS

FIGURES

CONTRIBUTORS

JAN BAETENS, University of Leuven

BART BEATY, University of Calgary

M. KEITH BOOKER, University of Arkansas

JAMES BUCKY CARTER, Independent Researcher and Educator

ALEXANDER DANNER, Emerson College

RANDY DUNCAN, Henderson State University

HUGO FREY, University of Chichester

DARREN HARRIS-FAIN, Auburn University at Montgomery

MARTHA KUHLMAN, Bryant University

DANIEL MAZUR, Art Institute of Boston; Brookline Arts Center

ESTHER BENDIT SALTZMAN, University of Memphis

MATTHEW J. SMITH, Radford University

STEPHEN E. TABACHNICK, University of Memphis

STEPHEN WEINER, Maynard Public Library

CHRONOLOGY

1697–1764	William Hogarth, painter, printmaker, cartoonist (*A Harlot's Progress*, *A Rake's Progress*)
1756–1815	James Gillray, caricaturist, printmaker (*John Bull's Progress*)
1756–1827	Thomas Rowlandson, artist, caricaturist (*Dr. Syntax*)
1757–1827	William Blake, poet, painter, engraver (*Songs of Innocence and Experience*, *The Marriage of Heaven and Hell*)
1799–1846	Rodolphe Töppfer, author, painter, cartoonist, caricaturist (*Histoire de Monsieur Jabot*)
1800–1862	Charles Philipon, caricaturist, editor of *Le Charivari*
1812–1887	Henry Mayhew, journalist, playwright, editor of *Punch*
1832–1908	Wilhelm Busch (*Max und Moritz*)
1863–1928	Richard Felton Outcault (*The Yellow Kid*, *Buster Brown*)
1871–1956	Lyonel Feininger (*Wee Willie Winkie's World*)
1871–1934	Winsor McCay (*Little Nemo in Slumberland*)
1880–1944	George Herriman (*Krazy Kat*)
1888–1955	Otto Nückel (*Schicksal: Eine Geschichte in Bildern/Destiny: A Novel in Pictures*)
1889–1972	Frans Masereel (*Mon Livre d'Heures/Passionate Journey*)
1891–1976	Max Ernst (*Une Semaine de Bonté/A Week of Kindness*)
1894–1947	Max Gaines (Maxwell Ginsburg) (*Famous Funnies*)
1895–1953	Milt Gross (*He Done Her Wrong*)

1905–1985 Lynd Ward (*Six Novels in Woodcuts*)

1907–1983 Hergé (Georges Prosper Remi) (*Tintin*)

1914–1992 Joe Shuster (*Superman*)

1914–1996 Jerry Siegel (*Superman*)

1917–1943 Charlotte Salomon (*Leben? oder Theater?/Life? or Theatre?*)

1917–1994 Jack Kirby (Jacob Kurtzberg) (*Young Love, X-Men*)

1917–2005 Will Eisner (*The Spirit, A Contract with God and Other Tenement Stories, Comics and Sequential Art*)

1922–1992 William Gaines (*Tales from the Crypt*)

1922– Stan Lee (*The Amazing Spider-Man, X-Men*)

1924–1993 Harvey Kurtzman (*Mad*)

1927–1995 Hugo Pratt (*Corto Maltese*)

1928–1989 Osamu Tezuka (*MW, Astro Boy/Mighty Atom, Buddha*)

1937– Tom Phillips (*A Humument*)

1938– Trina Robbins (*Wimmen's Comix*)

1939–2010 Harvey Pekar (*American Splendor*)

1941– Hiyao Miyazaki (*Nausicaä of the Valley of the Wind*)

1943– R. Crumb (*Fritz the Cat, Mr. Natural, The Book of Genesis Illustrated*)

1940– Gilbert Shelton (*The Fabulous Furry Freak Brothers*)

1946– Jacques Tardi (*C'était la Guerre des Tranchées/It Was the War of the Trenches*)

1947–2017 Jiro Taniguchi (*The Walking Man/Aruko Hito*)

1948– Aline Kominsky-Crumb (*Need More Love*)

1948– Art Spiegelman (*Maus*)

1952– Bryan Talbot (*The Adventures of Luther Arkwright*)

1953– Alan Moore (*Watchmen, V for Vendetta*)

1957–2007 Didier Lefèvre, photographer, journalist (*The Photographer/Le Photographe*)

1957–   Gilbert Hernandez (*Love and Rockets*)

1957–   Frank Miller (*Batman: The Dark Knight Returns, Sin City*)

1958–   Thierry Groensteen, theoretician (*Système de la Bande Dessinée/The System of Comics*)

1959–   David Beauchard (*L'Ascension du Haut Mal/Epileptic*)

1959–   Jaime Hernandez (*Love and Rockets*)

1960–   Neil Gaiman (*The Sandman*)

1960–   Scott McCloud, graphic novelist, theoretican (*Understanding Comics*)

1960–   Joe Sacco (*Safe Area Goražde*)

1962–   Frederic Lemercier (*Le Photographe/The Photographer*)

1962–   Étienne Robial, designer of the *Métal Hurlant* logo

1964–   Emmanuel Guibert (*The Photographer/Le Photographe*)

1966–   Guy Delisle (*Pyongyang, Shenzhen*)

1966–   Dylan Horrocks (*Hicksville*)

1967–   Chris Ware (*Jimmy Corrigan, Building Stories*)

1969–   Marjane Satrapi (*Persepolis*)

Introduction

The graphic novel – an extended comic book freed of commercial constrictions, written by adults for adults, and able to tackle complex and sophisticated issues using all of the tools available to the best artists and writers – is the newest literary/artistic genre and one of the most exciting areas of humanistic study today. Any teacher who has taught the graphic novel at the high school, undergraduate, or graduate levels, knows that students show enormous enthusiasm for this subject. Teachers no less than their students are excited because the graphic novel has attracted extremely talented writers and artists, and they have rendered powerful narratives, going far beyond the previous newspaper comics' light entertainment, superhero adventures, and children's stories. While they employ the same techniques as traditional comics, graphic novels' production values are much better, their content is much more complex and sophisticated, and (despite the obvious meaning of graphic "novel") they include non-fiction as well as fiction. It is now clear that there is no subject too profound or complex for the graphic novel to treat, as we see in Alan Moore's science fiction masterpiece *Watchmen*, which asks the question of whether or not it is possible to end war, and his *V for Vendetta*, a *1984* of the graphic novel; in the brilliant autobiography/biography *Maus* by Art Spiegelman, which deals with the travails of his parents during the Holocaust, and his psychological struggle as their son; in the disquieting *Persepolis* by the French-Iranian Marjane Satrapi, in which she reveals the difficulty of living under the Shah of Iran and then the Khomeini regime; in Doxiadis and Papadimitriou's *Logicomix*, a semi-fictional biography of Bertrand Russell which makes not only his life but his philosophical and even some of his mathematical achievements accessible; in David Beauchard's intense *Epileptic*, which explores the difficulty of dealing with his brother's chronic illness; and in Jiro Taniguchi's Zen-inspired *The Walking Man*, to name just a few of the outstanding works that are discussed in this volume.

Graphic novel adaptation of literary texts, including classic texts, is another area in which the new form has proven itself. There are superb adaptations of Homer, *Beowulf*, Shakespeare, Poe, *Moby Dick*, *The Picture of Dorian Gray*, Conrad, Proust, and Kafka, among many, many others. The use of such adaptations in the classroom along with the originals, prompts enthusiastic discussion of what, if anything, has been changed or not changed in the adaptation, and what such adaptation can bring to the interpretation of the original texts. While there are also film adaptations of many prose texts, the graphic novel remains a reading experience and is thus closer than a film to the original in its effect on the reader. But there are also excellent adaptations of graphic novels to film, such as that of Frank Miller's *Sin City*. Just as the graphic novel is close to prose texts because it too is a reading experience, it is also closer to film than literary texts are, because of the visual element in both media. So the graphic novel is truly a form for all seasons.

It is not by happenstance that the graphic novel, using words and pictures as opposed to earlier wordless woodcut novels by Frans Masereel, Otto Nückel, Lynd Ward, and others, has emerged during the past thirty-five years rather than earlier on. We can discern at least three main reasons for the rise of the graphic novel in our time.

First, there is the changing nature of reading itself. The graphic novel demands a hybrid kind of reading which involves viewing as well as reading per se. The internet, PowerPoint, film, HDTV, the presence of pictures everywhere in newspapers and magazines, texting, and email, have profoundly altered reading patterns. Indeed, it seems that we are in the middle of a permanent change in the nature of reading itself, which can be noticed among college students, who have much less patience for reading a prose novel of even reasonable length than an earlier generation had. With a graphic novel, there is no need for lengthy descriptions of settings and characters' physical features and gestures, and therefore the reading experience is much shorter than that needed for a prose work, even though the content is comparably sophisticated. Indeed, part of the intensity and appeal of reading a graphic novel arises from the fact that it can be done in a concentrated manner, in one sitting if need be.

The second reason arises from the unique combination of words and visual images in graphic novels as opposed to other visual media. Words can do things that visual images cannot – for instance, portray complex inner mental states or complex philosophical meditations – and visual images can do things that words cannot, such as capture subtle facial expressions. An excellent graphic novel combines the best of both the verbal and the visual worlds. But unlike the situation in a drama or film or a television show, which employ spoken words and ever-changing visual scenes and movements, in a graphic novel we have written words and drawn images presented on a page. When powerful written words are combined with powerful drawn images, and the reader can stay focused on any page or panel that he or she chooses for any amount of time, the result is a unique, hypnotic form of poetry available only in the graphic novel. Add to this the fact that the reader can turn backward or forward in the work at will and quickly look at the past or future of the story, and the advantage of a graphic novel over a film or drama becomes clear, at least in that respect. That is one reason that we have some films, such as Ari Folman's excellent *Waltz with Bashir*, about the first Israel–Lebanon war, that have been made into graphic novels.

But perhaps the best reason for the ever-growing popularity of the graphic novel is simply this: the graphic novel now offers many unique, outstanding international fictional and non-fictional works, and most of them are available in no other medium, despite cinematic adaptations of some of them. In short, anyone interested in important contemporary reading material simply cannot ignore the graphic novel. And scholars looking for new material to write about are excited to have an open, relatively unexplored field, while teachers now have the possibility of offering courses devoted exclusively to the graphic novel, or of including graphic novels in courses on contemporary prose literature.

The reader will find discussion of all of these aspects of the international graphic novel and more in this volume, which offers concise, expert analyses of the most important areas in this burgeoning field, including its techniques, the history of its development and acceptance, and the influence of important international cultural traditions, as well as subgenres, adaptations, and related pedagogy. The reader will find both surveys of important developments, and in-depth analyses of outstanding works.

The volume begins with a chapter on how the graphic novel works, in which Randy Duncan and Matthew Smith show how this old-new literary and artistic form is based on techniques developed in the popular comics, and they sometimes employ concepts from the new field of comics theory to make their case. In particular, they explore four technical elements, the panel, the sequence, the page, and the narrative, showing how each one contributes to the overall effect, sometimes unconscious, on the reader of a given graphic novel. Their insights provide a basis for an understanding of why the graphic novel has become a powerful literary and artistic form, and help illuminate the subsequent discussions of individual works.

In the second chapter about the development of the comics from William Hogarth to Will Eisner, Stephen E. Tabachnick gives the reader a concise survey ranging from the origin of comics in eighteenth-century England and Switzerland through the mid-twentieth century, including the wordless graphic novel form begun by the Belgian Frans Masereel and continued by Lynd Ward, Milt Gross, Otto Nückel, and Max Ernst, among others, to the pioneering work of Will Eisner, who stated as early as the 1940s that comics could become a serious literary and artistic genre rather than simply a venue for superheroes and children's stories. In his semi-autobiographical *Contract with God Trilogy* and *To the Heart of Storm* as well as *The Plot*, about the anti-Semitic forgery *The Protocols of the Learned Elders of Zion*, Eisner proved his earlier claim that the graphic novel could become what it is today – a respected literary and artistic form capable of tackling any subject, no matter how serious or complex – and in doing so provided a model for future graphic novelists.

In the third chapter, Stephen Weiner presents a chronologically based survey of the development and acceptance of the graphic novel from Eisner's work up to the present moment. He reveals the struggle the new form faced for acceptance by publishers, libraries, and the public at large, as well as its final arrival as a part of the cultural scene. He discusses many of the subgenres of the graphic novel ranging from the re-envisioned, more neurotic superhero and other forms of fiction to the autobiography, including Satrapi's *Persepolis*, among others. The reader gains an overview of the work of many very talented creators and their exciting contributions as well as their sometimes difficult paths to permanent acceptance by important social institutions.

The international graphic novel forms the subject of the fourth chapter, by Dan Mazur and Alexander Danner, in which they offer a survey of important examples from the major non-American graphic novel-producing cultures including especially, but not only, France and Japan. They discuss Jacques Tardi, Marguerite Abouet, and Clément Oubrerie from France, Hugo Pratt from Italy, Osamu Tezuka and Jiro Taniguchi from Japan, as well as Dylan Horrocks from New Zealand and Rutu Modan from Israel, among many other important artists and writers from around the world, often revealing the interaction between different national artistic traditions and individual artists from different countries, particularly in view of the fact that the graphic novel has become a global phenomenon.

In the fifth chapter, Hugo Frey analyzes the ways in which graphic novelists have made use of history to write fiction. Frey discusses the types of and trends in historical fiction, including the semi-biographical accounts in Chester Brown's *Louis Riel* and Kyle Baker's *Nat Turner*, as well as superhero comics fiction making use of genuine historical events, such as *Magneto Testament* about the character Magneto's travails during his time in a Nazi concentration camp, and Will Eisner's fictional *A Contract with God*, which reveals some of the problems faced by immigrants in New York City in the 1930s. He concludes that historical fiction has become a very important sub-genre of the graphic novel, even displacing autobiography and reportage to some extent.

In the sixth chapter, Darren Harris-Fain takes up the topic of revisionist superheroes. After a discussion of the several types and aspects of revisionism in literary texts, he looks at the ways in which some traditional comic book characters, for instance Batman, have been made more complex, subtle, and realistic by recent graphic novelists, especially Frank Miller, and how familiar Marvel heroes have even been relocated to the early seventeenth century by Neil Gaiman. He discusses the revision not only of individual characters but of the genre conventions that previously framed them, and concludes that the results of such re-envisionings "are often among the most original of graphic novels, and the graphic novel canon would be diminished without their presence."

Martha Kuhlman's seventh chapter covers two of the most important sub-genres of the graphic novel, autobiography and biography. She finds that the reason for our fascination "with autobiographical comics lies in the unique intersection between autobiographical narrative and the particularities of the text/image combination in comics, raising intriguing questions about authorship, authenticity, and the representation of trauma." Among other autobiographies, she analyzes several works about severe medical conditions, such as Pekar and Brabner's *Our Cancer Year*, Marisa Marchetto's *Cancer Vixen*, and David Beauchard's *Epileptic*, and demonstrates the value of the graphic novel perhaps more than any other genre of literature or art to portray health issues. She also discusses semi-fictional biographies by Chester Brown, Jacques Tardi, and Doxiadis and Papadimitriou, as well as works that combine autobiography and biography, such as Spiegelman's *Maus*, to determine the qualities that underlie their success.

In the eighth chapter, Jan Baetens discusses other important forms of non-fiction graphic narrative, including works of reportage such as Joe Sacco's *Safe Area Goražde* about a Muslim enclave surrounded by Serbs during the Bosnian conflict, and his *Palestine* about the Arab-Israeli struggle; and Emmanuel Guibert, Didier Lefèvre, and Frederic Lemercier's *The Photographer*, which tells the story of the work of Doctors Without Borders in war-torn Afghanistan, and which constantly intersperses photographs and drawn panels. He analyzes these works in depth, revealing their techniques and also explaining why the graphic novel has become a powerful and accepted journalistic form, which can add considerable depth to usual newspaper accounts as well as to television news.

Esther Saltzman, in the ninth chapter, examines graphic novel adaptations of H. G. Wells' *The Invisible Man*, Richard Stark's *Parker: The Hunter*, Robert Louis Stevenson's *The Strange Case of Dr. Jekyll and Mr. Hyde*, and Jonathan Swift's *Gulliver's Travels* in order to show what each contributes to an understanding of the original text. She begins with a discussion of the concept of adaptation, including the idea of fidelity to the original text, and compares the methods that the creators of these graphic novels have used to transform pure prose texts into a visual experience that goes far beyond what usual book illustrations have brought to such texts.

The tenth chapter, by M. Keith Booker, explains what film adaptations of graphic novels in many subgenres have brought to the graphic novels on which they are based, as well as on what the graphic novel brings to film, given the visual bases of both media. He considers a wide variety of film adaptations of graphic novels, including those of Daniel Clowes' *Art School Confidential*, Alan Moore's *V for Vendetta*, Harvey Pekar's *American Splendor*, and Frank Miller's *Sin City*, and concludes that such films "indicate a rich future for graphic novel adaptations to film, though the ultimate impact of such adaptations on the graphic novel form itself remains to be seen."

In the eleventh chapter, Bart Beaty examines the reasons that three outstanding works by Lynda Barry, David Beauchard, and Jiro Taniguchi respectively have been relatively underappreciated and denied the classic status that accrues to other, similarly excellent graphic novels. While his study of these international examples demonstrates just how subtle and profound they are, he also reveals that a tendency to assess the complexity of graphic novels through the narrow lens of academic literature scholarship often causes scholarly underestimation of important works, and he offers a caution about what to avoid when assessing the quality of graphic novels in order to arrive at a fair judgment. He also provides a stimulating discussion of the definition of the term "graphic novel" and the weakness of the definition as currently used.

Finally, in the twelfth chapter, James Bucky Carter offers his own methods for teaching the graphic novel in university classrooms. On the basis of his own experience as well as educational theory, he puts forward many excellent techniques for teaching this new form of art and literature to expand students' consciousness of themselves and the world around them. These techniques include having students themselves attempt to draw comics, and teaching them the reading techniques unique to graphic novels.

Hopefully this volume's focus on these important topics will be of use to teachers, students, and general readers who wish to engage with this new and exciting literary/artistic form. Its chapters offer broad and comprehensive as well as in-depth insights into a new area of the humanities which is now impossible to neglect in any informed consideration of the arts.

I

RANDY DUNCAN AND MATTHEW J. SMITH

How the Graphic Novel Works

Graphic novels are the long-form of a mode of communication called comics. Comics appear in single-panel cartoons like those on editorial pages, daily comic strips like Scott Adams' *Dilbert*, webcomics such as those published on Thrillbent.com, periodical comic book magazines like Marvel Comics' *Amazing Spider-Man*, and graphic novels like Marjane Satrapi's memoir, *Persepolis*. Comics are built using combinations of symbols in a medium fixed in time. Typically, these symbols are rendered through hand-drawn artwork, though artists have communicated using photography as well as montages and mash-ups of various images to achieve the same effect. Comics rely on the interaction of symbols to create meaning, possibly by the interaction of different kinds of symbols (say, pictures and words placed together) or by a sequence of images in relationship to one another. Comics are a collaborative medium in which the creator reduces the ideas that the creator wants to communicate into a finite set of symbols and the reader adds in additional information in the process of decoding the presentation. Thus, comics are both reductive and additive, as both the source and the receiver in the exchange contribute to the dynamics of meaning making. This first chapter explains how comics in general – and by extension those in graphic novels – function to facilitate the creation of meaning between creators and readers.

Graphic novels may be created by single storytellers or by a team among which the tasks of producing writing, line artwork, coloring, and so forth are divided among multiple contributors, a bit like an assembly line where workers perform different tasks in order to produce a single product, like a car. Such is the case for the example page used in this chapter to illustrate just a few of the basic principles of comics (fig. 1.1). This simplistic golden age superhero comic book is a far cry from the sophisticated graphic novels of today, but it does provide, on a single page, very clear examples of the basic components of the comics form, from which even the most literary of graphic novels is constructed. Figure 1.1 is a page taken from a fifteen-page

8

Fig. 1.1 Writer Ken Crossen and artist Jerry Robinson created "The Making of the Mightiest Man" in *Atoman* no. 1 (1946). The complete story is in the public domain and may be read at the Digital Comic Museum: http://digitalcomicmuseum.com/.

story in the 1946 premiere issue of *Atoman*, written by Ken Crossen and drawn by Jerry Robinson. Crossen was a science fiction author, noted for creating another more successful superhero, the Green Lama, and Robinson was famously one of Bob Kane's many ghost artists for *Batman*, and he is credited with the creation of the most significant supervillain of all time, the Joker. *Atoman* did not fare as well, and the series lasted only two issues. It came along in the post-war period during which the initial popularity in the superhero genre of comics was declining; however, it was developed at a time when many of the standards of Western comics storytelling were well established, if in some of their simplest forms, and for these reasons serves as a helpful reference.

This essay will discuss four key elements to the functioning of graphic novels: the panel, the sequence, the page, and the narrative, and is thus divided into corresponding sections. (At the initial level of the panel, composition takes into account consideration of a subset of elements that include framing, blocking, acting, and *mise-en-scène*, as will be discussed below.) A word of caution: this partitioning is somewhat arbitrary and concepts discussed under each heading may overlap and support one another in the actual creation of meaning.

The Panel

The fundamental unit of comics is the panel; a panel is defined as an area on the page (or screen, if one were to view webcomics, for instance) that captures a distinct moment or scene. The task of the creator is to determine how to encapsulate, or capture, the key moment(s) or scene into a panel. Comics are not film and typically do not enjoy the relative luxury of devoting storytelling space to capturing every nuance of movement; instead, comics display key movements, evidencing the reductive nature of comics storytelling. Effective storytellers have to be gifted at discerning what to include – and consequently what to leave out – in order to communicate with the audience.

Unlike photography, where the camera lens captures a single moment in time, the comics panel may capture a period of time much longer than the instantaneous wink of a camera's shutter. Thus, two characters might have an entire exchange in back-and-forth dialogue in the same panel that features a single static image. For example, in the fifth panel of the *Atoman* page, the heroic Atoman and his nemesis, Mr. Twist, are engaged in a conversation, but it is unlikely Atoman held his hand in mid-air throughout the length of both of their comments. Rather, Robinson probably selected that moment as the most dramatic pose in the midst of their exchange. It is not at all unusual for a panel to capture the visual information of activities that would take some time to perform in reality, and thusly show both cause and effect in the same panel. The fourth panel in the *Atoman* example illustrates this beautifully: even though Atoman may be moving at superhuman speeds, he still enters the room, strikes one henchman hard enough to knock him off his feet, and races across the room to intercept Mr. Twist's acid bath, all in the space of just one panel.

In assembling a panel, creators have a host of decisions to make. Cartoonists Jessica Abel and Matt Madden identify four compositional issues involved in producing a panel: framing, blocking, acting, and *mise-en-scène*, each of which is examined in turn hereafter.[1]

Framing

Panels are defined by a border called a frame. Most frames are rectangular, as the rectangular forms of the printed page (and computer screens) are easily divided into smaller, similar shapes. The very frame itself can communicate ideas about the conditions of what appears within them. Typically, frames are defined by black lines that surround the image, although variations are possible. Panels outlined in this typical fashion can communicate a common setting and, when in sequence with other panels, the steady progression of the story. A thick or jagged line can connote an unusual setting or, in the context of a story, a decisive moment of action or reaction. A frame composed of a scalloped line might suggest that the contents are part of a memory, and so on.[2] Note that in the *Atoman* page, five of the six panels are framed with typical solid lines, moving the story along, while only the first one is presented without a traditional frame. In this instance, the choice to present a panel without the typical frame helps to communicate the unbounded freedom that comes with Atoman taking flight.

When it comes to frames, size matters. Some panels comprise a mere fraction of the page (or screen) while others lay claim to the entire available space. (Cartoonist Jim Steranko famously once produced a Nick Fury story that contained a four-page panel by continuing the artwork over as many pages, but such practices are unusual.) In fact, one of the crucial differences between the motion picture and comics media is the ability comics has to alter the size of its frame. Filmmakers are constrained to one aspect ratio (the proportion between the height and width of their screens), but comics storytellers have the freedom to alter these from panel to panel. This presents an advantage in design, pacing, and emphasis.[3] Note in the *Atoman* example how radically the size of the frames shifts between the third and fourth panels. The third panel, where Mr. Twist begins to splash acid on Miss James, can be rendered in a smaller panel than the one that precedes it with only Mr. Twist's hand present, because we already know from the previous panel who is holding the acid. Besides, the tight space suggests the close proximity of the threat to Miss James. But in the fourth panel, Atoman's heroic entry, attack, and rescue are aided by the wider space given over to his dynamic actions.

Among the choices that are available to the creator in designing the panel is to determine what distance the objects in the frame will appear to be from the viewer. This is similar to where filmmakers place the camera in order to film a particular shot in movie-making. Some distances place the viewer far away from the activity: such long shots are ideal for defining the setting of a new scene (and, indeed, are also called establishing panels). The first and third panels in our example are long panels; the first shows the hero in flight over a cityscape and the third shows a room's-length of action. In most panels, the viewer is more situated at a middle distance between extremes. Such medium panels usually capture one or two characters from the waist up. In reality it is how we commonly see people in social settings, and thus when used in comics comes to represent most commonplace interactions. Note that the second and fifth panels in our example depict conversations between two characters and are medium views. Creators can also bring the viewer close in to the characters or focus on some object in detail. Such close-up panels help focus the viewer's attention on some emotional response or recognize some clue. In our example, panel three most definitely wants us to focus on the peril of the spilling acid and Miss James' alarmed reaction to it in a classic close-up. Panel six is also a close-up, a choice here used to focus on Atoman as he espouses his individual credo.

Creators can also sway a reader's reactions by manipulating the angles from which the objects in the panel are viewed. A straight-on panel at eye level suggests realism, as that is how most of us see the everyday world.[4] Panels two and four are examples of eye-level panels, even if the actions of the characters in these panels are not entirely realistic. In fact, most of the other panels here adopt more dramatic angles to heighten the drama of the Atoman adventure. In particular, panels one, three, five, and six cast the viewer at a low angle. Low-angle panels can make the objects in view seem more imposing, for awe or fear. Certainly, panels one and six could be attempting to put us in awe of Atoman's superpowers and resolve respectively, while panels three and five attempt to make us fear Mr. Twist's villainy. Although not depicted here, additional angles include high angles, which can suggest an all-knowing, godlike perspective over the objects, and a tilt angle, which can suggest uneasiness about the scene.

Skilled artists can also make the panel visually interesting by being aware of several other elements of effective design. For instance, there is the rule of thirds, which suggests that within any frame, the eye finds it most pleasing when the composition places key elements off-center. Imagine dividing up panel six with three evenly spaced horizontal lines and three evenly spaced vertical lines. The rule of thirds would suggest that the best place to put Atoman's face would be at the intersection of any two of these lines, which Robinson has done, rather than center his face perfectly in the middle of the panel. Another technique for ideal composition is called spotting the blacks, that is, using shadows to direct the reader's attention. Note how in panel five Atoman's figure is outlined by the thick curtains around him, casting a focus on him, say, rather than Mr. Twist's henchman, a relatively unimportant character who almost fades into the curtains himself. With all of these considerations in mind, it should be obvious that each panel is an act of communication unto itself; indeed, "The frame is always an invitation to stop and scrutinize."[5]

Blocking

Creators can also influence meaning depending on where they place characters within the frame. In theater and film such placement is called blocking. Blocking can reveal things about the relationships between objects in the frame.[6] For instance, in panel two, Mr. Twist appears in the foreground and is much larger than Miss James, signifying his power over her in her captive position. In panel four, Mr. Twist's henchman is positioned between the door and Miss James, allowing Atoman to demonstrate his speed and power with two superpowered acts in one panel. Creators are making conscious choices about who to depict within a frame and how to place them therein. They are also determining what (re)actions to have them put on display.

Acting

Characters are not only placed strategically within the panel, but they are also given the opportunity to emote. The great comics innovator, Will Eisner, believed that his craft drew strongly from the tradition of stage acting.[7] Accordingly, he emphasized the importance of the human figure in communicating mood in comics storytelling. Eisner called this emphasis "expressive anatomy," referencing how "body posture and gesture occupy a position of primacy over text."[8] Body posture and gesture are often widely recognized within a given culture, even though the same gestures may mean different things to people from different cultures; however, research into human facial expressions by psychologist Paul Eckman has identified six universal expressions which correspond to distinct human emotions: happiness, surprise, anger, fear, disgust, and sadness. Whether culturally dependent or universal, though, it is clear that creators can convey important information through the way their characters act. Consider Miss James' expression in panel three: even if you did not read Mr. Twist's threat, you can recognize the terror on her face by the positioning of her eyebrows and the shape of her mouth.

Cartoonists who have worked in more abstract styles have developed additional means for revealing the inner states of characters using a set of symbols that cartoonist Mort Walker called emanata.[9] For instance, a floating heart over a character's head might indicate she is in love. Another innovation that cartoonists have developed are the motion lines or "zip-ribbons" used to depict motion. Comics are a static medium and can only infer motion, not depict it like film, television, and video games can. Lines rendered behind a character are meant to communicate momentum. Interestingly, Robinson did not choose to use the technique of motion lines in panel three to show the quick movement of Atoman across the room; instead, he elected a less common technique of rendering several after-images to suggest that the speed with which the character was moving was so fast that the eye would perceive multiple images in that instant. In manga, speed is often depicted in an entirely different technique called subjective motion, where the object in motion is in focus and everything else in the surrounding environment is blurred or streaked. Such conventions allow the character to put forth a performance that further refines the creator's message.

Mise-en-Scène

Within each panel, the creator makes strategic decisions about what elements to present to the reader. In film analysis, such a totality of elements is discussed using the French term *mise-en-scène*, meaning "to put in the scene." *Mise-en-scène* takes into account the characters, backgrounds, dialogue, and sound effects appearing with the frame. Sometimes the *mise-en-scène* can vary from panel to panel, even in the same setting, if altering it helps focus the storytelling. Consider the condition of Mr. Twist's lair. When Atoman enters in panel four, it seems as though he is entering through a typical doorway into a cavernous empty room with no discernable divide between the floor, walls, or ceiling. Yet in panel five, there are clearly defined draperies hung on the walls and an exposed beam on the ceiling that was not visible just one panel earlier. Readers familiar with the conventions of comic book storytelling probably don't pause to wonder why Mr. Twist's décor fades in and out; rather, they can accept that such background detail in panel four would have distracted them from Atoman's dynamic entrance. Blurring the background detail in this panel punctuates the action all the more. When the pace slows down in the next panel to a conversation between the hero and villain, the restored details allow the scene to be more visually interesting even when not much physical activity is taking place.

Arguably, the most essential element to *mise-en-scène* appearing inside the comics panel are words. Experts such as Robert C. Harvey argue that words are central to the definition of comics, but numerous examples of wordless comics abound, from woodcuts by Frans Masereel in the early twentieth century to Andy Runton's silent *Owly* kids' comics today.[10] When words are used, they are used to complement the images, filling in for one another what the other cannot.[11] Words can reduce the polysemy, or multiple meanings possible within images, thereby anchoring them.[12] When words are juxtaposed against images, one begins to manipulate meaning. For instance, Abel and Madden present the example of a picture of an apple.[13] By itself it might symbolize health or the harvest, but label it with some word like "New York" and the meaning is directed in a particular fashion. Label that same picture "temptation" and another set of meanings grounded in biblical connotations for those familiar with them come up.

There are four common ways comics use words: as dialogue, thoughts, sound effects, and captions. Characters' dialogue usually is captured in word balloons that float around them. Eisner suggests that they come from a tradition of one's breath, which you can see as vapor on a cold day.[14] In fact, the Italian word for comics, *fumetti*, is named because of word balloons. The tradition can be traced back to medieval manuscripts, where scrolls, not balloons, trailed from characters' mouths with their words printed upon them. In contemporary practice, the speaker is indicated by a tail leading off of the balloon and pointing toward the speaker. Note in panel six how the tail of the word balloon above Atoman's head points to him; Mr. Twist isn't depicted in that panel, but the direction of the tail of the balloon points back to his position in the previous panel. A jagged shaped balloon could indicate shouting or mechanically reproduced speech such as a voice emanating from a radio or television.

Comics can also make us privy to the inner thoughts of characters through thought balloons. These are usually depicted by scalloped balloons with a trail of cloud-like puffs connecting the speaker to the balloon. Atoman's monologue in panel one could have just as easily been internalized by changing his speech balloon to a thought balloon in that panel, but like so many of us, apparently he just talks to himself out loud.

Sound effects other than human speech also float in the panel, although usually not in balloons. Such sounds are called onomatopoeia. Some sound effects are conventions while others are purely innovations of the creators. Conventionally, a fired gun produces a "BLAM" and the sound of a fist hitting a jaw makes a "POW" on the printed page, but anyone who has ever heard a real gun fire or witnessed a brawl knows these are not necessarily the phonetically accurate sounds of these violent actions, but they try to represent the presence of sound in the environment in an attempt to heighten the realism of the experience. Interestingly, the creators of *Atoman* resisted the temptation to make the pouring acid in panel three "SPLASH" or the sound of Atoman's fist "POW" when he strikes in panel four.

Both dialogue and sound effects take place within the world of the story; they are sounds accessible to the characters (called diegetic sound); however, there are also words sometimes placed in boxes called captions (a type of non-diegetic sound). These are typically the words of a narrator or a character off panel superimposed over the panel for explanation or effect. Panel two in our example has an unseen narrator explain to us the transition from Atoman's location to Mr. Twist's.

Comics theorist Scott McCloud outlined seven relationships between the use of word and image.[15] The most common in contemporary comics story-telling, and perhaps most interesting, is an interdependent relationship where words and images work together to convey information that neither could do alone. Eisner stated a preference for a more picture-specific combination where the image conveyed most of the meaning. In contrast to that style are more word-specific combinations, where the text contains most of the information and the visuals merely illustrate it. Such is the case in panel six, where Atoman's face stands as little more than an illustration to his speech.

Sometimes words and images repeat identical messages in duo-specific combination. This kind of repetition occurs a lot on the example page, including when the narrator explains Atoman's motion in panel four. At other times words and images can be additive in nature, where images help words or words help images. In panel one we already know Atoman is flying, but his words make clear his destination. At still other times words and images might seem to be parallel combinations, as the pictures tell one story and the images develop another. Even montages are possible where the words become part of the images.

Eisner's expressed preference for visuals doing most of the work in communicating through comics is a sentiment echoed by other professionals and summed up in the counsel to would-be cartoonists: show, don't tell.[16] Our

Atoman example comes to us from an era when comics made heavier use of words than contemporary comics storytelling, and should be viewed in historical context rather than as a model of current practice.

One masterful panel in a graphic novel comes from Alison Bechdel's *Fun Home*. On page 17, with shocking juxtaposition of words and imagery, she reveals that her father, Bruce, was a pedophile. The panel appears at the top of a page and contains a wide, eye-level, medium view of the Bechdel family facing forward in the pews of an ornate church with stained-glass windows and hanging chandeliers. Bruce is blocked into the center, as if he were separating whatever lies on either side. His expression is blank, his head bowed, but his eyes glance to the left side of the panel, as if he were cautiously checking out what lies to his side; to the right is his family in their Sunday best, kids looking bored to be there. To the left, in the direction of his glance, is a procession of young acolytes. A caption representing the words of Bechdel as narrator is positioned above the border and reads, "He appeared to be an ideal husband and father, for example." A second caption within the frame adds, "But would an ideal husband and father have sex with teenage boys?" These words appear to have an additive relationship with the image, setting up a contract between appearance and inner character. Bechdel chose to place that revelation in the most incongruous context imaginable, cracking the veneer of their perfect family in the most unexpected setting.

It is possible to communicate all of the above phenomenon in a stand-alone panel, such as those that typically appear as political cartoons or so-called "gag" cartoons in newspapers (for example, Bil Keane's *The Family Circus*). The multi-panel comic strip – and the long-form storytelling vehicles that build on it – introduces additional phenomena to comics when two or more panels are placed in relationship to one another.

The Sequence

Following on from the panel, the sequence is the next key element in the functioning of the graphic novel. Sequences arise when panels are placed in relationship to one another, or juxtaposed. Even adding a second panel begins to build a story, especially as it affords greater opportunity for conflicts within and between characters.

It would be impractical for creators to show every moment in the progression of a story and so they encapsulate, or select, the key moments of the narrative into segmented images. Eisner explained that a host of choices lay at the creator's discretion, and the effectiveness of one's storytelling abilities was often a reflection of one's ability to choose among the many possibilities of just what to depict and what to leave to the reader's inference. For instance, in creating the *Atoman* page, Crossen and Robinson determined that we needed to see Mr. Twist threaten Miss James with the open container of acid *and* splash it in her direction in two separate frames (see panels two and three), probably to heighten the drama of his menace. However, Atoman's flight to her rescue is only rendered in a single panel, even though, presumably, he would have to fly some distance from his point of origin to Mr. Twist's lair. Perhaps because nothing remarkable happened on the way, the creators felt no need to expend valuable story space on Atoman's travels. For storytelling purposes, it suffices to encapsulate his flight in one panel and move on.

When two panels are situated, or juxtaposed, next to one another, the space between the panels creates what is called a gutter. As is the case in the *Atoman* example, typically the gutter is a white space on the printed page bounded by the borders of any two adjacent panels. Sometimes a simple line and no white space divides them. At times there may be no space at all as the artwork from one panel bleeds or blends into the panel of the next moment in the story. Whether formal boundaries are presented or simply inferred, the gutter serves a remarkable function that invites even greater reader participation in the creation of meaning.

Within the gutter, the reader performs what McCloud has called closure.[17] This is a process whereby the reader infers information not expressly depicted by the creator. For instance, it seems that between panels four and five Mr. Twist must have stopped trying to splash acid on Miss James and stepped back from his assault. That motion is not expressly depicted in any of the artwork or explained by the narrator, but it is a reasonable inference based upon the information that is presented, most notably the difference in his posture and position in the two panels.

Each panel in a sequence relates to the ones before it and the ones that follow it in the sequence (with the exception that the first panel in a story does not have an antecedent nor does the final panel have anything that follows it).[18] These relationships exist because creators put these panels into the sequence and because readers weave together meanings throughout the sequence. Thus when Atoman shows up in Mr. Twist's penthouse in panel four, they carry over information gleaned in panel one; even if the villains are surprised by the hero's entrance, no reader should be surprised by his arrival – even though they may be pleased by his fortunate timing in saving Miss James. After all, they had gained the information that his rescue was underway back in panel one.

Because panels are prone to skip moments in the storytelling, each gutter presents a transition, some more subtle than others, that the reader must negotiate. Continuous elements carried over from one panel to the next certainly help, although when the setting changes entirely the reader can be jarred by the discontinuity. According to McCloud, the three most common types of transitions practiced in American comics storytelling are action-to-action, subject-to-subject, and scene-to-scene. Action-to-action occurs when a single subject progresses, such as when a character looks both ways on a street corner in one panel and then steps into the street in the next. Subject-to-subject transitions stay within a scene but change the subject, such as when in our example page the panels move from Miss James' peril in panel three to Atoman's dramatic rescue in panel four. Scene-to-scene transitions involve moving distances in time and space, such as exhibited in the transition from Atoman in panel one to Mr. Twist's penthouse in panel two. These three types of transitions tend to be the most common because they are the most action-oriented.

There are other types of transition too. Moment-to-moment transitions require limited inference because so little changes from one panel to the next. Aspect-to-aspect wanders about a scene with different focuses. These two are practiced more commonly in Japanese manga than in American comics. McCloud's sixth category, non-sequiturs, exhibit little logical connection. To McCloud's list Abel and Madden add symbolic transitions, which occur when one panel is juxtaposed against another that sets up a visual metaphor between the two.[19] For example, a man tripping in one panel and a cracked egg in the next suggests a particular symbolic relationship. As should be evident, varying degrees of inference need to be exercised across these options, but they all invite readers to do what their minds are prone to: impose meaning on juxtaposed stimuli.

When panels appear in relation to one another in sequence (as opposed to single panel cartoons), the rhythm and pacing of the story are informed by the number, size, and placement of the panels within a strip.[20] Indeed, as Eisner counseled, a creator can suggest the sensation of compressing time by adding many relatively small panels, or elongate time by widening a frame. Note that in *Atoman*, panel three is the slenderest panel on the page, and rightly so for the act of throwing the acid container at Miss James takes just an instant.

When panels occur in sequence, they also afford creators the opportunity to manipulate the reader's experience of the scene through movement of their perceived position in relation to the action. As discussed above in the previous section, each panel can be manipulated in terms of the reader's distance from the action and the angle from which they view it. When placed in sequence, creators have additional options. Zooming is when the objects come closer and closer (or farther and farther) from the viewer panel-to-panel. Tracking can be achieved as an object in motion is followed through its background in successive panels. Panning occurs when a wider scene is revealed across successive panels.[21] None of these effects are attempted in *Atoman*, but had Robinson divided panel four by placing a gutter between Atoman's striking the henchman and his rescue of Miss James, a panning sequence could have been created.

Skillful creators are also aware that sequenced panels are less likely to jar the reader when they observe action flow continuity.[22] When action continues from panel to panel moving in relatively the same direction and from a similar orientation to the reader, it services the story. Filmmakers know this as the 180-degree rule, which suggests keeping the characters on the same side of an imaginary axis. In *Atoman*, note that the reader's view never crosses over from Miss James in panels two through five; we always see her in front of us, but not from her perspective, as that could be disorienting. This rule can be violated, of course, but should be done so with care and in the service to the story, such as when a character changes the direction of their journey and, literally, turns around.

One skillful application of contemporary sequencing practice takes place in *Dotter of Her Father's Eyes*, written by Mary M. Talbot and drawn by Bryan Talbot. On page 49 of this memoir, the creative team foregoes borders and formal gutters between panels in the sequence, and relies instead on separating panels by manipulating the size of the characters and background shading. The first panel is a close-up on Miss Fenn the dance instructor, lecturing about proper movement while pointing to a diagram to our right. Flush against that chart is the second panel, comprised of a long shot of two girls awkwardly attempting to mimic dance poses. The third panel in the sequence is a close-up of another pig-tailed student asking a question. One of her pig-tails overlaps the elbow of one of the students in the second panel, suggesting that she is in a separate image entirely. Between each of these three panels, we experience subject-to-subject transitions, as a dance lesson is given by the teacher and then interpreted by different sets of her students. The one panel of the instructor lecturing is equal in size to the combined two panels of her students, with such space allocations alluding to her authority.

The Page

The third element to consider is the page itself. Printed comics are bounded by the spatial limitations of the physical page, a condition that encourages creators to arrange panels into strips of panels, or tiers. As scholar Thierry Groensteen explains, a creator might conceive of a story as unfolding in a continuous ribbon, but the page demands that the creator exhibit an awareness of effective layout to aid the reader's progression through the story.[23]

In the West, people are trained to read in a Z-pattern, starting at the top left of the page, proceeding left to right, then down and left to the next tier, and so forth. A basic grid is the simplest and easiest to follow layout; it is also the most bland. Note that the *Atoman* page is laid out following a grid that divides it into three vertical tiers with one to three panels in each tier. For many contemporary creators this proposes a design challenge to them, as they attempt to vary layout from page to page in order to maintain enough visual variety to engage an audience. Overlapping panels can help emphasize their reading order. A poor layout, say perhaps one that makes use of a mishmash of panels that alternate in flow between horizontal and vertical order, may make it hard for viewers to know what sequence to put the panels into. Confusing layout threatens to take readers out of the world of the story, frustrating one of the effective creator's chief aims.[24]

A creator can take advantage of the space the page provides to use an entire page as a single panel. Such "splash" pages are sometimes used at the beginning of a story to offer a dramatic introduction; sometimes they are reserved to mark dramatic moments later in the story. However, over-use tends to deteriorate the effect; used sparingly, it can have a substantial impact. In *Watchmen*, Dave Gibbons assiduously followed a three-tiered grid for hundreds of pages, and then made a shocking departure by using several full-page splashes in the graphic novel's final chapter to stunning effect to show the sprawling devastation of New York at the climax of the story.

Because of the way books are printed, creators can also take advantage of a diptych of pages printed side-by-side, creating a double-page spread.[25] Such practices knowingly acknowledge that a reader can take in two whole pages anytime they flip a leaf. Even cautious readers can have their peripheral vision pick up information on facing pages. Savvy creators then can control major reveals by judiciously spacing them on to subsequent pages.

A part of page layout involves how frames are constructed. Barbara Postema outlines variations that creators use to construct panels.[26] The first type involves panels framed by lines with blank spaces separating them, such as in our *Atoman* example. A variation on this involves no spaces, just lines separating one panel from its neighbor. Panels without drawn borders have the artwork from one panel adjacent to that of its neighbor. The previously discussed full-page panel is still another option. And creators can choose to place a smaller panel inset within a larger panel. This variation suggests an even stronger relationship between panels, as the larger provides some context for the actions highlighted in the smaller one.[27]

Even the space on the page outside the framed area can communicate, as the margins can carry information, too.[28] This so-called hyperframe has been used to creative effect in *Mad* for peripheral doodles, in Marvel Comics of the 1970s for solicitations, and in other comics to provide information about the title, issue, story, or page number. There is not much creative use being put to the hyperframe in the *Atoman* example, though.

One of the most interesting and challenging manipulations of the page comes from a J. H. Williams III and Mick Gray construction working from a script by Alan Moore in *Promethea, Book Two*. In this two-page spread, the character of Promethea is having a conversation with her predecessor along a pathway that twists itself into a Möbius strip (that is, the symbol for infinity). Their conversation, curiously, comments on the repetitious nature of their experience, and indeed they can "see" themselves appearing across panels earlier and later in the sequence. Moore and Williams take full advantage of the diptych here even while playing with the conventions of sequence and the expectations of panels in this piece that challenges our understanding of how comics work.

The Narrative

The fourth and final element to consider in the functioning of graphic novels is the narrative. It is certainly possible to establish rudimentary narratives at the level of the single-panel cartoon; however, graphic novels are able to develop the complexity of their storytelling over dozens, if not hundreds, of pages.

Going back to Aristotle in ancient Greece, we know that successful storytelling contains five essential components: a protagonist, the spark, escalation, climax, and denouement.[29] The protagonist is the character at the center of the story, such as Atoman. Readers should be able to empathize with a protagonist; the protagonist should have a clear sense of motivation and some ability to meet the challenges before the character.[30] Whether readers find him empathetic or not, Atoman seems to have the hallmarks of the same "All-Americans" he was aiming to appeal to in his audience of the time. Atoman's speech in panel six makes his motivation clear and his possession of superhuman abilities would suggest that he can meet the challenge posed by the acid-tossing Mr. Twist.

Early on in a narrative, a spark, or an inciting incident, changes the normal routine and starts the story's progression. The spark in the Atoman narrative took place several pages before our example page, when the villainous Mr. Twist sets in motion his plan to steal atomic secrets from the research facility where Atoman works in his alter ego. The next step in the narrative, then, is that one thing after another happens to complicate the narrative and challenge the protagonist. Our example page doesn't depict all the escalation in the *Atoman* story, but you do see that the confrontation raises the stakes for the characters involved. Stories are served by characters' internal and external desires and conflicts: Mr. Twist wants the secret of atomic power and Atoman wants to keep it out of Twist's hands. Ultimately, all of the conflicts reach a climax, which in *Atoman* occurs just a few pages after this one, when Atoman confronts Mr. Twist in an aerial dogfight that results in Mr. Twist's fiery crash. The brief, final phase of the narrative is a denouement, which follows the climax and usually depicts the new or renewed status quo afterwards. In *Atoman*, it occurs as a safe Miss James asks a departing Atoman if she will see him again, which he assures her will be the case.

Stories, of course, have themes or major ideas that they communicate across the span of their narration. For *Atoman* this may well be the necessity of protecting nuclear secrets or the triumph of the forces of justice over greed. Comics make available opportunities to sustain visual metaphors, repeated elements that drive home a major point through images. In *Atoman* that might be that heroes shine (Atoman's costume is yellow and red) and that villains clothe themselves in the trappings of respectability (note the suits worn by Mr. Twist and his henchman). Successful stories also balance convention with invention, or, as comics creator Carl Potts explains it, "Give the readers what they expect, but not in a way they expect it."[31] *Atoman* only lasted a couple of issues, in part because the hero was unremarkable, much like most other superhero titles of his time, and his writer failed to deliver an original take on the type of story, or genre.

The same elements hold forth in the modern graphic novel, of course. In the murder mystery *Whiteout*, creators Greg Rucka and Steve Lieber introduce us to Carrie Stetko, a US Marshall stationed in Antarctica. Carrie has committed a professional offense that has landed her with an assignment at the bottom of the world, but she is a smart detective and driven by her duty. The story is sparked into motion when a mutilated body is discovered at an isolated camp. The action escalates as Carrie's investigation proceeds, including several additional murders and an attempt on her own life. At the climax, Carrie identifies the killer and confronts that individual. In the denouement, Carrie stands on the ice and watches as the perpetrator is flown off to jail. The final page displays a keen symmetry with the graphic novel's opening page, where Carrie had been in a plane flying in to the crime scene. Rucka and Lieber also chose to produce the graphic novel without color, and the amount of white space throughout the story helps to perpetuate the visual metaphor of Antarctica as a cold and desolate setting.

The art of comics as made manifest in graphic novels results from attention to detail at many levels. Effective manipulation of the medium involves the knowledge and ability to capture one's message efficiently in panels, sequences, pages, and the narration. It also calls upon the reader to make interpretations that complete the process of getting across sensations and ideas. The remainder of this volume explores how this process has been – and continues to be – carried forth, in this exciting form of human communication.

Works Cited

Abel, Jessica, and Matt Madden. *Drawing Words & Writing Pictures: Making Comics: Manga, Graphic Novels, and Beyond.* New York: First Second, 2008.

Bechdel, Alison. *Fun Home: A Family Tragicomic.* New York: Houghton Mifflin, 2007.

Crossen, Ken, and Robinson, Jerry. *Atoman.* Spark Publications, 1946. Accessed at digitalcomicmuseum.com

Eisner, Will. *Comics and Sequential Art.* Tamarac, FL: Poorhouse Press, 1985.

Groensteen, Thierry. *The System of Comics.* Trans. Bart Beaty and Nick Nguyen. Jackson, MS: University Press of Mississippi, 2007.

Harvey, Robert C. *The Art of the Comic Book: An Aesthetic History.* Jackson, MS: University Press of Mississippi, 1996.

The Masters of Comic Book Art. Dir. Ken Viola. Perf. Will Eisner. Ken Viola Productions, 1987. Film.

McCloud, Scott. *Understanding Comics: The Invisible Art.* New York: Harper-Collins, 1993.

Moore, Alan, and Dave Gibbons. *Watchmen.* New York: DC Comics, 1987.

Moore, Alan, J. H. Williams III, and Mick Gray. *Promethea, Book Two.* La Jolla, CA: America's Best Comics, 2000.

Postema, Barbara. *Narrative Structure in Comics: Making Sense of Fragments.* Rochester, NY: RIT Press, 2013.

Potts, Carl. *The DC Comics Guide to Creating Comics: Inside the Art of Visual Storytelling.* New York: Watson-Guptill Publications, 2013.

Rucka, Greg, and Steve Lieber. *Whiteout.* Portland, OR: Oni Press, 2007.

Talbot, Mary M., and Bryan Talbot. *Dotter of Her Father's Eyes.* Milwaukie, OR: Dark Horse Books, 2012.

Walker, Mort. *The Lexicon of Comicana.* Port Chester, NY: Comicana, Inc., 1980.

NOTES

1 Jessica Abel and Matt Madden, *Drawing Words & Writing Pictures: Making Comics: Manga, Graphic Novels, and Beyond* (New York: First Second, 2008), 151.

2 Will Eisner, *Comics and Sequential Art* (Tamarac, FL: Poorhouse Press, 1985), 47.

3 Carl Potts, *The DC Comics Guide to Creating Comics: Inside the Art of Visual Storytelling* (New York: Watson-Guptill Publications, 2013), 17.

4 Eisner, *Comics*, 89.
5 Thierry Groenstein, *The System of Comics*, trans. Bart Beaty and Nick Nguyen (Jackson, MS: University Press of Mississippi, 2007), 54.
6 Abel and Madden, *Drawing Words*, 151.
7 Quoted in *The Masters of Comic Book Art*, dir. Ken Viola, performer Will Eisner (Ken Viola Productions, 1987).
8 Eisner, *Comics and Sequential Art*, 103.
9 Mort Walker, *The Lexicon of Comicana* (Port Chester, NY: Comicana, Inc., 1980), 28.
10 Robert C. Harvey, *The Art of the Comic Book: An Aesthetic History* (Jackson, MS: University Press of Mississippi, 1996), 3.
11 Barbara Postema, *Narrative Structure in Comics: Making Sense of Fragments* (Rochester, NY: RIT Press, 2013), 79.
12 Groenstein, *System of Comics*, 129.
13 Abel and Madden, *Drawing Words*, 16.
14 Eisner, *Comics*, 26.
15 Scott McCloud, *Understanding Comics: The Invisible Art* (New York: Harper-Collins, 1993), 153–55.
16 Potts, *DC Comics Guide*, 29.
17 McCloud, *Understanding Comics*, 63.
18 Groenstein, *System of Comics*, 110.
19 Abel and Madden, *Drawing Words*, 44.
20 Abel and Madden, *Drawing Words*.
21 Potts, *DC Comics Guide*, 66.
22 Ibid., 27.
23 Groenstein, *System of Comics*, 59.
24 Potts, *DC Comics Guide*, 50.
25 Groenstein, *System of Comics*, 91.
26 Postema, *Narrative Structure*.
27 Groenstein, *System of Comics*, 86.
28 Ibid., 30.
29 Abel and Madden, *Drawing Words*, 128.
30 Ibid., 129.
31 Potts, *DC Comics Guide*, 101.

2

STEPHEN E. TABACHNICK

From Comics to the Graphic Novel

William Hogarth to Will Eisner

In this chapter, we will discuss the nature of the graphic novel and how it developed from the comics. The graphic novel has little in common with traditional comic books which in the 1950s in America, for instance, largely consisted of the adventures of Superman and Batman, *Tales from the Crypt*, and *Archie*. For one thing, graphic novels are as thick as regular prose books, and they are printed on better paper and with better ink than usual comic books. Also, even though they are called graphic "novels," implying that they deal only with fiction, the term graphic novel includes not only fiction, but also serious non-fictional historical and political issues, and graphic novels are often autobiographical or biographical. If they do feature superheroes, it is a new kind of superhero – like Frank Miller's portrayal of Batman as the Dark Knight – psychologically complex, often neurotic, and self-questioning. Clearly, something significant has happened to comic books, which in the form of the graphic novel have become something much more like full-length prose novels or non-fictional prose works. In contrast to the popular mass-market comics, which have usually been severely restricted in both form and content by commercial constraints, the graphic novel is an extended comic book freed of all restrictions on form and content and capable of tackling all of the issues that writing and art for adults have always dealt with, using all of the literary and artistic resources available to any writer or artist. But it is a form that is clearly based on the techniques of comics, and readers have to read both words and pictures to make sense of it. Moreover, as Scott McCloud has written, comics, because they are composed not only of individual panels, but of empty spaces, or gutters, between the panels, force the reader to fill in those empty spaces with his or her imagination.[1] So this is both a traditional, highly interactive form that relies on techniques developed over the last two-and-a-half centuries in order to entertain and amuse, and a new form that is capable of using those techniques and newer, more sophisticated ones, in the service of the intellect.

The comics medium as we know it – and here I exclude hieroglyphics and cave drawings, which are sometimes cited as the origins of comics – began not in America, but in England in the eighteenth century. There William Hogarth, James Gillray, and Thomas Rowlandson were creating very interesting artworks containing some elements of what would become the comics: Hogarth, for instance, often shows the decline of a respectable member of society into a social outcast in a series of engravings – as in his "A Harlot's Progress" and "A Rake's Progress" – which are sequential panels. Similarly, Gillray, in his "John Bull's Progress," showed in four panels the journey of a citizen representing England itself – John Bull – from a life as a healthy and happy man to a soldier returning home with many wounds because of foreign wars. And Gillray in other features actually used word balloons within the panels. Rowlandson, in his illustrations to William Combe's *Tour of Dr. Syntax*, was the first to use the same character in several narratives with panels.

In addition to these three wonderful eighteenth-century proto-comics artists, we should not overlook Laurence Sterne's great eighteenth-century novel, *Tristram Shandy*. Unlike most illustrated books – such as Robert Louis Stevenson's *Treasure Island*, which has been illustrated numerous times – the visual elements in *Tristram Shandy* are not added on or extraneous interpretations of aspects of the book by people other than the book's creator. Rather, in *Tristram Shandy* the visuals (for instance, a completely black page and a completely blank page, as well as a group of asterisks and other typographical aberrations) are included by the author himself, are intrinsic to the pages on which they appear, and are absolutely essential to an understanding of the book. If the reader skips the illustrations in *Treasure Island* he or she will not miss any part of the story or its characters. If, however, the reader skips the visuals in *Tristram Shandy*, he or she is definitely missing parts of its story and its meaning. In other words, there is a case to be made that at least in its visual parts, featuring unusual typography, *Tristram Shandy* is not simply an illustrated book, but rather a proto-graphic novel. William Blake, the eighteenth-century poet, must also be mentioned in this context, because his poems, such as "The Sick Rose" (1794), were often accompanied by his own illustrations, and these illustrations and the texts modify one another, and neither would be as powerful if printed alone.

So the eighteenth century in England is crucial to the development of the comics. But the next major and indeed defining step takes place not in England but in Switzerland in the early nineteenth century, at the hands of Rodolphe Töpffer, a schoolteacher and later professor of literature at the University of Geneva. In his *Histoire de Monsieur Jabot* and other stories created in the 1820s and 1830s, for the first time we see a narrative rendered in dynamic and sketchy rather than full-bodied drawings, and which uses panels of different sizes. Because of this, Töpffer's stories look much like many of the comics we know today. The use of a series of pictures, word balloons, the continuous focus on a single character, differing panel sizes, and sketchy drawings, and indeed the use of caricature – as pioneered by Hogarth, Gillray, Rowlandson, and Töppfer – all become part of the form of the comics. That form is further developed in the nineteenth century by the magazines *Le Charivari* in France, *Punch* (which displayed the cartoons of John Tenniel, known for his illustrations to *Alice in Wonderland*, among other brilliant artists) and *Judy* (in which, as Alan and Laurel Clark point out, Charles Ross' character Ally Sloper began, and which, according to Roger Sabin, had a circulation of 350,000 per week at its peak) in England, and by a creator like Wilhelm Busch in Germany, whose very popular comic *Max und Moritz*, about two naughty boys, is largely responsible for the connection between comics and children.[2] This association was followed up in American comics in the late nineteenth and early twentieth centuries by such pioneer creators as R. F. Outcault in his *Hogan's Alley* (about a slum child) and *Buster Brown* (about a rich kid), Lyonel Feininger in his *Wee Willie Winkie's World*, and Rudolph Dirks in his *Katzenjammer Kids* (see Judith O'Sullivan for a full discussion of these and other American comics artists).[3] While amusing, this connection between children and comics has also helped keep comics from being thought of as a serious genre of literature and art. The work of Outcault, Feininger, and Dirks is all part of the first period of American comics, which lasts from approximately 1890 to 1930, and which was started by newspaper barons Joseph Pulitzer and William Randolph Hearst in New York City to boost circulation among an immigrant audience which did not yet know English well. Because they were considered entertainment for immigrants and children, and because they began in the newspapers, comics in America, as elsewhere, have too often been ephemeral throwaway productions, whose content has usually been restricted to the innocuous treatment of a limited range of socially acceptable subjects. Despite these commercial restrictions, there always were some truly extraordinary creators even in this early period of American comics. Feininger, for instance, was to become an important Cubist painter as well as a noted comics artist. Winsor McCay, with his *Little Nemo in Slumberland*, created a wonderful surrealistic journey into the dream world, while George Herriman's *Krazy Kat*, detailing an impossible love triangle between a cat, a dog, and a mouse, is rendered in very poetic language and pictures. It is important to note that despite their association with children and restrictions on their content, the comics have often treated important matters, albeit usually mildly and light-heartedly. For instance, in this early period of the

American comics, which was a time of massive immigration into the US, the difficulties of new immigrants when trying to fit into American society was a major topic. George McManus' *Bringing Up Father* showed humorously what happened when a simple Irish immigrant workman and his wife became nouveau-riche socialites, while Milt Gross' *Nize Baby* gently satirized his characters' Yiddish-inflected accents.

After the early period from around 1890 to 1930, there comes the second period of the American comics, from 1930 to 1950, during which superheroes were invented and flourished. Again, serious topics were sometimes treated, but this time literally in a masked manner. The development of superheroes in particular was perhaps to be expected in an era of the Great Depression, Al Capone, and then the Second World War. Big and unavoidable social and political issues demanded big characters like Superman, Batman, Wonder Woman and Captain America to handle them, and so the gods were born; and these gods dealt with the problems of crime and conflict and evil – especially Hitler – in a reassuringly straightforward and decisive way, as Christopher Knowles points out in his investigation of superheroes, *Our Gods Wear Spandex*.[4] Undoubtedly there was something very American about these secular gods, who reflected America's conception of itself as a superpower, even or especially in the midst of these troubles.

After the Second World War, attention turned from war to more usual topics such as romance, crime, horror, and sci-fi, with such titles as *Young Romance*, *Crime Does Not Pay*, *Tales from the Crypt*, and *Weird Fantasy* coming into prominence. Because some of this new material was thought to be deleterious to youth, especially by a congressional committee egged on by notorious anti-comics psychologist Fredric Wertham, author of *Seduction of the Innocent*, the Comics Code Authority, a self-regulatory censoring body established by the comic book industry itself in 1954, came into being. No longer could comics show sweat, depict scenes of bloodshed, or even use the words horror or terror in their titles.

Seen in retrospect, this was a fortunate development in the long march of the popular comics toward the graphic novel, because the usual result of censorship – a counter-reaction – occurred during the third period of the comics, which runs from around 1945 through 1975. The magazine *Mad* was born in 1952 as a wacky satirical look at the media and other American institutions. Because he called it a magazine, indicating that it was presumably for adults rather than children, William Gaines, its publisher – whose father Max had invented the comic book in 1933 – had fortunately placed it beyond the scope of the Comics Code Authority. As reading matter for grown-ups (although often read by teenagers and even children too), *Mad* was free of the restrictions on the other comics. Under the editorship of the great Harvey Kurtzman, *Mad* produced unrestrained satire on American society; everything, including the anti-Communist Joseph McCarthy congressional hearings – which often degenerated into a witch hunt – advertising, and popular films, was fair game for it. And as a result, although *Mad* always stayed more or less within the bounds of good taste, it is one of the important instigators of the 1960s and 1970s cultural revolution.

One aspect of that revolution, inspired in part by *Mad* and the comics censorship code was the advent of counter-culture comix – deliberately spelled with an x as a sign of rebellion against standard social conventions. Sex, drugs, and rock 'n' roll formed the basis of many of these revolutionary comix, whose major intention was simply to break as many taboos as possible, as Dez Skinn points out in his *Comix: The Underground Revolution*.[5] Anti-social characters, outrageous satire, overt political pronouncements, and formerly out of bounds topics characterized these comics. Gilbert Shelton's "Little Annie Amphetamine," based on Little Orphan Annie; and Dan O'Neill's *Air Pirates Funnies*, which showed Minnie and Mickey Mouse having sex, are just two of the more famous (or infamous) of these wild productions. O'Neill was sued by Disney and after a long legal battle settled with them, but as Skinn notes, "Unbelievably," after the case was settled, "O'Neill was hired by New York's Disney merchandising art department"; this was perhaps a recognition that a new age had come to the comics.[6] By breaking the ban on the unrestrained treatment of controversial issues that had governed the American popular comics since their inception, these works were freeing the comics from their decades of commercial restrictions as well as the decade of censorship imposed by the Comics Code Authority.

So it had taken the comics over half a century to truly free themselves from commercial and other restrictions, and to open the door for the ascendance of the graphic novel. But we should remember that already in the early twentieth century, in Belgium, Frans Masereel had published many wordless, extended comics narratives in book form. His most famous, *Passionate Journey* (1919), shows the tumultuous pilgrimage through life of an individual man – most likely himself, since the book begins with the engraving of an artist at work – with all of his triumphs and tragedies.[7] The man arrives in a large city by train, walks around it, viewing its various aspects, goes to bed with a prostitute, helps an old lady cross the street, tells stories to children, finds a girl he likes but experiences her death, goes to the beach, drives a car, runs from the rain, goes to a dance, drinks, gets into a fight, goes to church, saves a drowning person, declines an award for that, urinates on the city from a high rooftop, visits Africa, returns to Europe and insults a crowd which then chases him, and finds refuge in a house and then in a forest, where he finally dies and becomes a dancing skeleton. The novel closes with the words of Belgian author Hendrik Conscience, "They shall not tame him." As Thomas Mann writes in his introduction to this book, the protagonist is following his heart beyond all claims of class and other allegiance; he is a free artist. Masereel tells this story in black-and-white wood engravings that are nearly, but not quite, iconic, in that we can recognize the protagonist's face, but it is iconic enough for us to be able to identify with him. Mann calls Masereel's work a film in book form, but in fact, despite its lack of panels on each page, it is what we can now recognize as completely in comics form, in which each page can be seen as a panel in itself. Moreover, because it has no words and there is a large gutter between pages, it draws upon the reader's interactive imagination even more than the comics with text and pictures and several panels on each page do. How the reader interprets a given incident is more wide open than an interpretation of a prose novel or a usual comic.

Masereel's work was taken up by Americans Lynd Ward, who in the 1920s and 1930s drew six complex wordless woodcut novels, sometimes in several colors, and Milt Gross, the author of the comic strip *Nize Baby*, who in 1930 published the humorous, slapstick, and wordless woodcut novel *He Done Her Wrong* (which was subtitled *The Great American Novel*). This could be said to be the silent film era of the graphic novel.

Ward was the creator of *Gods' Man* in 1929, the first woodcut novel by an American, and the first of six that he would draw. *Wild Pilgrimage* (1932), the third, is one of the best. It tells the story of a factory worker who aspires to a less confined life. He wanders, witnesses a lynching, sexually attacks a farmer's wife, runs away and meets and learns from a hermit, and finally undertakes an unsuccessful revolt at his factory, during which he is badly beaten and killed by the police. In the second drawing in the book, a worker holds a hammer and sickle sign as the workers file into the factory, and the revolt seems to be the ultimate and unsuccessful outcome of communist ideology. The protagonist's dreams appear in orange coloring as opposed to the black and white of the other engravings. Essentially, he is trying to reconcile these dreams and his reality, without success. His pilgrimage is wild because it involves violence, some of it caused by him, and because it has no specific direction. No one in the novel, including the protagonist who is outright ugly, appears handsome or pretty, nor do the settings, which are usually dark and menacing or drawn in orange, as if consumed in fire. Often, the protagonist's face is tortured and nowhere does he appear at ease except perhaps when he is tilling the soil. For Ward, life is not a pleasant, pretty, or easy journey, and often does not end in happiness or success. From the first, unlike the popular comics, the graphic novel dealt with serious issues, including the meaning of life itself.

Fig. 2.1 The protagonist in Otto Nückel's *Destiny* jumps out of a window to her death as a policeman shoots at her. Eisner has stated that Nückel as well as Frans Masereel and Lynd Ward, other creators of graphic novels without words, were major inspirations for his own work. By permission of Dover Publishing.

Milt Gross' *He Done Her Wrong* (1930) tells the story of love between a frontiersman and a saloon singer, which is interrupted by an unscrupulous robber baron from the city who tells her that the frontiersman is dead and proceeds to marry her. After their marriage falls apart, she seeks work without great success, while the frontiersman finds his way to the city. After missing each other on several occasions, they are reunited, while the rich man is held accountable for his crookedness and exiled to a Middle Eastern land where he serves as a slave for all intents and purposes. The frontiersman, it turns out, rather than the rich man, is the father of the singer's children and they enjoy an idyllic existence together, along with her father. Gross' style is like that of a Sunday comic, very open, iconic, and unrealistic. In his introduction to the volume, Craig Yoe compares Gross' characters to Chaplin and Keaton, and his graphic novel as a whole to "the exaggerated villain-twist-his-mustache melodrama so popular in movies at the time" but "with a sardonic twist that propels the story like a rushing freight train."[8] These two American graphic novels can be seen as the predecessors of the word-and-picture graphic novels that would follow.

Also important is the German Otto Nückel's 1930 wordless woodcut novel *Destiny* (in English translation), showing the sad journey through life of an orphan girl who becomes a prostitute, then a single mother, then a criminal, and finally a suicide while being shot at by the police, experiencing love only once along the way (fig. 2.1).[9] Nückel's work almost does not have a single smile in it, and the always dark figures and backgrounds underline the sadness of the tale. The protagonist cannot extricate herself from a sea of troubles, which are not her fault. As in Lynd Ward's work, the silence makes the illustrations, drawn in an expressionistic style, even more powerful, and the reader's imagination is even freer than in comics with texts. These wonderful works were percolating below the surface and helped finally produce the graphic novel in word and picture.

In any discussion of the wordless graphic novel, Max Ernst's *Une Semaine de Bonté* (*A Week of Kindness*) must be mentioned. Published in 1934, this surrealistic collage novel captures the psychological undercurrents of sexuality by juxtaposing women and men who have animal heads, women with bat wings with men or other women, water on which some people walk while others drown, and male lions who dominate women, among many other images (fig. 2.2). While none of the major comics artists between 1934 and 1978, when Will Eisner's *A Contract with God* was published, seem to openly acknowledge Ernst's influence on their work, this famous masterpiece is always there in the background, demonstrating how the unconscious can be visibly portrayed and how men and monsters can be combined to form a meaningful character. In Alan Moore's 1987 graphic novel *Watchmen*, the character Dreiberg's essay, "Blood from the Shoulder of Pallas," references Ernst's graphic novel in order to point to the world's mysteries, writing that "When we stare into the catatonic black bead of a Parakeet's eye we must teach ourselves to glimpse the cold, alien madness that Max Ernst perceived when he chose to robe his naked brides in confections of scarlet feather and the transplanted monstrous heads of exotic birds."[10] And in *Epileptic* (2005), David Beauchard is influenced by Ernst's collages to create his own "men with animal heads."[11]

In addition to these well-known wordless graphic novels, the American Giacomo Patri's *White Collar* (1938) and the Canadian Laurence Hyde's *Southern Cross* (1951) also deserve mention. Along with Masereel's and Ward's novels discussed above, they are available in *Graphic Witness: Four Wordless Graphic Novels*, edited by George A. Walker. But there are many more such novels, including works by Werner Gothein, Carl Meffert (also known as Clément Moreau), and James Reid, and they must all be seen as predecessors, albeit often unacknowledged, of the graphic novel. In 1941–43, Charlotte Salomon, while hiding from the Nazis in southern France, created her autobiography from 769 of her paintings with transparent word overlays, and this work, *Life? or Theatre?*, can also be seen as an important precursor of the graphic novel as we know it today.

Although no technical obstacles prevented it from happening earlier, perhaps surprisingly the combination of words and pictures in an extended

Fig. 2.2 Painter Max Ernst's wordless *Une Semaine de Bonté*, a "surrealistic novel in collage," is also an important precursor of the graphic novel with words. By permission of Dover Publishing.

comic book did not happen until around the 1970s. Although they were not called by that term, which was coined by writer Richard Kyle in 1964, Gil Kane and Archie Goodwin's *Blackmark* (1971), Richard Corben's *Bloodstar* (1976), and Jim Steranko's *Red Tide: A Chandler Novel* (1976), were what we would today call graphic novels.[12] But it was in 1978 that Will Eisner, who had drawn the comic strip *The Spirit* about a masked vigilante crime-fighter (which lasted from 1940 to 1952), and who had said as early as 1941 that the comics could produce a full-scale novel comparable to those written in text alone, came out with the first important graphic novel, *A Contract with God and Other Tenement Stories* (1978), using both words and pictures. In his preface to *The Contract with God Trilogy* (2006), Eisner writes that "In 1978, encouraged by the work of the experimental graphic artists Otto Nückel, Frans Masereel and Lynd Ward, who in the 1930s published serious novels told in art without text, I attempted a major work in similar form ... I called it a 'graphic novel'."[13] As Mazur and Danner point out, while Eisner's works were not the first works about which the term term graphic novel was used, his "literary ambition and drive to bring serious comics – outside the conventional genres of superhero, science fiction or fantasy – into the broader mainstream did much to popularize the term and to jump-start the re-branding of comics as an art form for grown-ups."[14] Here, in the career of one creator, we see the leap from a popular, cartoony private eye to something far more serious. And something more serious than Dirks' *Katzenjammer Kids* and McManus' *Bringing Up Father*, which treated the American immigrant experience lightly and humorously. His trilogy details the struggles of European immigrants to survive in 1930s New York City. It is serious, it is honest, it is not always pleasant, and it convincingly portrays real people and their day-to-day struggles. Eisner not only drew very expressively but wrote well. Interestingly, he comments about the first novel in the trilogy, *A Contract with God*, that although "no major publisher would touch it at the time, this novel has remained in print for twenty-seven years, and has been published in eleven different languages."[15] This shows the difficulty the graphic novel faced in terms of recognition, and is a tribute to Eisner's persistence and the progress of the graphic novel genre itself.

A Life Force, the second of the novels, like the other two novels in the trilogy reveals the difference between Eisner's approach and that of the traditional comics. Eisner focuses on one Jacob Shtarkah (whose last name means "strong" in Yiddish), who after being commissioned to add a room to a synagogue is unemployed and suffers a heart attack. He also suffers love difficulties when he helps bring an old girlfriend from Germany to New York who soon leaves for Palestine to be with her daughter. He is then reunited with his wife, whom he wanted to divorce. His daughter is in love with a

Protestant stockbroker who has fallen on hard times, and Jacob's business with the Italian immigrant Angelo is threatened by their unknowing acceptance of stolen goods. At one point in the story, Jacob sees eye to eye with a cockroach, and although everything works out well for Jacob in the end, he learns that only the "life force," like that of the cockroach, will enable people to survive. As the story ends, he saves a cockroach from extermination. We are clearly out of the realm of the Sunday comics, which were largely confined to the exploits of straightforward, handsome superheroes, light humor, and children's characters. Eisner's very solid, black-and-white drawing style, which is realistic rather than iconic, complements his serious story.

Eisner is not only a pioneer in using the graphic novel medium for fiction, but for autobiography and non-fiction as well. The stories in *A Contract with God* are based on New York neighborhoods that Eisner knew from his youth, and his *To the Heart of the Storm* was described by Eisner himself as "frankly autobiographical."[16] In this work, we see the young Eisner, or Willie, as he heads south as a draftee toward an army base in 1942 during the Second World War, all the while thinking of his parents Sam and Fannie (their real names) and the stories about anti-Semitism which his father told him about his own life in Vienna circa 1910, and which his mother told him about her father arriving in New York in 1880 from Romania. He also remembers his youthful friendship with one Buck, who later revealed himself as an anti-Semite. He also describes other warring national tribes in New York, when Irish and Italian workmen get into a fight, and shows how his mother, while herself Jewish, has prejudices against German Jews. His companion on the train journey, Mahmid, formerly a Turkish Muslim but now an American Christian, understands Willie's problems with prejudice, having suffered it himself. Willie and Mahmid arrive at their base and head off in a line just as a storm, symbolic of the Second World War, is breaking. This autobiography is at once a painful statement about prejudice, and a look at Eisner's own struggle to become a man and an artist. His drawing is realistic and open, with few panels with borders and some large "splash" pages, and this free-flowing style combined with his fluid use of black and white, allows us to witness Willie's frequent transitions from the present to memories of the past, and helps create the convincing honesty of this work.

In *The Plot* (2005), which Eisner completed after twenty years of work just before he died at the age of eighty-seven, he helps develop the non-fictional graphic "novel," in this case by revealing the history of the notoriously anti-Semitic and false *Protocols of the Learned Elders of Zion*, a product of the Czarist secret police intended to convince the Czar that the Jews were behind a plot to modernize Russia, and therefore to influence him to cease his own modernizing efforts. In one of the final chapters, titled "1993," Eisner shows himself doing the research for this work, and in a chapter titled "2002," he gives proof of the continued publication of the *Protocols* despite all of the evidence that it was false, including the first unmasking, by British reporter Philip Graves in the London *Times* in 1921, who showed it was a plagiarism of satirist Maurice Joly's attack on Napoleon III of France, as well as a report by Senators Dodd and Keating in 1964 condemning it. He shows Graves comparing actual passages from Joly's work to actual passages from *The Protocols* in order to provide clear proof of the falsity of *The Protocols* and to enable the reader to see that for him or her self. Eisner shows the strong emotions and cunning looks of several of the conspirators against the Czar's modernizing tendency, but when he depicts Mathieu Golovinski, the opportunist who wrote the *Protocols*, and more recent anti-Semites, he refrains from cartoony exaggerations of their faces or an attempt to present them as pure evil. His realistic black-and-white style convinces us that they were simply ill-intentioned people seeking their own good at any price, and that he is telling a true story. Here, as in his earlier work, Eisner deserves praise as the first important graphic novelist, who proved himself capable of creating superb fictional, autobiographical, and historical works, which, as I have pointed out in *The Quest for Jewish Belief and Identity in the Graphic Novel*, were inspired by his own personal experience of growing up in New York City as the son of European Jewish immigrants, as well as by his cognizance of the painful history of the Jews in Europe based at least in part on his parents' testimony.

Following Eisner's example, the graphic novel began to grow in popularity and respect, with Art Spiegelman and Alan Moore, among others, also tackling sophisticated topics, such as Spiegelman's life as the son of Holocaust survivors in his *Maus*, and Moore's science fictional exploration in *Watchmen* of a failed attempt to end war. Whether the subject is neurotic superheroes or adaptations of classic literary works, including Martin Rowson's brilliant parody of T. S. Eliot's poem *The Waste Land*, biographies such as David Mairowitz's and Robert Crumb's life of Franz Kafka, expositions of important non-fictional works such as Sid Jacobson's and Ernie Colón's graphic adaptation of the 9/11 report, or a desperately satirical travel narrative like Guy Delisle's *Pyongyang* (as well as the vast variety of international works discussed by Mazur and Danner in their chapter in this book and in their own book), the graphic novel today has evolved into an exciting literary and artistic genre that is equal to any other genre of literature, art, or film in terms of its range and quality.[17] And like all other genres in these media, it retains its own special characteristics that make it especially compelling to its readers. The graphic novel represents the maturation, after two hundred years, of the work of Hogarth, Gillray, Rowlandson, and Töppfer, as well as that of Masereel, Ward, Gross, Nückel, and Ernst, and the underground comix artists, and we can only praise all of the wonderful creators who have made this leap possible.

Works Cited

B.[eauchard], David. *Epileptic*. Trans. Kim Thompson. New York: Pantheon Books, 2005.

Clark, Alan, and Laurel Clark. *Comics: An Illustrated History*. London: Green Wood, 1991.

Corben, Richard. *Bloodstar*. New York: Morning Star Press, 1976.

Delisle, Guy, and Helge Dascher. *Pyongyang: A Journey in North Korea*. Montreal: Drawn & Quarterly, 2005.

Eisner, Will. *The Contract with God Trilogy: Life on Dropsie Avenue*. New York: W. W. Norton, 2006.

 To the Heart of the Storm. New York: W. W. Norton, 1991.

 The Plot: The Secret Story of The Protocols of the Elders of Zion. New York: W. W. Norton, 2005.

Ernst, Max. *Une Semaine de Bonté: A Surrealistic Novel in Collage*. New York: Dover, 1976.

Gross, Milt. *He Done Her Wrong: The Great American Novel*. Seattle, WA: Fantagraphics Books, 2005.

Hyde, Laurence. *Southern Cross: A Novel of the South Seas*. Montreal: Drawn & Quarterly, 2007.

Jacobson, Sid, and Ernie Colón. *The 9/11 Report: A Graphic Adaptation*. New York: Hill & Wang, 2006.

Kain, Gil, and Archie Goodwin. *Blackmark*. New York: Bantam, 1971.

Kaplan, Arie. *From Krakow to Krypton: Jews and Comic Books*. Philadelphia, PA: Jewish Publication Society, 2008.

Knowles, Christopher. *Our Gods Wear Spandex: The Secret History of Comic Book Heroes*. New York: Weiser Books, 2007.

Kyle, Richard. "The Future of 'Comics'." *Richard Kyle's Wonderworld* 2 (Nov. 1964): 3–4. www.thecomicbooks.com. Web.

Mairowitz, David, and Robert Crumb. *Introducing Kafka*. London: Totem Books, 1990.

Mann, Thomas. Introduction, in Frans Masereel, *Passionate Journey: A Novel Told in 165 Woodcuts*. London: Penguin, 1998.

Masereel, Frans. *Passionate Journey: A Novel Told in 165 Woodcuts*. London: Penguin, 1998.

Mazur, Dan, and Alexander Danner. *Comics: A Global History, 1968 to the Present*. London: Thames & Hudson, 2014.

McCloud, Scott. *Understanding Comics: The Invisible Art*. New York: Harper Perennial, 1994.

Moore, Alan, and Dave Gibbons. *Watchmen*. New York: DC Comics, 1987.

Nückel, Otto. *Destiny: A Novel in Pictures*. New York: Dover, 2007.

O'Neill, Dan, et al. *Air Pirates Funnies*. San Francisco, CA: Hell Comics, 1971.

O'Sullivan, Judith. *The Great American Comic Strip: One Hundred Years of Cartoon Art*. Boston, Toronto, and London: Little, Brown and Co., Bulfinch Press, 1990.

Patri, Giacomo. *White Collar: A Novel in Linocuts*, in George Walker, ed. *Graphic Witness: Four Wordless Graphic Novels by Frans Masereel, Lynd Ward, Giacomo Patri and Laurence Hyde*. Buffalo, NY: Firefly, 2007.

Rowson, Martin. *The Waste Land*. HarperCollins, 1990.

Sabin, Roger. *Adult Comics: An Introduction*. London and New York: Routledge, 1993.

Salomon, Charlotte. *Life? or Theatre?* Amsterdam: B.V. Waanders, 1999.

Shelton, Gilbert. "Little Annie Amphetamine," in *The Collected Adventures of the Fabulous Furry Freak Brothers*. San Francisco, CA: Rip Off Press, 1971.

Skinn, Dez. *Comix: The Underground Revolution*. New York: Thunder's Mouth Press, 2004.

Spiegelman, Art. *The Complete Maus*. New York: Pantheon Books, 1996.

Steranko, Jim. *Red Tide: A Chandler Novel*. New York: Pyramid, 1976.

Sterne, Laurence. *The Life and Opinions of Tristram Shandy, Gentleman*. London: Penguin, 2003.

Tabachnick, Stephen E. *The Quest for Jewish Belief and Identity in the Graphic Novel*. Tuscaloosa, AL: University of Alabama Press, 2014.

Walker, George A., ed. *Graphic Witness: Four Wordless Graphic Novels by Frans Masereel, Lynd Ward, Giacomo Patri and Laurence Hyde*. Buffalo, NY: Firefly, 2007.

Ward, Lynd. *Gods' Man: A Novel in Woodcuts*. New York: Dover, 2004.

Wild Pilgrimage: A Novel in Woodcuts. Cleveland, OH, and New York: World, 1960.

Wertham, Fredric. *Seduction of the Innocent*. New York: Rinehart, 1954.

Yoe, Craig. Introduction, in Milt Gross, *He Done Her Wrong: The Great American Novel*. Seattle, WA: Fantagraphics Books, 2005.

NOTES

1 Scott McCloud, *Understanding Comics: The Invisible Art* (New York: Harper Perrenial, 1994).

2 Alan Clark and Laurel Clark, *Comics: An Illustrated History* (London: Green Wood, 1991); Roger Sabin, *Adult Comics: An Introduction* (London and New York: Routledge, 1993), 19.

3 Judith O'Sullivan, *The Great American Comic Strip: One Hundred Years of Cartoon Art* (Boston, Toronto, and London: Little, Brown and Co., Bulfinch Press, 1990).

4 Christopher Knowles, *Our Gods Wear Spandex: The Scret History of Comic Book Heroes* (New York: Weiser Books, 2007).

5 Dez Skinn, *Comix: The Underground Revolution* (New York: Thunder's Mouth Press, 2004)

6 Ibid., 148.

7 Frans Masereel, *Passionate Journey: A Novel Told in 165 Woodcuts* (London: Penguin, 1998).

8 Craig Yoe, Introduction to Milt Gross, *He Done Her Wrong: The Great American Novel* (Seattle, WA: Fantagraphics Books, 2005), unpaginated.

9 Otto Nückel, *Destiny: A Novel in Pictures* (New York: Dover, 2007).

10 Alan Moore and Dave Gibbons, *Watchmen* (New York: DC Comics, 1987), chapter 7, 30.

11 David B.[eauchard], *Epileptic*, trans. Kim Thompson (New York: Pantheon Books, 2005), 215.

12 See also Stephen Weiner's chapter in this volume for additional 1970s works that can be considered graphic novels.

13 Will Eisner, Preface to *The Contract with God Trilogy: Life on Dropsie Avenue* (New York: W. W. Norton, 2006), xiii–xiv.

14 Dan Mazur and Alexander Danner, *Comics: A Global History, 1968 to the Present* (London: Thames & Hudson, 2014), 181.

15 Eisner, *Contract with God Trilogy*, xiv.

16 Will Eisner, *To the Heart of the Storm* (New York: W. W. Norton, 1991). For the quote, see Arie Kaplan, *From Krakow to Krypton: Jews and Comic Books* (Philadelphia, PA: Jewish Publication Society, 2008), 159.

17 Mazur and Danner, *Comics: A Global History*.

3

STEPHEN WEINER

The Development of the American Graphic Novel

From Will Eisner to the Present

The "graphic novel," a complete story told in cartoon format, emerged, it seemed, fully grown in the United States' comic book and trade publishing world in the early 1970s. Over the next several decades and into the new millennium, the graphic novel format would attract traditional comic book as well as mainstream readers to stories told in cartoon format, inspire the film industry, and win prestigious literary awards.

The 1970s

One of the earliest American practitioners of the graphic novel format (and the one who popularized the term "graphic novel") was cartoonist Will Eisner, who pitched his semi-autobiographical cartoon short story collection, *A Contract with God and Other Tenement Stories*, to an editor at Bantam Publishing in 1975, telling the editor that he was holding a new literary form, a "graphic novel."[1] Eisner was tapping into an impulse in the American comics bloodstream that preceded his book by several decades. In the late 1920s and 1930s, picture book artist/writer Lynd Ward had created a series of "woodcut" (picture) novels, the most famous being *Gods' Man* in 1929. In 1950, Arnold Drake and Leslie Waller's illustrated mass-market paperback, *It Rhymes with Lust*, appeared, attempting to bring the comics medium to adult readers by telling a kind of comics film noir. In 1968, artist/writer Gil Kane self-published a book-length genre story, *His Name is...Savage*. Kane followed with a second book-length cartoon fantasy, *Blackmark*, in 1974 written by Archie Goodwin. Both of Kane's books were aimed at non-traditional comics readers. Other early graphic novel attempts included Walt Kelly's fantastic *Prehysterical Pogo (in Pandemonia)* (1967) and artist/writer Jim Steranko's 1976 publication, *Red Tide: A Chandler Novel*, an illustrated novel based on Raymond Chandler's *Red Tide*.

Eisner's vision of a "graphic novel" rose from his belief that comics could tell mature stories and from the impulse of the underground cartoonists, notably R. Crumb, who used comics to make personal and political statements as opposed to telling regurgitated genre tales. The first underground "graphic novel," Justin Green's *Binky Brown Meets the Holy Virgin Mary*, was a forty-four-page treatise appearing in 1972. In *Binky Brown* and the work of other underground cartoonists, Eisner saw the possibility of using the cartoon format to reach readers outside of comics. *A Contract with God and Other Tenement Stories* was eventually published in 1978 by Baronet Press and carried in bookstores, but it sold poorly. In 1979, Eisner's one-time protégé, Jules Feiffer, published *Tantrum*, a black-and-white splashy graphic novel about a man refusing to accept middle age, with trade publisher Alfred Knopf. Eisner eventually republished *A Contract with God* with comics publisher Kitchen Sink Press in 1985. In the years following *Contract with God* until his death in 2005, Eisner published over twenty stand-alone literary graphic novels, making him the single cartoonist in America most dedicated to the graphic novel form and the person most closely connected to it.

Despite Eisner's vision for the graphic novel form, with the exception of Feiffer's *Tantrum*, few "art" graphic novels emerged in the years following *A Contract with God*, although clever genre storytellers were quick to capitalize on the graphic novel form. Husband and wife creative team Richard and Wendy Pini produced the well-done fantasy series about elves called *ElfQuest*. *ElfQuest* issues were collected into books, each being a "graphic novel." Through shrewd marketing these books were carried in comic book specialty shops and in bookstores, a very unusual accomplishment at the time. *ElfQuest* had made it out of the comic book ghetto but it didn't tell the compelling adult story that Eisner had dreamed of. Marvel Comics followed suit with a line of graphic novels featuring stories of established heroes, some invoking slightly more mature themes. Other serialized books such as Dave Sim's *Cerebus the Aardvark* and Kevin Eastman and Peter Laird's *Teenage Mutant Ninja Turtles* (both initially parodies of action comics) thrived in the graphic novel format but did little to promote comics as an art form.

The 1980s

During the early 1980s the graphic novel format made significant headway within the alternative comics industry, an outgrowth of the underground comics. A segment of the comics readership had matured and responded positively to more mature stories. One such story was *Love and Rockets*, a self-published black-and-white magazine by brothers Mario, Jaime, and Gilbert Hernandez, which told stories of life in the Latino community. Set in the fictional town of Palomar, the characters loved and hated, drank and worked, and schemed and dreamed. First appearing in 1981, *Love and Rockets* was picked up by Fantagraphics Books. The book was special in part because the Brothers Hernandez told a kind of story unusual in comics: naturalistic, literary fiction. They brought punk aesthetic and ethics previously unheard of to comics. Also, the visual appearance of the stories was arresting as the brother-cartoonists had very different art styles: Gilbert's was slightly simple and Jaime's voluptuous and volatile.[2] *Love and Rockets* was also singular because the stark drawings mirrored the stark, economically deprived lives of the characters. This brought in new readers, particularly women. Still being published in the new millennium, *Love and Rockets* has proved to be one of the great ongoing bodies of work in the comics medium's history.

Another book critical to the blossoming graphic novel format within the alternative comics community was Harvey Pekar's *American Splendor*, depicting Pekar's mundane life as a file clerk. Illustrated by various artists, including R. Crumb, *American Splendor* attracted the attention of Doubleday Publishing, and an *American Splendor* collection was released in the mid-1980s.

Husband and wife Robert (R.) and Aline Kominsky-Crumb were vitally active at this time. Both had been around comics since the late 1960s, when R. Crumb created the underground comix sensation, *Zap Comix*, thus becoming one of the few superstars in comics. By the 1980s, the Crumbs were editing (and contributing to) the alternative comic *Weirdo*, recognized for its alternative sexual culture as well its outsider art. *Weirdo* also proved to be the launch pad for many alternative cartoonists.

It wasn't until 1986, however, with the publication of Art Spiegelman's *Maus: A Survivor's Tale*, that Eisner's two-part vision for the graphic novel format was realized. *Maus* used stark cartoons to tell a brutal adult story: the incarceration of Spiegelman's parents in German concentration camps, their subsequent arrival in America, and Spiegelman's mother's suicide. Originally appearing sequentially in Spiegelman's own magazine, *RAW*, *Maus* was collected and republished by Pantheon Books. Part of Spiegelman's impetus was to tell his parents' story and part was to help move the comics medium forward: Spiegelman felt that if comics were to survive, the form had to join the art world.[3] A couple of other adult-oriented genre graphic novels also made significant noise at the same time as *Maus*: Frank Miller's *Batman: The Dark Knight Returns* and Alan Moore and Dave Gibbons' *Watchmen*, both politically charged superhero reinventions espousing vigilante justice.[4] Both superhero graphic novels were published by DC Comics. All three books appeared in 1986, and the recognition they received went outside the traditional comic book readership. The graphic novel format was on its way.

The comics industry began to recognize its own achievements as well and the "Will Eisner Comic Industry Awards" were created in 1988, acknowledging excellence in a variety of aspects of comic book creation and culture. These awards were given out annually at a convention in San Diego known as the San Diego Comicon.

In the wake of *Maus, Watchmen, and Batman: The Dark Knight Returns*, mainstream and alternative comics publishers sought the attention of new readers, and played with storylines and presentation formats that they hoped would reach the readers of *Watchmen, Dark Knight,* and *Maus.* Not all these efforts were successful, but even if these new approaches made only a small impact on the general readership, they affected the publishing industry, because the success of *Maus* had been noticed. Sporadic reviews of "graphic novels" popped up in industry journals, in part because prior to the creation of the graphic novel format there was no reviewable comics publishing format.

The entertainment industry noticed the changing role of comics as well. The first group of *Batman* films, beginning in 1989, attempted to capture the dark moodiness of Frank Miller's *Batman: The Dark Knight Returns.* These films paved the way for the crashing wave of superhero films that followed a decade or so later.

The 1990s

The 1990s brought important changes to the comics industry, many spurred by the new graphic novel format. Small publishers targeted older readers with more mature stories told in comics form. One example was *Kings in Disguise*, a Depression-era story with Huck Finn overtones written by James Vance and illustrated in black-and-white stark tones by Dan Burr. Brought out first as a "limited series" (finite as opposed to ongoing) and then collected into a graphic novel by Kitchen Sink Press in 1990, the book was awarded an Eisner for best new series. *Kings* was also positively reviewed by the trade book publication *Publishers Weekly.* The graphic novel form allowed trade publications access into the comics industry where the periodical format had not. The early 1990s brought increased recognition for the graphic novel format as well: Art Spiegelman had completed a second memoir entitled *Maus II: A Survivor's Tale: And Here My Troubles Began* in 1992. Spiegelman was awarded a Pulitzer Prize that same year for *Maus.* The book eventually became so well respected that it became a staple of many high school and university classrooms.

New comic book publishers sprang up in response to the changing industry. Dark Horse Comics, formed in the mid-1980s, lured top mainstream creators such as Frank Miller and John Byrne through their doors in an effort to challenge "mainstream" companies Marvel and DC Comics. Dark Horse promised more creative freedom and royalties on books where the major companies didn't, as well as offering incentives such as more frequent royalty checks. Dark Horse varied their product from hero stories such as John Byrne's colorful *Next Men* to Frank Miller's dark detective series *Sin City*, to comic book versions of successful movies such as *Star Wars*. Perhaps the most successful of the Dark Horse books was Mike Mignola's moody, back-door graphic novels series featuring the hero-devil Hellboy. What made *Hellboy* so appealing was the world Mignola created and the main character. A devil determined to be good, Hellboy had the wise guy character of Dashiell Hammett's Sam Spade and the tired punch of the Hulk. The fantasy world he inhabited was populated by characters familiar from folktales such as Baba Yaga and King Arthur. The writing was sparse and the subtly colored illustrations evocative rather than overwhelming. *Hellboy* proved so popular that it became a mini franchise, branching out into a series of ancillary comic books and graphic novels as well as prose novels and feature films.

Another new company formed in the early 1990s was Image, which was created by a group of highly successful cartoonists because they wanted to create new characters and retain ownership of their creations. Both Marvel and DC Comics did not allow ownership. Image focused initially on presenting a new line of heroes, vying for the audience of Marvel and DC Comics. Over time the company expanded into art graphic novels as well.

The comics industry was changing, riding in part on the promise of the graphic novel. Because comics were sold through comic book specialty shops, with a repeating clientele, it was possible to appeal directly to specific kinds of readers. As a result, micro-publishers sprang up: very small companies such as Kitchen Sink Press or even smaller, self-publishing companies, started by the cartoonists themselves to publish and promote their own work. Two of the most successful of the self-publishing companies were Cartoon Books and Abstract Studios. In 1993, Abstract Studios produced Terry Moore's ongoing periodical *Strangers in Paradise*, initially about a love triangle between Francine, David, and Katchoo, involving gay and heterosexual themes. To thicken the plot, Moore threw in a murder mystery and made one of the central characters a fugitive. *Strangers in Paradise* was produced in black and white, and the magazine was often text heavy and complemented by uncluttered, clear illustrations. Moore creatively integrated song lyrics into the text and, in few instances, used photography. The periodicals were then collected into a series of graphic novels, each with its own point of departure and its own resolution, so it was possible to read one *Strangers in Paradise* graphic novel without reading others. The series ran from 1993 to

Fig. 3.1 Cartoonist Terry Moore experimented with minimalist imagery for an early graphic
novel cover, *Strangers in Paradise*. By permission of Abstract Studios.

2007, and was collected in several graphic novel formats over the fourteen-year period (fig. 3.1).

Bone, written and drawn by Jeff Smith, was another self-published black-and-white periodical, proving even more successful than *Strangers in Paradise*. Beginning in 1991, *Bone* told the story of three slapstick Bone cousins, one goofy, one well-intentioned, and one scheming but loyal. On the run, the three cousins land in a pre-technological fantasy world with a war about to erupt. Smith was a master cartoonist and effortlessly moved back and forth from drama to humor, sometimes in the same panel. Produced bi-monthly, the first story arc was republished as a graphic novel, *Out from Boneville*, in 1993, selling fifty thousand copies in eighteen months.[5] Prior to this, there had been some doubt as to the viability of the graphic novel as a commercial enterprise. A large part of the revenue generated within the comics industry was fueled by the collectible market, making out-of-print comic book issues, resold at high prices. A "graphic novel," which kept older issues in print and at an affordable price, threatened that aspect of comics' revenue. However the sales of the first *Bone* graphic novel, *Out from Boneville*, produced by a tiny company, was a powerful demonstration of the emerging graphic novel format. *Bone* became one of the most celebrated comic book series, winning forty-one awards for a storyline running fifty-five issues long. The entire story was collected into nine graphic novels. After the story was completed in 2004, the nine graphic novels were collected into one volume running more than 1,300 pages, creating another graphic novel format, the "omnibus." While compiling the omnibus, Smith corrected inconsistences that had appeared in the course of producing the *Bone* issues and graphic novels.

The combined momentum of *Bone* and *Strangers in Paradise* began a "self-publishing movement" which branched out beyond the two graphic novel series. Many self-publishers banded together and toured comic book specialty shops, in part to promote their individual comics and graphic novels, and in part to convince comic book specialty store owners to embrace the graphic novel format. These efforts positively promoted that format.

Will Eisner remained a vital force in the industry, publishing one completely fictional or semi-autobiographical graphic novel every year-and-a-half to two years throughout the decade. The 1990s were a particularly productive time for Eisner even though he was in his late seventies, as he published six fictional graphic novels, most of them in part autobiographical.

The term "graphic novel" did not confine itself to fictional works. A "graphic novel" had come to mean any book-length text in cartoon form. In fact, many of the best recognized graphic novels were non-fiction works, Art

Spiegelman's *Maus* serving as the most famous example, but there were several others as well. One very important non-fiction graphic novel was Scott McCloud's *Understanding Comics*, published in 1993 by Kitchen Sink Press. Part discussion of how comics and cartoons work, partly exploring the links between cartooning and other art forms, and partly a rumination on the nature of art, *Understanding Comics* burst onto the comics readership as an "original" graphic novel, meaning it hadn't been serialized prior to its publication in book form. Presented in black and white, with a cheeky cartoon version of Scott McCloud himself narrating, *Understanding Comics* became a sensation, selling ten thousand copies in the first month. Trade publisher HarperCollins successfully distributed the book to the general readership, demonstrating that a fruitful relationship could be formed when trade publishers selectively partnered with the comic book/graphic novel industry.

One especially important comic book series that became a series of graphic novels as well was Neil Gaiman's *Sandman*, published by DC Comics from 1988 to 1996. Writer Gaiman reimagined Sandman, a hero originally appearing in the 1940s, who used sleep gas to subdue criminals. In Gaiman's reimagining, Sandman's name was Dream (also known as Morpheus and Oneiros), and was a god-like force that ruled the dream world. Dream had six siblings that ruled transitional states as well such as Death, Destruction, Desire, and so on. Because the Dream characters were older than time, all human history was fair game in *Sandman*, and characters such as William Shakespeare and Marco Polo had repeating roles.

Gaiman was a very literate comic book writer, and classical and fantasy references and influences could be felt in his storylines. He was also able to ascertain the particular skills of each artist he worked with and wrote stories to specifically utilize the talents of each of his collaborators. One result of this practice was that each story arc in the *Sandman* series was highly individualistic. Winning multiple Eisner awards, *Sandman* ran for eight years – a total of seventy-five issues. These issues were collected into ten graphic novels. When Gaiman chose to leave *Sandman*, DC Comics made the unprecedented decision to cancel the immensely popular series rather than have it continue with another writer at the helm, a policy unheard of at the time.

Mainstream comics publishers Marvel and DC Comics were changing in other ways as well. They more actively supported the graphic novel format than they had previously, by making greater efforts to collect completed story arcs of ongoing heroes into several graphic novel series. The two companies also experimented, presenting more mature stories featuring those same popular characters in graphic novels aimed at more mature readers, in an attempt to capture a piece of the *Sandman* audience.

New developments were riding on the back of the graphic novel format. One significant change was the way graphic novels were sold from comic book distributors to comic book stores. Trade publishers allowed book-stores to return unsold books, but comic book distributors, when selling to comic book specialty shops, did not. This made comic book retailers some-what reluctant to invest in the graphic novel as it was a new format, and the books were non-returnable at first. However in 1996, DC Comics changed their policy, making graphic novels returnable. Now retailers felt free to sell graphic novels. This change on the part of a major comics publisher indi-cated that the collectible market, a focal point of the comics industry, was weakening, and that the graphic novel format was the direction in which the industry was headed.

These changes within the comic book industry triggered changes outside of it. Public libraries, which had limited themselves to comic strip collections such as Charles Schulz's *Peanuts* and Hergé's *Tintin* books in the past, wel-comed works such as *Maus*, *Watchmen*, *Understanding Comics*, and *Bone* into their collections. Where the periodical format had proved too challeng-ing, the graphic novel form made it possible for public libraries to place these books on their shelves. The new format also allowed librarians to see that comics could be about more than superhero slugfests and funny animal stories.

Public library graphic novel collections in the 1990s were primarily inte-grated into the Young Adult collection, because of the stigma that comic books, and by extension, graphic novels, were only for children and teenage boys. The fact was that by the mid-1990s, the average customer in a comic book specialty shop was in his mid-twenties or older. Librarians may have been catching up with changes in terms of graphic novel content, but their understanding of the changing face of the graphic novel readership came years later.

In order for librarians to collect graphic novels, these books had to be reviewed by publications used for collection development purposes. *Pub-lishers Weekly* had been reviewing selected graphic novels as early as 1989, but in the 1990s, collection development magazines aimed specifically at librarians, such as *Voice of Youth Advocates*, *Library Journal*, and *Book-list*, began including graphic novel reviews in their columns. These reviews advertised the ways that some graphic novels were changing the content of comic book storytelling. Just as positive reviews advertised graphic novels to librarians, the inclusion of graphic novels in public library collections adver-tised the changing comics field to the wider culture, giving graphic novels a new respectability.

The media played a part as well. Since the splash made by the triumvirate of *Maus*, *Watchmen*, and *Batman: The Dark Knight Returns* had garnered attention in 1986–87, occasional articles on the changing face of the comics industry appeared in publications as diverse as *Time*, *Rolling Stone*, and *The New York Times Book Review*. Many of the articles were written by cartoonists themselves, especially Will Eisner, hoping to gain respectability for the graphic novel form.

New respectability was the buzzword as the 1990s turned toward the new millennium. Fantagraphics Books scored a big hit with Dan Clowes' book *Ghost World* (1997), which told the story of Josh, Enid, and Becky as their high school years closed. First appearing as a serialized story, and illustrated in soft colors, *Ghost World* exuded a delicious wistfulness as well as a lost adolescent quality, as the questions the book asked were as big as the future in store for the young protagonists. *Ghost World* became a cult classic and was reimagined as an art film in 2001.

Comics and graphic novels were having an impact on a few prose novelists as well. Serious use of comics mythology had been explored as early as 1977, when Robert Mayer published *Superfolks*, an examination of superhero conventions and clichés. Jay Cantor creatively used the newspaper cartoon in his "novel in five panels," *Krazy Kat*, in 1988, but neither of these books had the weight of Michael Chabon's novel, *The Amazing Adventures of Kavalier and Clay*, depicting immigrant cartoonists during the early days of the comic book industry. Chabon's novel won the Pulitzer Prize for Fiction in 2001, as well as being a PEN/Faulkner Award for Fiction and a National Book Critics Circle Award finalist in 2000, and brought a literary sheen to the graphic novel front.

2000–2010

As the new century turned, American graphic novel expansion continued. Chris Ware's book, *Jimmy Corrigan: The Smartest Kid on Earth*, a tale of present-day middle-aged Jimmy's first meeting with his father, as well as a parallel story featuring Jimmy's grandfather suffering under his abusive father set against the backdrop of the 1893 World's Fair, was an enormous critical and commercial success. Ware had been awarded multiple Eisner and Harvey awards previously (the "Harvey" Award was named in honor of Harvey Kurtzman, the creative force behind *Mad* magazine) but it was a surprise when *Jimmy Corrigan* was awarded the *Guardian*'s First Book Award in 2001, the first time a graphic novel won a major prize in the United Kingdom outside the comics industry. Ware's bleak story wasn't new, but his presentation was: the drawings moved inward, giving the reader a claustrophobic feeling which echoed the emotional state of the protagonist. The panels themselves were organized in such a way as to purposely disorient the reader, making him or her cast off assumptions about storytelling itself. The award cemented Ware's reputation and put him on the path to international stardom.

Another development was the introduction of the international graphic novel market to American readers. Marjane Satrapi's black-and-white, picture bookish, two-volume graphic novel *Persepolis* (a semi-autobiographical tale of growing up under the Shah and the Islamic Revolution in Iran) became a bestseller and opened the door; but more generally, there was a foreign invasion afoot: French graphic novels such as Satrapi's little masterpiece and David B.'s autobiographical *Epileptic*, thrilled American readers, and manga, or Japanese comics, were making a big impact on American readers and on the work of American creators such as Bryan O'Malley (*Scott Pilgrim*). America had joined the international graphic novel community.

The march toward respectability continued. YALSA, the young adult division of the American Library Association, sponsored a day-long graphic novel symposium in 2002. Guest speakers included writer Neil Gaiman and cartoonists Art Spiegelman, Jeff Smith, and Colleen Doran. Librarians also presented at the conference, discussing issues that both hindered and aided graphic novel collection development. The Public Library Association conference, also held in 2002, featured a graphic novel program as well. Both were well attended and were covered by the media. Sensing a change, booksellers began studying how to best integrate graphic novels into their trade book collections. In October 2002, a meeting attended by booksellers, trade publishers, and comic book publishers was held in New York City to discuss ways to best utilize graphic novels in bookstores. The keynote speakers were Art Spiegelman and Jules Feiffer. In addition, book vendors sponsored panels consisting of librarians to learn better ways to distribute graphic novels to bookstores and public libraries.

The combined effect of these programs sent a message to the American publishing community: in the same way that librarians had engaged with graphic novels, the trade readership might also engage. This inspired several trade publishing houses to start their own graphic novel imprints. Prior to this the only consistent graphic novel trade imprint was the line at Pantheon Books, which had brought out *Maus*.

Graphic novels were now a hot commodity, infusing new energy into a publishing industry struggling with the changing methods of book delivery and a reading public clamoring for something new. One advantage the graphic novel had in this environment was that it was particularly important to hold the physical graphic novel as opposed to reading it electronically.

Most graphic novels released through trade publishers had experienced prior success within the comic book industry, such as *Maus* and *Understanding Comics*, so relatively few new graphic novels were published by trade publishing houses at this time. In addition, comics publishers, sensing a wider audience, made attempts to reach readers outside of the comic book industry with a broader range of graphic novels often employing a more accessible artistic style.

Another force moving the graphic novel into the cultural forefront was the movie industry. Sporadically offering superhero films and television programs as early as the 1940s, with efforts primarily focused on heroes from the DC universe, the film industry now broadened its approach. With the success of Marvel Comics' *X-Men* (2000), Marvel's film division began, creating *X-Men* sequels as well as films featuring other Marvel heroes. *Spider-Man* (2002) grossed close to a billion dollars worldwide, and cemented the superhero film as a cornerstone of the film industry. Over the next decade, superhero feature films were released on an average of one every sixty days. The new film genre was strong enough also to produce film adaptations of art comics such as Kevin Smith's feature film, *Chasing Amy* (1997), which focused on co-creators of a successful alternative comic book; Harvey Pekar's *American Splendor* (2003); and Dan Clowes' *Art School Confidential* (2006); as well as parodies such as *My Super Ex-Girlfriend* (2006).

The graphic novel industry continued to bask in its growing respectability. In 2003, Top Shelf, a small art comics publisher, brought out Craig Thompson's *Blankets*, a 600-page black-and-white semi-autobiographical graphic novel centered on growing up in an Evangelical Christian household. The book recounted Thompson's childhood, his first love, and his early adult years. The serious tone of *Blankets* contrasted nicely with Thompson's earlier work, the short, playful *Good-bye, Chunky Rice* (1999) featuring a turtle and a mouse. *Chunky Rice* received a Harvey Award for best new talent, but *Blankets* received eight prizes within the comics industry, including multiple Harvey and Eisner awards in 2004, as well as ranking number one on *Time*'s graphic novel list. This momentum pushed *Blankets* out of the comic book field and into bookstores, and it eventually received international recognition. *Blankets* was one more example of how graphic autobiographical stories such as *Maus* and *Persepolis* fascinated trade book readers.

By this time the media had latched firmly onto graphic novels and information about them seemed to be everywhere: serious reviews and articles about graphic novels appeared in publications ranging from *Time* to *Rolling Stone* to *The New York Times* to the *English Journal*.

The interest in graphic novels expanded to an appreciation of comic strips as well. In 2004, Fantagraphics Books began releasing the entirety of Charles

Schulz's *Peanuts* chronologically in a hardbound collectible graphic novel format, with each volume covering roughly two years of the newspaper strip. The series was a tremendous success, landing on *The New York Times* bestseller list.

In 2005, Scholastic launched its own graphic novel imprint, Graphix, and the first effort was to republish Jeff Smith's cartoony epic *Bone*, which had concluded in 2004. Originally *Bone* was aimed at the adults who frequented comic book shops, but Scholastic refocused *Bone* as a children's book. To do this *Bone* was colored and released as a 6″ × 9″ (15.2 × 22.9 cm) standard book size, rather than the original black-and-white 7″ × 10″ (17.8 × 25.4 cm) format, and sold through school book fairs as well as bookstores. Each of the nine books of *Bone* was released at six-month intervals. *Bone* became a phenomenon and was used in classrooms as well as becoming a bookstore bestseller. The success of *Bone* and the books that followed in the Graphix line empowered other publishers to create their own lines of children's graphic novels.

Cartoonist Charles Burns' *Black Hole*, distributed by Pantheon Books, was another significant step for the American graphic novel. Originally published by Kitchen Sink Press and Fantagraphics Books serially from 1995 to 2005, *Black Hole*'s success within the comic book industry forced it out of that industry, and a hardcover edition was distributed by Pantheon Books in 2005. A metaphor for sexual awakening and adolescence, *Black Hole* was illustrated in menacing, meticulous, black-and-white drawings, and told the story of 1970s-era teens in Seattle who contracted a mysterious disease called "the bug," which caused physical deformities, making them into social outcasts.

Alison Bechdel's *Fun Home: A Family Tragicomic* was released by Houghton Mifflin in 2006, without prior publication within the comics industry. Bechdel was best known for her ongoing comic strip, *Dykes to Watch Out For*. Autobiographical in tone, *Fun Home* depicted Bechdel's attempts to untangle her childhood, come to terms with her own lesbianism, and learn whether or not her remote father, who may have committed suicide, was gay. One important contribution the book made was bringing gay and lesbian issues to the forefront using the comics format. As a result, *Fun Home* was lauded and landed on many of the year's "Best" lists and was a finalist for the 2006 National Book Critics Circle Award, in the Autobiography/Memoir category. In 2007, *Fun Home* won the GLAAD Media Award for Outstanding Comic Book, the Stonewall Book Award for non-fiction, the Publishing Triangle–Judy Grahn Nonfiction Award, and the Lambda Literary Award in the Lesbian Memoir and Biography category. *Fun Home* was nominated for the 2007 Eisner Awards in two categories, Best

Reality-Based Work and Best Graphic Album, and won the Best Reality-Based Work award.

The support for literary graphic novels brought out important new works that expanded the range of material over the next several years. Chinese-American cartoonist Gene Yang produced *American Born Chinese*, which was published by First Second in 2006 without prior serialization. Drawn with a cartoony simplicity, the book told parallel stories: the Chinese legend of the Monkey King and two stories of Chinese Americans. *American Born Chinese* was another sophisticated, well-executed graphic novel detailing a story Americans hadn't really heard before. Like *Black Hole* and *Bone*, *American Born Chinese* was also noteworthy because it was not autobiographical. It was very well received and won the Printz Award offered by the American Library Association. Other important books published exclusively by trade publishers in the years to follow included picture book writer/illustrator David Small's *Stitches* (2009) a memoir about his childhood bout with cancer which left him mute and led to his running away from home at sixteen, hoping to become an artist; and R. Crumb's opus, *The Book of Genesis* (2009) a faithful adaptation of the Book of Genesis, noted in part for its racy sexuality, and drawn in Crumb's traditional cross-hatching style. The book reached number one on *The New York Times* Graphic Novels Bestseller List and was awarded Harvey and Eisner awards, and was published by the respected academic trade house W. W. Norton & Company.

2010–2015

One exceptional graphic novel brought out by trade publisher Gotham Books in 2012 was cartoonist Ellen Forney's black-and-white, strangely accessible memoir, *Marbles, Mania, Depression, Michelangelo, and Me: A Graphic Memoir*. *Marbles* recounted Forney's diagnosis of bipolar disorder at the age of thirty, and her years-long struggle to gain mental stability while remaining vitally creative. In doing so, Forney studied the work and lives of artists such as Sylvia Plath and Georgia O'Keefe, whom she believed to have bipolar disorder, all the while trying to answer the question of whether or not bipolar disorder was a necessary ingredient of creativity. The result was an examination of creativity itself and of the myth of the crazy artist. *Marbles* received positive notices from National Public Radio, *Time*, was named a "Best Graphic Novel" by *The Washington Post*, and was winner of the National Association for the Advancement of Psychoanalysis 2013 Gradiva Award, indicating the wide reach of the expanding graphic novel form (fig. 3.2).

Fig. 3.2 Cartoonist Ellen Forney conveys a conflicted mind through a myriad of words and a single illustration. Page 22 from *Marbles, Mania, Depression, Michelangelo, and Me: A Graphic Memoir* (2012). By permission of Gotham Books.

It had taken almost forty years, but the graphic novel, the long cartoon form that Will Eisner had placed so much faith in, had arrived: graphic novels were now rooted in the American fabric, influencing other branches of the entertainment industry, winning prestigious awards that had been previously denied them, and showing up in public libraries and classrooms both at the public school and university level. Graphic novels covering a broad range of topics were being released from an ever-expanding publishing base, reaching out of the specialized comic book readership and into the heart of American culture.

Works Cited

Bechdel, Alison. *Fun Home: A Family Tragicomic.* New York: Mariner Books Reprint Edition, 2007.

B.[eauchard], David. *Epileptic (L'Ascension du Haut Mal, 1996–2004).* Trans. Kim Thompson. New York: Pantheon Books, 2005.

Burns, Charles. *Black Hole.* New York: Pantheon Books, 2005.

Byrne, John. *Next Men.* Vol. 1. San Diego, CA: IDW Publishing, 2011.

Cantor, Jay. *Krazy Kat.* New York: Vintage, 2004.

Clowes, Dan. *Ghost World.* Seattle, WA: Fantagraphics Books, 2001.

Crumb, Robert. *The Book of Genesis Illustrated by R. Crumb.* New York: W. W. Norton, 2009.

Zap Comix No. 0. Chicago, IL: Apex Novelty, 1967.

Drake, Arnold, and Leslie Waller. *It Rhymes with Lust*. Milwaukie, OR: Dark Horse Reprint Edition, 2007.

Eastman, Kevin, and Peter Laird. *Teenage Mutant Ninja Turtles: The Ultimate Collection*, Vol. 1. San Diego, CA: IDW Publishing, 2012.

Eisner, Will. *A Contract with God and Other Tenement Stories*. Racine, WI: Kitchen Sink Press, 1985.

Feiffer, Jules. *Tantrum!* Seattle, WA: Fantagraphics Books, 1997.

Forney, Ellen. *Marbles: Mania, Depression, Michelangelo, and Me: A Graphic Memoir*. New York: Gotham Books, 2012.

Gaiman, Neil, et al. *The Sandman: Preludes and Nocturnes*. New York: DC Comics, 1993.

Green, Justin. *Binky Brown Meets the Holy Virgin Mary*. San Francisco, CA: McSweeney's, 2009.

Hernandez, Jaime, and Gilbert Hernandez. *Love and Rockets*, Vol. 1: *Music for Mechanics*. Seattle, WA: Fantagraphics Books, 1995.

Kane, Gil. *Blackmark*. Seattle, WA: Fantagraphics Books, 2002.

 Gil Kane's Savage! Seattle, WA: Fantagraphics Books, 1982.

Kelly, Walt. *Prehysterical Pogo (in Pandemonia)*. New York: Simon and Schuster, 1967.

Mayer, Robert. *Superfolks*. New York: St. Martins, Griffin Reprint Edition, 2005.

McCloud, Scott. *Understanding Comics: The Invisible Art*. New York: Harper Perennial, 1994.

Mignola, Mike, and John Byrne. *Hellboy*, Vol. 1: *Seed of Destruction*. Milwaukie, OR: Dark Horse Books, 2004.

Miller, Frank. *Batman: The Dark Knight Returns*. New York: DC Comics, 1997.

 Sin City, Vol. 1: *The Hard Goodbye*. Milwaukie, OR: Dark Horse Books, 2010.

Moore, Alan, and Dave Gibbons. *Watchmen*. New York: DC Comics, 2014.

Moore, Terry. *Strangers in Paradise*, Vol. 2. Austin, TX: Abstract Studios, 1999.

Pekar, Harvey, and Kevin Brown. *American Splendor and More American Splendor: The Life and Times of Harvey Pekar*. New York: Ballantine Books, 2003.

Pini, Wendy, and Richard Pini. *The Complete ElfQuest*, Vol. 1. Milwaukie, OR: Dark Horse Books, 2014.

Sabin, Roger. *Comics, Comix, and Graphic Novels: A History of Comic Art*. London: Phaidon, 1996.

Satrapi, Marjane. *The Complete Persepolis*. New York: Pantheon Books, 2003.

Schumacher, Michael. *Will Eisner: A Dreamer's Life in Comics*. New York: Bloomsbury, 2010.

Sim, Dave. *Cerebus*, Vol. 1. Ontario: Aardvark-Vanaheim, 1991.

Small, David. *Stitches: A Memoir*. New York: W. W. Norton, 2009.

Smith, Jeff. *Bone: The Complete Cartoon Epic in One Volume*. Columbus, OH: Cartoon Books, 2004.

Spiegelman, Art. *Maus I: A Survivor's Tale: My Father Bleeds History*. New York: Pantheon Books, 1986.

 Maus II: A Survivor's Tale: And Here My Troubles Began. New York: Pantheon Books, 1992.

 MetaMaus. New York: Pantheon Books, 2011.

Steranko, Jim. *Red Tide: A Chandler Novel*. New York: Pyramid, 1976.

Thompson, Craig. *Blankets*. Atlanta, GA: Top Shelf Productions, 2003.

Vance, James, and Dan Burr. *Kings in Disguise*. Racine, WI: Kitchen Sink Press, 1990.

Ward, Lynd. *Gods' Man: A Novel in Woodcuts*. New York: Dover, 2004.

Ware, Chris. *Jimmy Corrigan: The Smartest Kid on Earth*. New York: Pantheon Books, 2003.

Weiner, Stephen. *Faster than a Speeding Bullet: The Rise of the Graphic Novel*. New York: NBM, 2012.

Wright, Bradford W. *Comic Book Nation: The Transformation of Youth Culture in America*. Baltimore, MD: Johns Hopkins University Press, 2001.

Yang, Gene Luen. *American Born Chinese*. New York: First Second, 2006

NOTES

1 Michael Schumacher, *Will Eisner: A Dreamer's Life in Comics* (New York: Bloomsbury, 2010), 200.

2 Roger Sabin, *Comics, Comix, and Graphic Novels: A History of Comic Art* (London: Phaidon, 1996), 204.

3 Art Spiegelman, *MetaMaus* (New York: Pantheon Books, 2011), 203.

4 Bradford W. Wright, *Comic Book Nation: The Transformation of Youth Culture in America* (Baltimore, MD: Johns Hopkins University Press, 2001), 273.

5 Stephen Weiner, *Faster than a Speeding Bullet: The Rise of the Graphic Novel* (New York: NBM, 2012), 45.

4

DAN MAZUR AND ALEXANDER DANNER

The International Graphic Novel

The "international graphic novel" is perhaps a redundant concept, as the graphic novel is, and has largely always been, an international form, boasting rich international cross-pollination. As we will show, the concept of the graphic novel goes back to the very earliest days of comics publishing. It may make sense to speak broadly, in the context of English-language comics, of an evolution from comics to graphic novels; in a European or Japanese context, however, such a linear progression is clearly more difficult to claim.

The European and Latin American Graphic Novel, from Töpffer to L'Association

Seeking "firsts" in comics history is a questionable pursuit, but there is no doubt that the work of Rodolphe Töpffer in the early nineteenth century marked a major development in the history of comics as a whole, and of the graphic novel as format and concept. Töpffer, a Swiss writer, painter, and schoolmaster based in Geneva, drew sequential, satirical stories, initially for the amusement of his students; he published the first of these, *Histoire de Monsieur Jabot* (1833), at a little over fifty pages, in a horizontal format. To describe this apparently new form of expression, Töpffer used the term "littérature en estampes" ("literature in prints," anticipating the term "graphic novel").[1] His comics featured most of the recognizable formal elements of the medium, with the exception of speech bubbles (text in Töpffer's work is generally limited to hand-written passages below each image).

Through the 1840s, Töpffer completed seven *histoires en estampes*, ranging in length from fifty-two to ninety-two pages. With dry wit and slapstick humor, Töpffer satirized such contemporary follies as social climbing (*Histoire de Monsieur Jabot*), bourgeois pedagogical trends (*Histoire de Monsieur Crépin*, 1837), romantic infatuations (*Les Amours de Monsieur Vieux Bois*, 1837), scientific ineptitude, and political hysterias (*Monsieur Pencil*,

58

1840). His books were republished in pirated editions, and widely read throughout Europe and the United States.

For the rest of the century, artists experimented with the "novel in prints." Among the best known are Gustave Doré and Cham (Amédée de Noé) in France, Wilhelm Busch in Germany, Fritz von Dardel in Sweden, and George Cruikshank in England. The most ambitious vision for the young art form was probably that of the French Caran d'Ache (Emmanuel Poiré), who in 1894 embarked on a completely wordless graphic novel, *Maestro*. Intended to comprise 360 pages, the work remained unpublished until a partial version was discovered and released by the French Centre National de la Bande Dessinée et de l'Image in 1999 (fig. 4.1).

Unlike these nineteenth-century examples, European comics in the first six decades of the twentieth century were aimed almost exclusively at children, and confined to periodical publishing. In the post-war period, Franco-Belgian comics were dominant, under the influence of the two major stylistic "schools:" l'école de Bruxelles, which featured the clear-line style made popular by Hergé, Edgar P. Jacobs, and others in *Le Journal de Tintin*, and the more elastic and rounded cartooning style seen in l'école de Marcinelle (also referred to as l'école de Charleroi), typified by artists such as Jijé and André Franquin in the journal *Spirou*. The republication of the most popular series in hardcover albums became an increasingly common practice.

Among South American countries, Argentina had perhaps the richest tradition of comics and cartooning during the first half of the twentieth century; the Second World War and its aftermath brought in an influx of talent from Italy, a group of young artists and writers that included Hugo Pratt, contributing to a widely acknowledged "golden age" of Argentinian comics, or *historieta*. The towering creative figure of these decades was writer Héctor Germán Oesterheld. Working with artists like Pratt, Francisco Solano López, and Alberto Breccia, Oesterheld brought a sense of maturity, humanism, and moral depth to the medium. Though he worked in conventional adventure genres such as westerns (*Sergeant Kirk*, 1953–56) and war (*Ernie Pike*, from 1957), Oesterheld avoided simplistic good versus evil plotting. With Solano López drawing, Oesterheld created one of the most famous of all Argentinian comics, the science fiction epic *El Eternauta*. Originally serialized in the journal *Hora Cero* from 1957 to 1959, *El Eternauta* follows a small band of men from all walks of life as they resist an overwhelming alien invasion in Buenos Aires. While fulfilling the requirements of the sci-fi action genre, *El Eternauta* focuses on the inner lives of its characters and on serious themes raised by the invasion. *El Eternauta* has become a true icon of Argentinian comics; in 2010, the anniversary of its initial publication was chosen as a national holiday celebrating the medium.

Fig. 4.1 Caran d'Ache (Emmanuel Poiré) (1858–1909) *Maestro*, 1894. A proposed 360-page wordless graphic novel about a musical prodigy by the great 19th-century French cartoonist Caran d'Ache, *Maestro*, had it been completed, might very well have been a landmark in comics history. Instead, the project was known of only through an 1894 letter by the artist, pitching the book to the newspaper *Le Figaro*. That he had actually drawn at least 100 pages of *Maestro* remained unknown until 1999, when the originals were discovered in a private collection and purchased by the Centre National de la Bande Dessineé et de l'Image in Angoulême, France.

An adult sensibility in European comics began to emerge in the early 1960s. In 1964, French publisher Eric Losfeld began publishing graphic novels for adult readers, which included the erotically tinged science fiction adventure *Barbarella* (1964) by Jean-Claude Forest, and Belgian Guy Peellaerts' *Les Aventures de Jodelle* (1966). In 1965, the Italian Guido Crepax began his series of stories featuring the character Valentina, initially introduced in the journal *Linus*. Like his Franco-Belgian contemporaries, Crepax combined eroticism and sophisticated storytelling, adapting the fragmented editing techniques of New Wave Cinema.

Hugo Pratt, back in Italy after his sojourn in Latin America, continued in the mode of his work with Oesterheld with *Una Ballata del Mare Salato* (*Ballad of the Salt Sea*, 1967), a South Seas adventure that introduced the globe-trotting mercenary Corto Maltese. First serialized in the magazine *Sergeant Kirk*, *Una Ballata del Mare Salato* reached 250 pages when published in book form. Pratt's work, though action-packed, generally emphasized morally ambiguous characters and situations.

Another Italian artist, Guido Buzzelli, had been primarily an illustrator of westerns for publishers in Italy and England, before turning toward a career as a serious painter in the early sixties. Dissatisfied with his ability to impart narrative and thematic ideas on his canvases, Buzzelli decided to employ the medium of comics for purely personal, expressive purposes. His forty-six-page science fiction/political allegory *La Revolta dei Racchi* (*The Revolt of the Ugly*), was completed in 1967. Eventually published in an Italian science fiction magazine, it was discovered there by Georges Wolinski, editor of the French comics journal *Charlie*. Wolinski published it in 1970, and continued with Buzzelli's subsequent graphic novels including *I Labirinti (Labyrinths)* (1970) and *Zil Zelub* (1972).

As the 1970s progressed, exposure to American underground comix encouraged European cartoonists and independent publishers to seek similar creative freedom by launching their own magazines; important examples include the French *L'Écho des Savanes*, started by Claire Bretécher, Nikita Mandryka, and Gotlib; *Métal Hurlant*, which showcased work by Moebius (Jean Giraud), Philippe Druillet, Chantal Montellier, and Nicole Claveloux among many others; and the feminist comics journal *Ah! Nana*. Dutch artists Joost Swarte and Evert Geradts created their own underground movement with *Tante Leny* and *Modern Papier*, while Spain, emerging from Franco-era repression, had *El Rrollo Enmascarado*, *Star*, and *Bésame Mucho*. Not all innovations came in periodicals; the independent French publisher Futuropolis broke with common *bande dessinée* custom by publishing comics in a variety of formats. Their 1974 large-format (30 x 40 cm) release of Jacques Tardi's dark, hallucinatory *La Véritable Histoire du Soldat Inconnu* (*The*

True Story of the Unknown Soldier), was a major statement for both artist and publisher.

Before long, the venerable Franco-Belgian publisher Casterman recognized the potential market for long-form *bande dessinée adulte*, in part thanks to the company's success with the 1975 French translation of Pratt's *Una Ballata del Mare Salato*. Casterman innovated further with the journal (*A Suivre*) (*To Be Continued*), which began publication in 1978. (*A Suivre*) was explicitly dedicated to long-form comics narrative aimed at a literate adult readership. Shortly before the phrase "graphic novel" would begin to be popularized in the United States by Will Eisner, Jean-Paul Mougin declared in an early editorial that the magazine's serialized stories should be considered "true comics novels [*romans en bande dessinée*], divided into chapters."[2] (*A Suivre*) introduced many important graphic novels of the late seventies and eighties, including major works by Tardi (*Ici Même, C'était la Guerre des Tranchées*) and a number of Hugo Pratt's Corto Maltese stories. The team of Benoît Peeters and François Schuiten contributed several of their *Cités Obscure* novels, a series of interrelated but independent fantasies built around imaginary cities. Another important body of work developed in the pages of (*A Suivre*) was the *Alec Sinner/Joe's Bar* cycle of stories by Argentinian expatriates José Muñoz and Carlos Sampayo.

By the end of the eighties, however, *la bande dessinée adulte* had become a victim of its own success as independent publishers were absorbed by corporate entities, and the francophone graphic novel became formulaic and genre-bound. This, at least, was the point of view of a new generation of artists. Jean-Christophe Menu, Lewis Trondheim, David B., Patrice Killoffer, Joann Sfar, Guy Delisle, and others, formed the nucleus of the publishing collective L'Association, which was founded in 1990. Other similar groups soon emerged, including the Belgian Freon, the French Ego comme x, which specialized in autobiographical comics, and Amok, founded by two second-generation French-African immigrants, Yvan Alagbé and Olivier Marboeuf.

For these younger artists, the creative stagnation of French comics was inextricably linked to the inflexible format of the forty-eight-page, color, hardcover "album," referred to as 48CC. As Menu wrote in his manifesto *Plates-bandes*, "since all that we stand against in BD is contained in the 48CC, our production must break with it completely."[3] Accordingly, L'Association published books only in black and white and soft-cover, but in a variety of sizes and formats, without fixed limits on page count.

Despite its origins in opposition to the commercialization of French comics, L'Association soon found that there was a considerable market for this new approach to *bande dessinée*; their successes included David B.'s *L'Ascension du Haute Mal* (*Epileptic*), Trondheim's series *Les Formidables*

Aventures de Lapinot (which was eventually taken over by publishing giant Dargaud), and most sensationally in terms of sales, *Persepolis*, the autobiographical graphic novel by Iranian-born Marjane Satrapi.

Though British graphic novelists of the modern era seem not to have cohered into recognizable movements or "schools" as did their continental counterparts, individual artists have excelled in the form in a more idiosyncratic fashion. Raymond Briggs, beginning as a children's illustrator, created several acclaimed book-length comics for young readers including *Father Christmas* (1973) and *The Snowman* (1978). Briggs then created the graphic novel *When the Wind Blows* (1982) using the same endearing, colored-pencil style, but for adult readers; it details the effects of a nuclear war on a retired British working-class couple.

Posy Simmonds' two graphic novels – *Gemma Bovary* (1999), a modernized retelling of *Madam Bovary*, and *Tamara Drewe* (2007), a satire of the ephemeral community of writing colonies – were serialized in *The Guardian* prior to their collection as complete volumes. Both are notable for her blending of forms, combining comics layouts with large chunks of text, the latter thoughtfully integrated into the visual composition, not merely presented alongside.

Other noteworthy British contributions to the graphic novel include Nick Abadzis' *Laika* (2007) a fictionalized account of the Russian 1950s cosmonaut dog, and Tom Gauld's 2012 *Goliath*, which retells the biblical story from the point of view of the hapless "giant."

The Graphic Novel in Japan, from 1933

Western-style cartooning was introduced in Japan in the late nineteenth century, and for several decades remained a phenomenon of the press: political cartoons, and short satirical gag strips appearing in newspapers and humor magazines. From the 1920s, popular Japanese children's comic strips were collected into hardcover editions. In 1933, Tokyo bookstore owner Sotaro Nakamura launched the Nakamura Manga Library, a series of original, hardcover comics for children, printed in color with a high production quality. The series ran to a hundred titles, before being discontinued during the Second World War. The best-known creator for this imprint was Noboru Oshiro, whose *Kasei Tanken* (*Voyage to Mars*, 1940), about the adventures of a boy and his dog and cat on Mars, included scientific information and actual photographs of space, as well as encounters with sentient tomatoes and other whimsical details. Oshiro's books would inspire many young readers destined to become post-war manga creators; Osamu Tezuka, Leiji Matsumoto, and Yoshihiro Tatsumi all later attested to the impact of his work.

After the war, monthly magazines based in Tokyo resumed publication of manga; this was the high end of the comics industry in Japan, while the low end, based largely in Osaka, consisted of cheaply printed books known as *akahon* (red books), sold at candy stores and train station stalls. It was in this format that Osamu Tezuka created his early groundbreaking works, which are generally considered the start of *sutori* (story) manga (as opposed to gag-oriented strips or political cartoons), though in many respects Tezuka was picking up where Oshiro and others left off before the war years. *Shin Takarajima*, (*New Treasure Island*, 1947), a full-length graphic novel drawn by Tezuka from a script by Shichima Sakai, sparked intense excitement, especially with its famous opening pages, a wordless sequence of the young protagonist speeding down the road in a car, for which Tezuka employed "cinematic" framing, with action broken down panel-by-panel, from different angles.

Perhaps even more important, Tezuka brought an unprecedented emotional and thematic depth to children's manga. The breakthrough in this regard was the madcap science fiction adventure *Chiteikoku no Kaijin* (*The Mysterious Underground Men*, 1948). What distinguished this *akahon* novel from previous children's manga was the dimensionality with which Tezuka imbues the supporting character of Mimio, a rabbit given the power of speech by scientists. Mimio insists that he's human, bristling when anyone calls him a rabbit. In the final scenes, having sacrificed his life to save the hero, Mimio's poignant dying words are, "am I...human?" Tezuka thus introduced a note of tragedy – an "anti-happy ending," as he later called it – to the cheery world of children's manga.[4] It is widely seen as "the first manga in which the naturalistic depiction of a character's psychology is integral to the story."[5] The theme of the quasi-human outsider struggling with their identity would remain an important theme in Tezuka's subsequent *akahon* novels such as *Metropolis* (1949) and *Kitarubeki Sekai* (*Nextworld*, 1951) – and in his most famous creation, Tetsuwan Atom (Astro Boy), which he originated after leaving the *akahon* world for the high-end manga magazines in Tokyo.

By the mid-1950s, a younger generation of manga creators launched a concerted effort to create comics for a more mature readership of teens and adolescents. Focusing on moody thrillers and action stories, this new style of manga, developed within a tight-knit group of very young artists including Masahiko Matsumoto, Yoshihiro Tatsumi, Takao Saito and others, would come to be known as *gekiga* (literally "dramatic pictures"). Like Tezuka's early work, *gekiga* emerged from the lowest level of the manga industry. Its first manifestations appeared in the *akahon* crime anthologies and *Kage* (*Shadow*, launched in 1956) and *Machi* (*City*, from 1957), distributed through the network of inexpensive rental libraries known as *kashihon.* Matsumoto's story *Rinshitsu no Otoko* (*The Man Next Door*), in the first issue of *Kage*, set the tone. A mystery in which a young cartoonist suspects his next door neighbor of murder, *Rinshitsu no Otoko* is still essentially juvenile, with a wink-to-the-reader happy ending, but Matsumoto's use of cinema-inspired paneling and pacing was taken further than Tezuka's had been to this point.

Over time, the material grew gradually darker. Tatsumi's *Kuroi Fubuki* (*Black Blizzard*, 1956) is a novel-length demonstration of this early *gekiga* aesthetic. A melodramatic and far-fetched thriller plot gave Tatsumi the opportunity to fully indulge his film noir-inspired *gekiga* vision; expressionistic lighting, atmospheric rain and snow effects abound, and while Tatsumi's early style was cartoony and crude, it's quite far from the rounded, cute, Disney-esque Tezuka style (to which Matsumoto's *Rinshitsu no Otoko* still owes some allegiance).

Meanwhile, an alternative form of graphic novel was developing in *shojo* manga, manga aimed at young female readers. Tezuka was a pioneer in this format as well; his *Ribon no Kishi* (*Princess Knight*, 1953) is considered the first *shojo* story manga, and established one of the fundamental themes of *shojo*; the fluidity or uncertainty of gender. A swashbuckling epic, initially serialized in the magazine *Shojo Club*, it tells the story of a princess born with both a male and female "heart" (due to a mix-up by a mischievous angel), causing her to swing between feminine and masculine personality traits.

In terms of its pacing and drawing style, *Princess Knight* is very much in keeping with Tezuka's work aimed at *shonen* (boy) readers. The work of another artist, Macoto Takahashi, on the other hand, continued the aesthetic tradition of pre-war *shojo* literature, with stories and artwork that emphasized emotion and beauty over action and plot. Takahashi's *Sakura Namiki* (*The Rows of Cherry Trees*, 1957), a 120-page novel set at a girls' school, focuses intently on the inner life, emotions, and anxieties of its young protagonist as she navigates the jealousies, rivalries, and unspoken rules of adolescent friendships. The quiet reflectiveness of Takahashi's story is light years from the fast-paced action and comedy of *shonen* manga; this tone persists as characteristic of *shojo* manga.

The hard-boiled *gekiga* style eventually became predominant in mainstream manga for boys and young men as the readership matured, and the prosperity of the 1960s made the *akahon* form and *kashihon* rental market obsolete. But while Takao Saito's slick, violent, long-running hit man series *Golgo 13* typified *gekiga*'s commercial development, *gekiga* branched off in another direction, that of the alternative manga journal *Garo*. Founded in 1964 by editor Katsuichi Nagai and manga artist Sanpei Shirato, *Garo* sought to evade the grip of major commercial publishers and retain the freedom of the vanishing, low-budget *akahon*.

In 1967, *Garo* published the groundbreaking short story *Nejishiki* (*Screwstyle*) by Yoshiharu Tsuge. *Nejishiki* broke sharply from anything in manga heretofore; an enigmatic dream-like account of a wounded young man wandering through bleak seaside and urban areas, meaning is derived from visual symbolism and metaphor. The narrative style is poetic rather than prosaic.

Tsuge's work influenced a generation of artists in *Garo*, who experimented with surrealism, psychedelia, magical realism, and searingly confessional personal stories. *Red Colored Elegy* (1971), a downbeat love story by Seiichi Hayashi was serialized in the magazine then released in novel form; its introspective, understated narrative and stylistic variability show the influence of Tsuge's comics, as well as that of 1960s New Wave Cinema. Tsuge's own crowning achievement was his 1986 graphic novel *Muno no Hito* (*The Useless Man*), a semi-autobiographical cycle of stories about an unemployed cartoonist attempting various futile business endeavors to support his family, while encountering assorted strange characters on the margins of modern life.

Shojo manga evolved too, as a young generation of women artists entered the previously male-dominated field. Known as the Year 24 Group (for the year Showa 24, corresponding to 1949, when most of them were born), this cohort brought an explosion of new themes and stylistic approaches to manga narrative. Riyoko Ikeda's *Bara no Bessayu* (*The Rose of Versailles*, 1972) was the group's first major commercial success. A melodramatic epic romance of the French Revolution, it demonstrates visual innovations including an open, collage-like approach to page structure that would become a hallmark of *shojo* manga.

The women of this generation also explored issues of gender ambiguity and same-sex relationships in works like Moto Hagio's *Thomas no Shinzou* (*The Heart of Thomas*, 1974), which harkens back to themes of adolescent friendship reminiscent of Takahashi's *Rows of Cherry Trees*, but with an undisguised eroticism and a shift in gender: *Thomas no Shinzou* explores the relationships of young male students at a European boys' academy. The fascination in girls' manga with attraction between beautiful boys and young men continues in the *yaoi* (boy's love) and *shounen-ai* (beautiful boy) genres to this day.

The 1980s brought a shift toward greater realism in comics, as publishers and creators attempted to appeal to the tastes and interests of readers who had once been enthusiastic consumers of childhood fantasy, but who now lived as salarymen and office ladies. One consequence of this shift was a boom in *joho*, informational manga, which ranged across diverse topics from cooking instruction to political essays, including such works as Shotoro Ishinomori's corporation-praising bestseller *Manga Nihon Keizai Nyuman (Japan Inc.: An Introduction to Japanese Economics)* of 1986.

Perhaps counter-intuitively, this trend toward greater realism also played a significant role in the popularization of futuristic dystopian fiction. Strongly influenced by French creator Moebius, Katsuhiro Otomo's *Akira* (1982–90) rendered an imaginative science fiction world – full of psychic battles and imaginary technologies – in a richly detailed and realistic urban landscape. The series was further grounded in familiar themes of Japanese life, tying intergenerational values and conflicts to the ever-present reality of post-war Japan; the Tokyo of *Akira* contains at its center a crater left by the last great war, a conflict the young protagonists never saw, although they are surrounded at all times by older survivors.

By turning a fantastical concept into something more easily perceived as serious and adult, Katsuhiro Otomo ushered in a trend toward grittier, more consequential science fiction, just as Alan Moore was soon to do for mainstream American comics. This confluence paved the way for manga's popularization with American readers – *Akira* was among the first Japanese works to earn wide American readership.

A so far less internationally impactful, if no less artistically important development of manga in this time was the birth of *josei* (women's) manga, which responded to the maturation of *shojo* readers and creators. *Shojo* of this era broadened its exploration of taboo relationships; the implied lesbian romances of earlier decades became unambiguous, while incest and mixed-age relationships also made their appearances. In nearly all cases, however, the sexual realization of these relationships was only alluded to, if not entirely postponed. These romances were mere flirtations, unsatisfying to older readers with active sexual lives – lives they wanted to see reflected less coyly in their reading. This desire was aided by the increasing role of female creators in manga, less beholden to the idealization of virginal maidenhood. The result was a launch of several *josei* magazines featuring creators visually influenced by the Year 24 Group's 1970s *shojo*, brought to bear on more complex, adult themes. Mariko Iwadate's *Uchi no Mama ga iu Koto ni wa (What Mama Says*, 1991), for instance, uses a light, thoughtful line and generous white space to detail the romantic and familial conflict of a young woman in love with a man she fears her mother won't grant permission for her to marry, followed later by examinations of the challenges of married life. *Josei* manga grew increasingly frank in its depiction of mature female sexuality in books such as Moyoco Anno's *Happy Mania* (1995–2001), Erica

Sakurazawa's melancholy relationship dramas *Koi no Okite* (*The Rules of Love*, 1993–94), and *Shitsu no Sukima* (*Between the Sheets*, 1995–96), or Kyoko Okazaki's *Pink* (1989), a screwball comedy about an office lady who moonlights as a call girl.

While American prudishness about female sexuality may explain the relative scarcity of translated *josei* manga, Japan is no stranger to moral outcry over depictions of sex in comics, experiencing effective anti-comics censorship campaigns as recently as the early 1990s. In the wake of this moral panic, which temporarily stifled the more sexually explicit manga work, Japanese publishers set out to achieve a more "respectable" form of manga. *Joho* manga played a substantial role in this, respectable for its educational value, as did a greater emphasis on upscale lifestyles – manga readership had grown considerably more affluent by this time, or at the very least, more financially aspirational.

Despite frequently tight editorial controls, distinct and ambitious creative voices still emerge, and have pushed manga in increasingly literary dimensions. Naoki Urasawa has earned respect in Japan and abroad by working within established, even flagging genres, to revitalize them with new ideas and an uncommonly nuanced approach. *Nijusseiki Shonen* (*20th-Century Boys*, 2000–6) follows a group of child heroes who fail in their destiny to save the world, and must spend the rest of their lives atoning for their mistakes. His best known work in the US has been *Pluto* (2003–9), which is billed as a posthumous collaboration with Osamu Tezuka, as it retells a classic *Astro Boy* story about a killer preying on robotic survivors of a great war. Part science fiction, part procedural investigation, part meditation on the damage war wreaks on the psyche of those who wage it, it demonstrates an insight and morally complex worldview that most Western readers haven't yet learned to associate with Japanese comics.

Graphic Novels in the International Age

The growing acceptance of the graphic novel in America in the 1990s and 2000s coincided with a new internationalism in comics. There were numerous reasons for this, including the sudden popularity of translated manga among younger readers throughout Europe, the United States, and Latin America; a burgeoning international avant-garde which saw European and Japanese comics translated in Art Spiegelman's and Françoise Mouly's *RAW* magazine and in R. Crumb's *Weirdo*, while serious cartoonists from the Americas and across Europe appeared in journals like the Swiss *Strapazin*; and the emergence of British comics creators as a key source of revitalization of the American mainstream industry.

Manga and Western Comics

While the stylistic influence of translated manga on a generation of Western comics readers and creators is widespread – Bryan Lee O'Malley's *Scott Pilgrim* series (2004–10) is one of the best known examples – the effects of Japanese–Western cross-pollination were not always as visibly apparent.

In the 1990s, Japanese publisher Kodansha commissioned original work from two important French comics artists, Baru (Hervé Barulea) and Edmond Baudoin. The different format and increased page count provided by manga publishing standards proved extremely fruitful for both, resulting in two important works which were shortly republished in French: Baru's *L'Autoroute du Soleil* and Baudoin's *Le Voyage*. The content didn't apparently reflect the Japanese originals; both books dealt with "road trips" across France, albeit of very different tone. In *L'Autoroute du Soleil*, two *banlieue* youths run afoul of drug dealers and flee across a landscape of industrial spaces, cheap motels, and beach resorts, while *Le Voyage* tells the story of a man leaving his job and family behind for a journey of self-discovery in which dream, fable, and fantasy intermingle with reality. Since Japanese serialization provided the opportunity for a much-increased page count, both of these works achieved a novelistic structure that was unusual at the time for francophone *bande dessinée*, as well as a "decompressed" style of narrative, including an increase in the number of wordless pages and panels. *L'Autoroute du Soleil* was published by Casterman in 1995 as a single volume at an unprecedented 425 pages, and went on to win the best album award at the Angoulême festival. *Le Voyage* was published by L'Association in 1996, and was awarded the "best scenario" prize at Angoulême the following year.

The lines of influence between manga and Western comics are not unidirectional. Moebius' importance for Otomo has already been noted; Jiro Taniguchi was another creator who took considerable influence from *bande dessinée*, an influence visible in the precise details of his historical fiction, such as *Botchan no Jidai* (*The Times of Botchan*, 1987–2006), but felt even more keenly in *Aruku Hito* (*The Walking Man*, 1990–92), a series of naturalistic vignettes about a man walking through his own neighborhood, appreciating the mundane pleasures of home and nature. It was a work perhaps too French for Taniguchi's audience – the book sold far better in Europe than in Japan. But this success led to an even more direct cross-cultural production: he collaborated with Moebius on *Icaro 1* and *2* (2003, 2004), a sadly unfinished science fiction trilogy.

Another artistically ambitious manga-ka (manga artist), Taiyo Matsumoto, prides himself on blending influences from across all the major comics cultures, Japanese, American, and European, alternating between stylish, yet substantive action stories (*Tekkon Kinkreet: Black and White*, 1993) and moodier literary fiction (*Blue Spring*, 1993). As Matsumoto describes the philosophy he works from, "American Comics are powerful and cool. European comics seem very intellectual. And Japanese comics are very lighthearted. If you could combine the best of all three, you could create some really tremendous work."[6] Matsumoto's *GoGo Monster* (2000) is a particularly striking work, a subtly surreal story of a lonely schoolboy, with a precise, unhurried pace and ominous tone.

Internationalism in the Anglophone graphic novel

Even work often thought of as part of the American graphic novel tradition draws substantially on the talents of Canadian and British creators. *Watchmen*, one of the first major commercial successes in the format, was only American insofar as it was contracted by an American publisher – both writer and artist are English.

The independent comics movement of the 1980s and 1990s – which led directly into the "graphic novel" mindset – freely embraced works from various English-speaking regions. Canada offered the meticulous nostalgia of Seth's *It's a Good Life, if You Don't Weaken* (serialized in *Palookaville*, 1993–96) and *Clyde Fans* (*Palookaville*, 1998–present), as well as the brutal introspection of Chester Brown's anthology *Yummy Fur* (1986–94), where he first serialized works like *I Never Liked You* (2002; serialized as *Fuck*, 1992). New Zealander Dylan Horrocks offered a more lighthearted form of self-referential nostalgia in his *Hicksville* (1998, following serialization in *Pickle*), which posits an imaginary town entirely devoted to the craft and curation of comics art. Such works added much to the alternative comics aesthetic reflected in the work of Americans like Chris Ware and Daniel Clowes, and the continuing tradition of independent "literary" comics (fig. 4.2).

At the same time, Canadian Dave Sim and collaborator Gerhard were producing the abrasive satirical fantasy satire *Cerebus* (1977–2004), which would define the black-and-white self-publishing movement of such creators as Jeff Smith, Colleen Doran, Carla Speed McNeil, and many others. In addition to challenging traditional publishing processes, *Cerebus* offered playful formal experiments such as allowing panels to spin across pages, looping through odd trajectories that evoked the central character's own journeys.

The British Invasion of the American Mainstream

In the mid-1970s, Kelvin Gosnell, a competitions subeditor at England's IPC, persuaded the publisher to launch a new science fiction comics anthology under the semi-futuristic title *2000 AD*, despite that such magazines were

Fig. 4.2 Canadian Jeff Lemire continues to produce compelling literary fiction set in rural Canada. This page from Lemire's multi-generational epic trilogy, *Essex County* (2009), shows an old man remembering his long-ago betrayal of his brother. *Essex County* © Jeff Lemire

in steep decline in the US. The magazine debuted in 1977, initially boasting a rehash of the aging *Dan Dare* adventure series, before finding its flagship in *Judge Dredd*, a satire of the violent justice of American fiction. In the years to follow, *2000 AD* and its imitators helped to launch the careers of many prominent artists and writers, such as Alan Moore, Neil Gaiman, Grant Morrison, Bryan Talbot, and others.

In the early 1980s, when Len Wein began looking for a new voice to revamp his and Bernie Wrightson's *Swamp Thing*, fellow editor Karen Berger pointed him in the direction of Alan Moore. Beginning in 1983, in collaboration with Steve Bissette, Moore turned the Swamp Thing from a campy monster into something much more otherworldly, framed by lyrical narration and pointed social commentary. American mainstream comics had only recently abandoned the structure of self-contained story issues in favor of ongoing continuity, allowing comics to explore greater complexities in plot and character; Moore went one better – he was also paying attention to *language*. And with that, a major trend toward writer-led comics serials was launched.

DC soon returned to the British talent pool, appointing Berger as the official liaison to the UK. She recruited artists as well, such as Brian Bolland and Dave Gibbons, but her focus was very much on writers, and she introduced American readers to Grant Morrison, Neil Gaiman, and Peter Milligan, among others. Where *Swamp Thing* brought Moore success, his collaboration with Dave Gibbons, *Watchmen* (1986–87), made him a comics superstar, and changed the direction of mainstream American comics for years to follow – often in ways that Moore himself found distasteful, to the point that he has expressed regret for having written it. Grant Morrison soon penned his own meta-fictional romp with *Animal Man* (1988–90), followed by the downright surrealist *Doom Patrol* (1989–93).

The end of the eighties brought two more series that would serve to crystallize movement in the direction of adult-targeted horror/fantasy: Jamie Delano's *Swamp Thing* spinoff, *John Constantine: Hellblazer* (1988–91), and a year later, Neil Gaiman's *The Sandman* (1989–96). In 1993, these titles became flagships for DC's new adult-targeted imprint, Vertigo, which was staffed almost entirely by British talent. Vertigo was appropriately put under the editorial stewardship of Karen Berger, who had recruited most of the talent filling the line.

Moore had departed DC by this time (objecting to DC's adoption of age ratings), but continued to produce new material through various independent publishers, including the book many would consider his magnum opus: *From Hell* (1999) is a dense historical fiction about London's Jack the Ripper, illustrated by Scottish/Australian cartoonist Eddie Campbell, who was otherwise best known for his semi-autobiographical *Alec* series. Campbell's tightly constrained, scratchy style was a perfect pair to Moore's delving into esoteric history and lore.

Although Bryan Talbot did not garner the same level of commercial notoriety in the US mainstream as his contemporaries, his influence was profound; the blend of atmospheric moodiness, politics and philosophy, and science fiction narrative that would define much of the British invasion could be found first in Talbot's subversive sci-fi adventure, *The Adventures of Luther Arkwright* (1978–89), prompting Warren Ellis to describe the book as "probably the single most influential graphic novel to have come out of Britain to date."[7] He built on this early achievement by moving in very different directions, such as into the more realistic and intimate story of a homeless teenager making her escape from an abusive home in *The Tale of One Bad Rat* (1994–95).

The Internet and the International Graphic Novel

Today, interest in international graphic novels is high, especially in the wake of the boom in manga. But no publisher can ever do as much to stoke interest in international comics as the growth of the internet has achieved. Even language barriers have been mitigated as "scanlation," the (technically illegal) fan practice of scanning and translating Japanese comics, then posting them to the internet, has made thousands of officially untranslated manga available to English-reading audiences.

But it is not the fans alone doing the work of bringing graphic novels to international audiences – creators themselves now have the option of self-publishing their work immediately to a global audience, neatly sidestepping the challenges of traditional international publishing. German Demian.5 (aka Demian Volger) was an early adopter of web publishing, serializing his wordless sex farce, *When I Am King*. At once funny, cute, lewd, and technically experimental, he garnered a larger audience than such works typically have access to, while making use of visual techniques unavailable to print cartoonists, such as limited animation within panels.

Canadian artist Emily Carroll found an enthusiastic international readership with the publication of her very first comics story, "His Face All Red" (2010), the first in a series of masterful dark fantasies that would grow her audience until she eventually published *Through the Woods* (2014), a collection of stories on her favored themes of isolated young women trapped by dark forces. For most creators, a collection of new shorts would be an indulgence – a minor work between larger novels – as such collections rarely sell well. But Carroll's book was highly anticipated, her online presence having built up a devoted fan base who saw the merit of her chosen form.

Rene Engström of Sweden similarly gained a spontaneous following when she began serializing her frankly sexy relationship dramedy, *Anders Loves Maria* (2006–10) – even the serialization added to the experience of the work, as it took a number of soap-operatic turns, keeping readers both hooked and vocal about the characters and their choices.

Graphic Novels in Translation

This new artistic revolution sparked by L'Association and similar groups in European comics, along with broadening interest in manga, has resulted in many important contributions to the internationalism of the graphic novel. Many of the successful translations of European graphic novels in the first decades of the twenty-first century have coincided with the rise of autobiography and non-fiction as dominant genres. David B.'s *L'Ascension du Haut Mal* (*Epileptic*), Joann Sfar's *Le Chat du Rabin* (*The Rabbi's Cat*), and Marjane Satrapi's *Persepolis* became bestsellers in multiple translations including English; the latter represents one of a handful of examples often cited to give validity to the entire concept of the graphic novel. Other excellent French works translated into English include Aristophane's *Les Soeurs Zabîme* (*The Zabime Sisters*), Emmanuel Guibert's *La Guerre d'Alan* (*Alan's War*), and Guy Delisle's travel chronicles, including *Pyongyang* and *Shenzhen*. Italian cartoonists have partaken as well, with Igort's *5 is the Perfect Number*, Gipi's *Notes for a War Story*, and Gabriella Giandelli's *Interiorae* notable examples. The trend continues in the second decade of the twenty-first century: Austrian Ulli Lust's 2009 memoir, *Heute ist der letzte Tag vom Rest deines Lebens* was released to acclaim in English as *Today is the Last Day of the Rest of Your Life* (2013), as was the dark fairy tale *Jolies Ténèbres* (*Beautiful Darkness*) by Fabien Vehlmann and Kerascoët the following year. In terms of historically important European comics, David Kunzle's 2007 English translation of the complete comics of Rodolphe Töppfer was an essential contribution.

While commercial manga has had a substantial international audience for some time, small publishers have also begun to make translations of the more artistic end of the Japanese comics world, including work by Taniguchi and Taiyo Matsumoto, as well as historically important manga by Tezuka, Hagio, Shigeru Mizuki, Tatsumi, Hayashi, and others.

Other areas of the world, such as Latin America and Eastern Europe, have yet to fully participate in the recognition of the graphic novel as an international phenomenon. As of this writing, an English-language edition of *El Eternauta* has been announced, the first such translation of Héctor Germán Oesterheld. We can certainly expect Africa, the Middle East, India, and other parts of Asia to take part in the international graphic novel movement, but so far little work from these regions has reached Western markets. French-African immigrants, however, have brought new voices to the form: apart from the aforementioned Yvan Alagbé, Ivorian-born writer Marguerite Abouet's series *Aya de Yopougon* (*Aya of Yop City*, 2005–10), drawn by Clément Oubrerie, depicts daily life in her native country. Similarly, the Middle East has been represented in graphic novels mostly through immigrant perspectives such as Satrapi's *Persepolis* and the work of French-Syrian cartoonist Riad Sattouf. One exception is the Israeli Rutu Modan, whose graphic novels *Exit Wounds* (2007) and *The Property* (2013) employ precisely drawn character dramas to explore themes of Jewish and Israeli identity, memory, and family.

For every translated work, of course, there are still many major works from many countries that remain unavailable to English readers; but gradually the panorama of international comics is being revealed to an anglophone readership, one that will, hopefully, continue to be increasingly receptive to foreign works.

Works Cited

Abadzis, Nick. *Laika*. New York: First Second, 2007.
Abouet, Marguerite, and Clément Oubrerie. *Aya de Yopougon* (*Aya of Yop City*). Paris: Gallimard, 2005–10.
Anno, Moyoko. *Happī Mania* (*Happy Mania*). Tokyo: Shōdensha, 1995–2001.
Aristophanes. *The Zabime Sisters* (*Les Soeurs Zabîme*) (1996). Trans. Matt Madden. New York: First Second, 2010.
B.[eauchard], David. *L'Ascension du Haut Mal* (*Epileptic*). Paris: L'Association, 1996–2004.
Baru. *L'Autoroute du Soleil*. Brussels: Casterman, 2002.
Baudoin, Edmond. *Le Voyage*. Paris: L'Association, 1996.
Briggs, Raymond. *Father Christmas*. New York: Coward, McCann & Geoghegan, 1973.
The Snowman. New York: Random House, 1978.
When the Wind Blows. New York: Schocken, 1982.
Brown, Chester. *I Never Liked You: A Comic-Strip Narrative*. Montreal: Drawn & Quarterly, 2002.
Yummy Fur. Toronto: Vortex/Montreal: Drawn & Quarterly. 1986–94.
Buzzelli, Guido. *I Labirinti* (*Les Labyrinthes*). *Charlie Mensuel* 24–33. Paris: Éditions Du Square, 1971.
La Revolta dei Racchi. Rome: Institute of Education, University of Rome, 1967.
Zil Zelub: Charlie Special 2. Paris: Éditions Du Square, 1977.
Campbell, Eddie. *Alec: The Years Have Pants (A Life-Sized Omnibus)*. Marietta, GA: Top Shelf Productions, 2009.
Carroll, Emily. "His Face All Red." *Emily Carroll Art & Comics*. Emily Carroll, 2010. June 17, 2015. http://emcarroll.com/comics/faceallred/01.html.
Through the Woods. New York: Margaret K. McElderry, 2014.

Crepax, Guido. *Ciao Valentina e altre storie* (1965–95). Milan: RCS Quotidiani S.p.A, 2007.

D'Ache, Caran. *Maestro*. Angoulême: Musée de la Bande Dessinée, 1999.

Delano, Jamie, and John Ridgway. *John Constantine: Hellblazer* (Series). New York: DC Comics, 1988–91.

Delisle, Guy. *Pyongyang*. Paris: L'Association, 2003.

Shenzhen. Paris: L'Association, 2000.

Demian.5. "When I Am King." *When I Am King*. June 17, 2015. www.demian5.com/king/wiak.htm.

Ellis, Warren. "Book Review: The Adventures of Luther Arkwright." *Artbomb.net.*, June 17, 2015. www.artbomb.net/detail.jsp?tid=201.

Engström, Rene. "Anders Loves Maria." *A Little Rene Engström*, June 17, 2015. http://reneengstrom.tumblr.com/. www.anderslovesmaria.com/

Forest, Jean-Claude. *Barbarella*. Paris: Le Terrain Vague, 1964.

Gaiman, Neil. *The Sandman*. New York: DC Comics, 1989–96.

Gauld, Tom. *Goliath*. Montreal: Drawn & Quarterly, 2012.

Giandelli, Gabriella, and José Avigdor. *Interiorae*. Bologna: Coconino Press, 2005.

Gipi. *Notes for a War Story* (*Appunti per una Storia di Guerra*). New York: First Second, 2007.

Gravett, Paul. *1001 Comics You Must Read before You Die*. London: Cassell Illustrated, 2014.

Manga: Sixty Years of Japanese Comics. London: Laurence King, 2004.

Guibert, Emmanuel. *La Guerra de Alan: Según los Recuerdos de Alan Ingram Cope* (*Alan's War*). Castalla-Alicante: Ponent Mon, 2004.

Hagio, Moto. *The Heart of Thomas* (*Thomas no Shinzou*) (1974–75). Trans. Matt Thorn. Seattle, WA: Fantagraphics Books, 2012.

Hayashi, Seiichi. *Red Colored Elegy* (1970–71). Trans. Taro Nettleton. Montreal: Drawn & Quarterly, 2008.

Holmberg, Ryan. "An Introduction to Gekiga, 6970 A.D." *The Comics Journal* 24 (March 2011). Web, June 17, 2015. www.tcj.com/AN-INTRODUCTION-TO-GEKIGA-6970-A-D/.

Horrocks, Dylan. *Hicksville*. Montreal: Drawn & Quarterly, 2001.

Igort. *5 è il Numero Perfetto* (*5 is the Perfect Number*). Bologna: Coconino Press, 2003.

Ikeda, Riyoko. *La Rose de Versailles* (*Bara no Bessayu/The Rose of Versailles*) (1972). Trans. Misato. Brussels: Kana (Dargaud-Lombard), 2002.

Ishinomori, Shōtarō. *Manga Nihon Keizai Nyuman* (*Japan Inc.: An Introduction to Japanese Economics: The Comic Book*). N.p.: Nihon Keizai Shinbun, 1986.

Iwadate, Mariko. *Uchi no Mama ga iu Koto ni wa* (*What Mama Says*). Tokyo: Shūeisha, 1991.

Kinsella, Sharon. *Adult Manga: Culture and Power in Contemporary Japanese Society*. Honolulu, HI: University of Hawai'i Press, 2000.

Lehmann, Timothy R. *Manga: Masters of the Art*. New York: Collins Design, 2005.

Lemire, Jeff. *Essex County*. Atlanta, GA: Top Shelf Productions, 2009.

Lust, Ulli. *Heute ist der letzte Tag vom Rest deines Lebens* (*Today is the Last Day of the Rest of Your Life*). Berlin: Avant-Verlag, 2009.

Matsumoto, Masahiko. *Rinshitsu no Otoko* (*The Man Next Door*). Tokyo: Shogakukan Kurieitibu, 2009.

Matsumoto, Taiyo. *Aoi Haru* (*Blue Spring*). N.p.: Shogakukan, 1993.

    Gogo Monsuta (*GoGo Monster*). N.p.: Shogakukan, 2000.

    Tekkonkinkreet (*Black and White*). N.p.: Shogakukan, 1993.

Mazur, Dan, and Alexander Danner. *Comics: A Global History, 1968 to the Present.* London: Thames & Hudson, 2014.

Menu, Jean-Christophe. *Plates-bandes*. Paris: L'Association, 2005.

Modan, Rutu. *Exit Wounds*. Montreal: Drawn & Quarterly, 2007.

    The Property. Trans. Jessica Cohen. Montreal: Drawn & Quarterly, 2013.

Moebius, and Jiro Taniguchi. *Icaro 1 & 2*. New York: IBooks, 2003, 2004.

Moore, Alan, and Eddie Campbell. *From Hell* (1999). Marietta, GA: Top Shelf Productions, 2006.

Moore, Alan, and Dave Gibbons. *Watchmen*. New York: DC Comics, 1987.

Moore, Alan, Stephen Bissette, John Totleben, and Rick Veitch. *Saga of the Swamp Thing*. New York: DC Comics, 1987.

Morrison, Grant, et al. *Animal Man*. New York: DC Comics, 1988–90.

    Doom Patrol. New York: DC Comics, 1989–93.

Mougin, Jean-Paul. "Editorial." (*A Suivre*), May 4, 1978.

Muñoz, José, and Carlos Sampayo. *Alack Sinner* (1975–2006). Collected in *Alack Sinner: L'Âge de l'Innocence*. N.p.: Casterman, 2007.

    Joe's Bar (*Nel bar*) (1981–2002). Trans. Jeff Lisle. New York: Catalan Communications, 2007.

Oesterheld, Héctor, and Solano López. *L'Eternaute* (*El Eternauta*) (1957–59). Paris: Vertige Graphic, 2008.

Oesterheld, Héctor, and Hugo Pratt. *Ernie Pike* (1957). N.p.: Casterman, 2001.

    Sergeant Kirk (*El Sargento Kirk*) (1953–61). Collected in *Sergeant Kirk: Deuxième Époch*. Paris: Futuropolis, 2008.

Okazaki, Kyoko. *Pink*. Tokyo: Magajin Hausu, 1989.

O'Malley, Bryan Lee. *Scott Pilgrim*. Portland, OR: Oni Press, 2004–10.

Oshiro, Noboru, and Taro Asahi. *Kasei Tanken* (1940). Tokyo: Shogakukan Creative, 2005.

Otomo, Katsuhiro. *Akira*. Tokyo: Kodansha, 1982–90.

Peellaert, Guy. *The Adventures of Jodelle* (*Les Aventures de Jodelle*) (1966). Trans. Richard Seaver. New York: Grove Press, 1967.

Peeters, Benoît, and François Schuiten. *Les Cités Obscure* (*The Obscure Cities*). N.p.: Casterman, 1983–2008.

Power, Natsu Onoda. *God of Comics: Osamu Tezuka and the Creation of Post–World War II Manga*. Jackson, MS: University Press of Mississippi, 2009, 19–37.

Pratt, Hugo. *Corto Maltese: La Ballade de la Mer Salée* (*Corto Maltese: Una Ballata del Mare Salato/Ballad of the Salt Sea*) (1967). Brussels: Casterman, 2005.

Saito, Takao. *Golgo 13*. N.p.: Shogakukan, 1968–.

Sakurazawa, Erica. *Koi no Okite* (*The Rules of Love*). N.p.: Shodensha, 1993–94.

    Shitsu no Sukima (*Between the Sheets*). N.p.: Shodensha, 1996.

Satrapi, Marjane. *Persepolis*. Paris: L'Association, 2001.

Schodt, Frederik L. *Manga! Manga!: The World of Japanese Comics*. Tokyo: Kodansha International, 1983.

Seth. *Clyde Fans*. Montreal: Drawn & Quarterly, 2004.

    It's a Good Life, if You Don't Weaken. Palookaville 4–8. Montreal: Drawn & Quarterly, 1993–96.

Sfar, Joann. *The Rabbi's Cat* (*Le Chat du Rabin*) (2001). Trans. Alexis Siegel and Anjali Singh. New York: Pantheon Books, 2005.

Sim, Dave, and Gerhard. *Cerebus*. Kitchener, ON: Aardvark-Vanaheim, 1977–2004.

Simmonds, Posy. *Gemma Bovary*. New York: Pantheon Books, 1999.

Tamara Drewe (2005–6). Boston and New York: Houghton Mifflin, 2007.

Smolderen, Thierry. *The Origins of Comics: From William Hogarth to Winsor McCay*. Trans. Bart Beaty and Nick Nguyen. Jackson, MS: University Press of Mississippi, 2014.

Strömberg, Fredrik. *Swedish Comics History*. Malmo: Swedish Comics Association (Seriefrämjandet), 2010.

Takahashi, Macoto. *Sakura Namiki* (*The Rows of Cherry Trees*) (1957). Tokyo: Shogakukan Creative, 2006.

Talbot, Bryan. *The Adventures of Luther Arkwright*. N.p.: Near Myths, 1978–89.

The Tale of One Bad Rat. Milwaukie, OR: Dark Horse Books, 1995.

Taniguchi, Jiro. *The Walking Man* (*Aruku Hito*). 1990–92. Trans: Shizuka Shimoyama and Elizabeth Tierman. Wisbech, Suffolk UK: Fanfare/Ponent Mon, 2004.

Botchan no Jidai (*The Times of Botchan*). Tokyo: Futabasha, 1987–2006.

Tardi, Jacques. *It Was the War of the Trenches* (*C'était la Guerre des Tranchées*) (1993). Trans. Kim Thompson. Seattle, WA: Fantagraphics Books, 2010.

La Véritable Histoire du Soldat Inconnu (*The True Story of the Unknown Soldier*) (1974). Paris: Futuropolis, 2005.

Tardi, Jacques, and Jean-Claude Forest. *You Are There* (*Ici Même*) (1978). Trans. Kim Thompson. Seattle, WA: Fantagraphics Books, 2009.

Tatsumi, Yoshihiro. *Black Blizzard* (*Kuroi Fubuki*) (1956). Trans. Akemi Wegmüller. Montreal: Drawn & Quarterly, 2010.

Tezuka, Osamu. *The Mysterious Underground Men* (*Chiteikoku no Kaijin*) (1948). Trans. Ryan Holmborg. Brooklyn, NY: PictureBox, 2013.

Princesse Saphir (*Ribon no Kishi*) (1953). Trans. Sylvain Chollet. Paris: Soleil Manga, 1977.

Tetsuwan Atomu (*Astro Boy*). N.p.: Kobunsha, 1952–68.

Tezuka, Osamu, and Shichima Sakai. *New Treasure Island* (*Shin Takarajima*) (1947). Tokyo: Shogakukan Creative, 2009.

Thompson, Jason. *Manga: The Complete Guide*. New York: Ballantine/Del Rey, 2007.

Töpffer, Rodolphe. *Monsieur Pencil* (1840). Trans. David Kunzle, in *Rodolphe Töpffer: The Complete Comic Strips*. Jackson, MS: University of Mississippi Press, 2007.

"Essai de Physiognomonie/Par R T. [Rodolphe Töpffer]" (1845). *Gallica*. June 17, 2015. http://gallica.bnf.fr/ark:/12148/btv1b8529034f.r=.langFR.

Les Amours de Monsieur Vieux Bois (1837). Trans. David Kunzle, in *Rodolphe Töpffer: The Complete Comic Strips*. Jackson, MS: University of Mississippi Press, 2007.

Trondheim, Lewis. *Les Formidables Aventures de Lapinot* (*The Spiffy Adventures of McConey*). Paris: Dargaud, 1993–2003.

Tsuge, Yoshiharu. *L'Homme sans Talent* (*Muno No Hito*) (1986). Trans. Kaoru Sekizumi and Frédéric Boilet. Angoulême: Ego Comme X, 2004.

"Screwstyle" ("Nejishiki") (1967). Trans. Bill Randall, *The Comics Journal* 250. Seattle, WA: Fantagraphics Books, 2003.

Urasawa, Naoki, and Osamu Tezuka. *Pluto*. N.p.: Shogakukan, 2003–9.

Urasawa, Naoki. *Nijusseiki Shonen (20th-Century Boys)*. N.p.: Shogakukan, 2000–6.

Vehlmann, Fabien, and Kerascoët. *Beautiful Darkness (Jolies Ténèbres)* (2009). Trans. Helge Dascher. Montreal: Drawn & Quarterly, 2014.

Yoshihara, Yuki. *Sheet no Sukima*. Tokyo: Shogakukan, 1995–96.

NOTES

1 Rodolphe Töpffer, "Essai de physiognomonie/Par R T" (1945), 13. http://gallica .bnf.fr/ark:/12148/btv1b8529034f.r=.langFR

2 Jean-Paul Mougin, "Editorial," (*A Suivre*), May 4, 1978.

3 Jean-Christopher Menu, *Plates-bandes* (Paris: L'Association, 2005), 28.

4 Osamu Tezuka, "Afterword (1982)," in Ryan Holmborg, ed., *The Mysterious Underground Men (Chiteikoku No Kaijin)* (Brooklyn, NY: PictureBox, 2013), iv.

5 Ryan Holmberg, "Osamu Tezuka and the First Story Manga," in Holmborg, ed., *Mysterious Underground Men*, x.

6 Quoted in Paul Gravett, *Manga: Sixty Years of Japanese Comics* (London: Laurence King, 2004), 162.

7 Warren Ellis, "Book Review: The Adventures of Luther Arkwright," www .artbomb.net/detail.jsp?tid=201.

5

HUGO FREY

Historical Fiction

"Last Kind Word Blues" can be found in the anthology *Before the Blues,
Vol. 2.* (Yazoo Records) and also in the soundtrack of *Crumb* (Rykodisc),
Terry Zwigoff's 1995 film about the misanthropic comix artist Robert
Crumb. Crumb is shown in a room lined with shelves of 78s; he picks one,
cues it up on the phonograph, and lies back on a daybed to let Geeshie Wiley
wash right over him. "When I listen to old music," Crumb says in voice over
as Wiley plays, "it's one of the few times I actually have a kind of love for
humanity. You hear the best part of the soul of a common people, their, you
know, their way of expressing the connection to eternity, or whatever you
want to call it."[1]

The quotation cited above is derived from Greil Marcus' writing about
Bob Dylan's ambiguous relationship with the North American folk music
tradition. It does not feature in the main text of his work but rather forms
part of the discography, being included as a note on the recording history
of the bluesman, Geeshie Wiley. One does not experience historical fiction
in the graphic novel in the same way as one listens to music, nor for that
matter as one reads a traditional novel or watches a film. Nonetheless, in
Robert Crumb's deeply felt admiration for Wiley's work, one is reminded
of how historical materials, reconstituted through cultural representation in
whatever form, commonly provide powerfully optimistic counterpoints to
the present-day world of uncertainty, existential angst or the more explicit
menaces of poverty, ill health, and war. While Crumb is famous and infamous for the lewd and grotesque humor of his underground comix strips,
his own oeuvre is punctuated with precisely this same kind of nostalgic historical reflection. For example, there is his historical–biographical treatment
on the story of the blues, "Patton," that was first published in *Zap Comix* 11
(1985), not to mention his numerous, lovingly detailed, one-page portraits of
bluesmen, country singers, bandsmen, and others from the 1920s and 1930s
that he created as a collection of trading cards and that were published as
Robert Crumb's Heroes of the Jazz Age.[2]

In the rest of this chapter I will explain that several variations on Crumb's vision of the past as a golden age are a common theme for historical fiction being published in the graphic novel. This does not mean that the medium has developed an especially saccharine perspective. On the contrary, the picture is a much more ambiguous and complex one than that. In several of the graphic novels discussed herein the past is a place littered with violence and defeat and, generally speaking, readers of historical fiction in graphic novels will learn to appreciate the survival of the little "ordinary people" as an example of the narrative of triumph over adversity. It is also the case that today these folkloric–realist tendencies are increasingly being marginalized when compared with autobiography and journalistic reportage. Significantly, it is in genre fiction and nuanced meta-fictional exposition of the processes of memory itself where renewed creative dynamism is currently found. Throughout this chapter I define "historical fiction" to mean story-telling about the past, or plots set in the past, which make only limited claims to either scientific accuracy or to any recognized academic or scientific truth. This does not mean accuracy or convincing *mise-en-scène* is not important in numerous graphic novels of the type discussed in this chapter. Simply, it means that in historical fiction the primary objective is to recount stories about real or invented people and events rather than to establish any other pact with the reader. While it may seem easier to define what historical fiction is not rather than what it is, in fact a number of relatively consistent dispositions have been established for the graphic novel, and it is to the first of these – folkloric realism – that I will next turn. This discussion will be followed by a consideration of the current fashion in the publishing of historical fiction in genre-inspired works. The chapter concludes with recognition of the rise of more meta-historical graphic novels that use memory as a theme or blur together the pre-existing tropes to which I will now turn.

The portrayal of history imagined as a golden age, an authentic time of genuine values, even if marred by violence, the time to fight the good fight, suffuses a compelling corpus of important groundbreaking graphic novels from the 1970s until at least the 1990s. This kind of folkloric realism was the mode that Will Eisner established in what many consider to be the first graphic novel – *A Contract with God* (1978). Therein through a series of short stories Eisner describes the struggle of a generation of migrants to New York. In addition, comparable material is returned to in Vance and Burr's *Kings in Disguise*; James Sturm's *America: God, Gold, and Golems*, as well as in his shorter work *Satchel Paige*; and it is also evidenced in Joe Kubert's hard-edged *Jew Gangster*. In this latter title Kubert pays his tribute to the earlier work of Eisner through the inclusion of lovingly created reproduction illustrations of the tenement buildings and people that featured so memorably in *A Contract with God*. In addition, Jack Jackson – writing as Jaxon – provides a Texan variation on the same themes. In *Comanche Moon*, and again in his later titles including *Los Tejanos and Lost Cause*, Jaxon created a series of stories that explore the people, history, and conflicts of the Texas–Mexico frontier.[3] In a period when literary fiction was too often tempted into sterile modernist experimentalism, each of these graphic novelists is returning to the traditional idea of emphasizing a strong sense of place and character. Susan Sontag once remarked of cinematic fantasies of Nazism in the 1970s, "the colour is black . . . the fantasy is death."[4] In these graphic novels the world is a bittersweet mixture of autumnal yellows and browns, leading to winter snows, and the fantasy is not death, but rather the survival of the individual, family, or community group in the face of adversity. The works are where Crumb's "soul of the common people" is repeatedly represented for readers to empathize with and support.

Art Spiegelman's explanation for his fascination with the old comic strips of the turn of the century as a point of solace after his experiencing the attacks on the World Trade Center and the beginning of the "war on terror" is a pertinent additional reminder as to what is at stake in the folkloric-realist interpretations of history. He writes: "The only cultural artefacts that could get past my defenses to flood my eyes and brain with something other than images of burning towers were old comic strips; vital, unpretentious ephemera from the optimistic dawn of the twentieth century."[5] The subjects, stories of adversity and survival, found in historical works by Jaxon, Eisner, and Kubert provide a comparable function to what Spiegelman is suggesting. Creators and their readers recall historical struggles to reassure themselves that contemporary crises can be survived. We turn to stories from the Depression, or of westward expansion, or to the building up of the great cities, to discover it was worse back then than it is today, or at least just as awful. Moreover, we can read and explore these words and images reassured in the knowledge that some decent ordinary people survived and even later thrived. Generally speaking, the fascination with the period of circa 1890 to 1950 is also because this period represents a time when political and moral categories appeared more fixed than they are today. It is the nostalgia for political and moral certainties that is provided in these historical graphic novels which makes them significant. In his fascinating writing on the wider themes of representation of Jewish belief and the Holocaust in graphic novels, Stephen E. Tabachnick has emphasized that even when depicting the most horrific examples of man's treatment of man, several of these graphic novels allow a space for theological interpretation and imply a world where there are not only clear moral dividing lines but where there is also a role for God.[6] One may add that commonly graphic novels working as folkloric-realist historical fiction also extend to include secular variations of the same narrative type. In both theological and secular cases there is a desire to explain terror, murder, and social oppression through the nobility of the victims or at the least the decency of normal people who are swept into the maelstrom of economic and political change. As a brief aside, few of these works focus on any characters associated with the forces of oppression or evil. The famous work in the graphic novel format that does in part depict the experience of being a violent persecutor is included in Stassen's account of the genocide in Rwanda, *Deogratias*.[7]

In addition, the dominant storyworld that I am discussing here allows for quite boldly critical political interpretation. For example, in Vance and Burr's *Kings in Disguise*, the writer and artist team portray the social consequences of the Depression on one family. To paraphrase, oppressive landowners and property speculators are shown stealing the common land, while police brutally shut down legitimate trade union strikes. Furthermore, Vance and Burr shed light on the social world of the hobo and homeless, noting too the violence of that world. Cleverly they also narrate one character's self-realization of his homosexuality and depict the homophobic subculture within the economically marginalized community. First published in 1990, just shortly after the end of the Reagan administration, *Kings in Disguise* is a powerful assertion of an American socialist vision.

The visual appeal of these works is also very important, and as I have explained when writing with Jan Baetens in *The Graphic Novel: An Introduction*, drawing style is a critical issue for all types of graphic novel, and the folkloric-realist historical fictions are no exception.[8] Each of the aforementioned creators (Crumb, Eisner, Sturm, Jaxon, Kubert, Vance and Burr) has developed their own style; however, there are some common properties that establish an underlying aesthetic for this group of works. As noted above, predominantly the works either use or evoke browns, yellows, greys, or shades of black and white. The color of the pages of the fantasy or superhero comics is thereby utterly rejected. Similarly, creators Crumb, Eisner, Jaxon, Kubert, and Burr all use a drawing style that emphasizes detail but still shows a clearly implied form of freehand sketching. This implies a further level of authenticity in their works, conveying the impression that the scenes being drawn are captured at first hand. As one might expect, throughout the works a high level of detail is employed, including inclusion of appropriate historical costumes and objects. Re-drawing of accurate advertising signage, or detailed landscapes and natural life, are commonplace. There is also importantly a regular organization of the page layout, with quite discreet selections being made here so that this framing pattern does not interfere with either narration or the detail of the visual content inside the panels. This is also the case for Eisner, who deliberately does not use panels but nonetheless provides very regular and unobtrusive designs for the material on the page. Crumb's historical influence should not be underestimated in all of this material, even if not everyone we are discussing indulges in the deep cross-hatching and pinpoint detail associated with his work. Another fascinating influence is the original illustrations found in a work such as Guthrie's *Bound for Glory*, though here I admit to be purely speculating.[9] What the unofficial, but mutually reinforcing, school of works all do achieve is a broadly common visual style that is naturalist and figurative and quite pointedly different from any other genre of the comic book (funny animals, superheroes, or detective fiction) and is equally a distinctive use of the graphic novel.

The inflection of a specific political commitment or the aesthetic of the drawing or page design are just two typical ways these graphic novels gain our attention as readers. These aspects are an important part of Chester Brown's *Louis Riel*, but they are not the main reason for its success.[10] Riel is a fascinating figure from the late nineteenth-century history of the Canadian frontier (rather typically for the corpus I am identifying, he is a folk hero, a pioneer with decades of legend and popular and academic interpretations attached to his resistance against British westward expansion in Manitoba). However, what makes Brown's work significant is its sheer intellectual audacity. The work compels our fascination because Brown's use of the graphic novel form is so intelligent. This effect is achieved by Brown's decision to publish detailed and important endnotes to support or contradict most of the content on the main pages of the work. Thus, the reader is invited to reflexively read the graphic novel and follow Brown's account of Riel's life and work, while also constantly exploring Brown's research notes that comment on his source materials. For example, when in the body of Brown's work a known historical fact is traduced for poetic reasons, the correct alternative scenario is simultaneously discussed in a written form via his extensive endnotes, of which there are twenty-five pages in total. It is the intellectual daring of *Louis Riel* that makes us want to know more about the real Riel, rather than any direct connection to the man or the place. *En passant*, one may add that multiplicity of view is also important in another worthy newer work, David Rakoff's *Love, Dishonor, Marry, Die, Cherish, Perish: A Novel*.[11] Therein, Rakoff addresses modern history as experienced by a group of individuals from the Depression up until the Aids crisis. However, he defies all existing conventions by merging a long narrative poem with full-page illustrations of his protagonists, contributed by Seth, and using an original production design of a hardboard jacket, created by graphic designer Chip Kidd.

While Chester Brown expanded the tradition of folkloric historical fiction through juxtaposing visual content (the body of the work) with discursive textual detail (the endnotes), two other artists have adopted the opposite strategy of an abandonment of most words altogether. Thus, Kyle Baker's *Nat Turner* recounts the events of the life of the eponymous slave revolt leader through predominantly page after page of images with very little accompanying text.[12] The words which feature are quoted directly from the original *Confessions of Nat Turner*, and the passages that are used are deployed to lend force to Baker's illustration and vice versa. At the end of the work the "Confessions" are repeated across two full pages, a repetition that further emphasizes Turner's own justificatory account of his actions. George A. Walker's *Written in Wood: Three Wordless Graphic Narratives* uses no words whatsoever.[13] It is composed of three collected historical wordless graphic novels that depict the death of Tom Thomson in 1917, the 9/11 attacks, and the life of Conrad Black, a controversial media executive.[14] Walker employs page after page of woodcut images to establish sequential storytelling (see figs 5.1. and 5.2). As readers we are so trained to need words to give us meanings that the interpretation of this work, without any such guidance, is a difficult and intense experience. It is as if Walker is forcing one to think through what links together the narrative meaning that connects each image and page. Here we have moved a considerable distance from the works of Eisner, Kubert, or Jaxon, although Walker shares their concern for achieving a sense of place and the individual or community (and woodcuts as a form emphasize portraiture or the positioning of people in their environment).

New works which align to the folkloric-realist tendency in historical graphic novels continue to be published. For example, recently there have been some titles that use the graphic novel to explore the biographies of notable country and western musical stars of the 1950s to 1980s.[15] In addition, there is sometimes an unusual or one-off work or series which does not conform to the general pattern identified herein but that offers something different for its subject (for example, Nick Abadzis' *Laika* of 2007, about the first dog sent into space by the Russians). However, such newer works of historical fiction in this mode are far outweighed numerically by graphic novels created as autobiography or reportage. Following the successes of Art Spiegelman, Marjane Satrapi, Joe Sacco, and many others, more often than not historical narratives are presented through these ways of talking about the past. The power of the eyewitness account is today so widely accepted that there seem to be fewer and fewer graphic novelists working in the tradition first set out by Eisner and Jaxon. Let me add that the experimental variations of Brown, Rakoff, Baker, or Walker are comparatively unusual

Fig. 5.1 Page 143 from George A. Walker, *Written in Wood* (Richmond Hill, Ontario: Firefly Books, 2014), "Book of Hours: A 9/11 Story." Images of daily life on 8/11 New York: the pictures in this silent work need no comment. Reproduced with permission from the Porcupine's Quill © 2015 George A. Walker.

when one surveys the shelves in bookstores dedicated to graphic novels. Two factors start to explain this change in fashion. First, it is as if putting oneself in the story somehow guarantees a greater level of authenticity than a more distanced third-person account, however realistic in detail and authentic in drawing style or original in visual approach. Second, the form of the graphic novel, the page after page of juxtaposed grids, greatly facilitates narration which provides flashback and flash forward from the point of view of a single narrator or autobiographical voice. The folkloric-realist graphic novels did not work with the depiction of time in this way.

Autobiography and reportage's increased monopoly on historical matters does not mean that historical fiction has ended completely. On the contrary, what is notable is that it has simply found different venues for its circulation and representation. Notably, the folkloric-realist current is being gradually

Fig. 5.2 Page 144 from George A. Walker, *Written in Wood* (Richmond Hill, Ontario: Firefly Books, 2014), "Book of Hours: A 9/11 Story." Images of daily life on 8/11 New York: an example of the power of "silence" in wordless graphic novels. Reproduced with permission from Porcupine's Quill © 2015 George A Walker.

replaced by genre fiction that is set in the past. Unlike the social-folklore realist school that is in a slow, but long-term decline, this new current of works, that are blending historical setting and genre fiction, is a vibrant industry, including numerous crime, horror, and detection graphic novels. Even time travel style science fiction works use and comment on history, a paradigm developed in Bryan Talbot's very early graphic novel, *The Adventures of Luther Arkwright*.[16] What is also important to underline in a general survey such as this one is that it has been Mike Mignola and his several collaborators who have developed some of the most prototypical treatments in their *Hellboy* graphic novels.[17] Through the now numerous titles from this series, Mignola has developed his own new version of a 1920s to 1950s weird tale that is a loyal reflection of that earlier narrative world and an example of original contemporary storytelling.

In addition, there have also been many reinterpretations of pre-existing, now historically significant superhero characters, wherein the famous protagonists are featured in historical settings. Three different variations on the idea of positioning traditional comic characters in new historical graphic novels are worthy of highlighting here.

1. There are several retellings of the founding moment of the superheroes' transformation or birth (the best of these remains Frank Miller and David Mazzucchelli's *Batman Year One*).[18] While these titles are entertaining, and even thrilling for fans, they do not merit much discussion here except to say that in the 1980s and 1990s it was the rebooting of *Swamp Thing* and *Sandman* that greatly assisted DC Comics in dominating the commercial sector of graphic novel publishing.

2. There are several works where the fictional superheroes have been transported into different historical contexts than those in which one would expect to find them, that is, their own storyworlds set up in the traditional comics. Thus, in addition to *Hellboy*, Mike Mignola has provided a 1930s Batman graphic novel, *Gotham by Gaslight*, and there are similar treatments for Nick Fury (*Max Fury: My War Gone By*) and the X-Men (*Marvel 1602*).[19] The titles are similar to the genre of academic history books where scholars imagine the past asking the question "What if?" In comparison to those vanity projects these titles enable writers and artists to comment on different periods while maintaining the core franchise hero. They allow for some intriguing remixes and mash-ups where historical visual styles are used to redraw the familiar heroes in new ways. In that sense they are comparable with those titles where the main comics houses have allowed underground comix artists or graphic novelists to play with their worlds.

3. A significant variant of the works discussed in 2. above are the very serious commemorative works in which the traditional comics characters have been incorporated into the context of the Holocaust. This is the case in two comparable works: *X-Men: Magneto Testament* and *Sgt Rock: The Prophesy*.[20] Therein the artists deploy quite a modest and cautious use of images so as to avoid sensationalism. Thus, relatively familiar or iconic images of the Holocaust feature in each work. For example, a double-page image of piles of victims' glasses is one important section in *Magneto Testament*. A similar restraint is used to represent a Sonderkommando worker. To achieve this the page is filled with written testimony that is set against a double page of black panels with no images at all. The tone established herein is deeply respectful and the underlying premise is educational. For this reason one cannot call these works "extreme" and

they are not comparable with such contributions where grotesque and shocking tactics are relatively normal (see, for example, the works of the British-based fine artists the Chapman Brothers, wherein toy soldiers, figurine toys from fast-food chains, and other popular culture ephemera are used to make large scale "toy" models of Holocaust camps and battlefields).[21]

Moving on, Alan Moore and Eddie Campbell's *From Hell* is an apropos graphic novel here because at its core it too also re-uses genre material.[22] Let me explain further: *From Hell* is an example of where a narrative rooted in the tradition of genre (pulp horror/crime) is explicitly elevated into something more distinctively elitist than these origins suggest. Almost a genre of its own, the "Ripper" case was first of all established and disseminated in sensational press coverage of the murders, and intermittently ever since has been subject to redepiction in popular crime and horror novels or films. Furthermore, it has become a popular subfield of conspiratorial "true crime" publishing. In *From Hell* this possibly unpromising popular context is rejected in favor of a strategy of elitism. Throughout the work Moore represents the Ripper case as an intellectual matter rather than a work in the subgenres of horror, crime, or true crime. For him the material is a chance to encounter "the vortex of fiction," a space to acknowledge and discuss how a horrible event becomes the subject of popular cultural and literary interest. Moreover, the work is presented as always being something more than just a meditation on the Ripper mythology. Notably, Moore suggests that the murders are a metaphor for the violence of the whole of the twentieth century, and it is on this note that he concludes the book when the detective Abberline ponders: "I think there is going to be another war."

Eddie Campbell's illustrations add to the overall effect of *From Hell* being entirely about its own seriousness and claim to something "higher" than the deeper pulp-genre contexts. Page after page of black-and-white sketching combines with carefully rendered maps, street scenes, and river vistas. Campbell's graphics offer a London for serious intellectuals, psycho-geographers of the city, people just like Moore himself, and not for the traditional horror fan (although of course the categories are not exclusive). Moreover, the depictions of the violence in *From Hell* are genuinely unpleasant because this is an important part of the subtext: this work is serious art and not trash horror, and it is for this reason that Campbell must show us everything and not just the typical clichés. Ironically, this is why the reader is given page after page of close-ups and intense imagery, precisely because it is not found in the traditional pulp genres. And, just in case we were ever unsure that *From Hell*'s real message is that this is all to be taken very

seriously indeed as a work of literature and art, then Campbell's anatomi-
cally detailed depictions of sexual intercourse underline the same message,
as do his occasional sequences of quasi-abstract illustration. In *From Hell*
everything is organized to be high art, recuperating the reader away from
the old populist sensationalism of the underlying material.

Moore and Campbell borrowed the Ripper mythology from numerous
sites of genre fiction. Whether or not their transformation of it into an intellectual and artistic new work is fully realized is a matter of opinion. The
least one can say is that *From Hell* lacks any of the spirit of humanity that
Crumb located in his stories of the blues, or Eisner, Jaxon, Kubert, Brown,
and others provided in their works. Perhaps it is the clinical appropriation
of genre fiction into the image of the high art realm that in the end limits the
piece. Finally regarding Moore, one can note briefly here that his later series,
The League of Extraordinary Gentlemen, illustrated by Kevin O'Neill, offers
a refreshingly light-hearted counterpoint to *From Hell*.[23] Therein the Victorian period is captured through an ironic filtering of some of its best-known
literary works.

The direct adaptation of pre-existing "old" genre fiction into new graphic
novels adds a further tranche of publications one may call historical fiction. For example, translated from the French, there are important works by
Jacques Tardi that retell the 1970s noir fictions of Jean-Patrick Manchette.[24]
Similarly, Darwyn Cooke has adapted crime fiction from Donald Westlake,
in three recent works, *Parker: The Hunter*, *Parker: The Outfit*, and *Parker:
The Score*.[25] Cooke's drawing style deliberately echoes the lines and shapes
of 1960s design and advertising culture. This visual tactic further historicizes
his work, as it is presented as if the graphic novel was made contempora-
neously with the original novel. For what it's worth it is also the case that
adaptations have moved in the other direction, that is from graphic novels
to different media, as when the director Sam Mendes adapted the graphic
novel *Road to Perdition* by Max Allan Collins for the cinema in 2002.

The folkloric-realist historical fiction is also being supplanted by a quite
different approach to the works discussed as using genre as a key device.
Thus, several graphic novelists continue to engage with historical themes
by emphasizing the process of discovering the past rather than discussing
or using a period of history per se. This updating of historical fiction has
much in common with the autobiographical graphic novel because it too
focuses on a present-day narrator recounting tales of how the past is shaping the present day. This strategy of self-reflexivity is well evidenced in the
series of titles by Kim Deitch, including *Alias the Cat!* and *The Search for
Smilin' Ed!*[26] Drawn and written in a mode close to magical realism, they

depict Deitch's obsession with the history of early television and animation, and repeatedly a cat-like character, Waldo. As with Crumb and Spiegelman, Deitch justifies his obsessions with the past on the grounds that the present day is deeply worrying. Thus in *Alias the Cat!* he proclaims: "at the dawn of a new century, and the world seems more full of greedy fucks, evil politicians, and empty headed flag-waving assholes than it ever was!"[27] It is also true that in works from Daniel Clowes and Charles Burns, past times frequently hover ominously over present-day protagonists, and this is communicated via the inclusion of extended images from previous periods. In both of their oeuvres little snippets of visual information, included in one or two panels, snap to life alongside the dramas of the contemporary plot. Generally speaking, Clowes offers a more contained and constrained approach to the idea of "history as memory," or meta-history, when compared to that developed by Burns. Throughout his trilogy – *X'ed Out*, *The Hive*, and *Sugar Skull* – there is a nightmarish weaving together of dark fantasies, historical memories, and a series of dysfunctional familial and sexual relationships.[28] Herein no one period (past, present, or future) is a stable or a dominant memory or setting. Instead, the reader is left to map through constantly juxtaposed images of different times so as to eventually understand what haunts the main protagonist.

Just occasionally there have been examples of work where some of the main tendencies in historical fiction that I have discussed in this survey have been productively blurred together in clever syntheses. For example, the first major graphic novel from Ben Katchor displays interesting intersections between the folkloric-realist mode and some aspects of those works that pastiche genre fiction. His *The Jew of New York* was published by Pantheon at the end of the 1990s and to some extent it signaled that important publishing house's re-engagement with the graphic novel post-*Maus*.[29] Katchor's work is a sophisticated composite of a number of themes and issues discussed in this chapter. Certainly it is drawn and narrated in a realist mode. For example, the social setting of the new migrants and their "small lives" matches very strongly the folkloric-realist graphic novels. So too does the inclusion of a political subtext that underlines an endemic culture of anti-Semitism. What is, however, also a critical element of the success of this work is Katchor's ability to present his material as a pastiche of folk tales and oral traditions of the period he tries to capture, and that is a move which is close to Mignola's appreciation of the old weird tales that inspired *Hellboy*. A further intersection with the faux-pulp graphic novels of a Mike Mignola is Katchor's careful balance between ironic distance and underlying respect for authenticity in the material. It is also the case that Katchor and Mignola share a fascination with (differing) versions of the uncanny and the surreal. Katchor provides a series of digressions on myths and legends about the development of New York and its hinterland: tall tales of mystics, magical schemes to make a fortune, and eccentric characters thrown into the maelstrom of a rapidly growing city. Similarly, Mignola's work is derivative from the weird tales tradition invented by H. P. Lovecraft and his contemporaries. In summary, Katchor achieves something quite remarkable in *The Jew of New York*: there is a deep sense of realism but this is wedded to an open eye for pastiche and irony.

In conclusion, the purpose of this chapter has been to explain the common shapes of historical fiction in the graphic novel. It has underlined the main paradigms through which the past is recounted in exemplary fictional works. It has underlined the importance of a folk-realist current of work in which a nostalgic view of the past is established by highlighting narratives of survival and triumph in adversity. The rise of autobiography and reportage in graphic novels has taken away much space from this approach and consequently, different reimaginings of the past have developed. Notably a substantial number of graphic novelists combine historical fiction with genres of horror, crime, and the superhero comics. Reflexive accounts on the nature of thinking about the past in the present day are also an increasingly rich area of creation.

By way of an epilogue, it is useful to very briefly underline two final aspects here. First, now that the graphic novel is an established cultural form, it is able to respond quite quickly to anniversaries and commemorative events of public importance. Witness the spate of new works of historical fiction being published to coincide with the hundredth anniversary of the outbreak of the First World War.[30] Second, as my brief earlier note on the importance of Tardi's work in English translation, *West Coast Blues*, intimates, francophone creators also commonly write historical fiction. Tardi's own prolific career is of course exemplary. However, his career is just one case among many where historical settings are critical for the *bande dessinée*. In fact, the story of the rise of the graphic novel in the English language is not complete without acknowledging the several early translations of French and Italian examples of historical fiction. After all, it was in precisely this format that Tardi, Hugo Pratt, Moebius, and Enki Bilal were introduced to North American readers.[31] When the translations of their historical fictions (*Corto Maltese*, *Blueberry*, *The Hunting Party*, and others) are read alongside those better remembered contributions from Will Eisner and Jack Jaxon, one starts to recognize just how significant historical fiction is for the graphic novel.

Works Cited

Augustyn, Brian, and Mike Mignola. *Batman: Gotham by Gaslight*. New York: DC Comics, 2013.

Baetens, Jan, and Hugo Frey. *The Graphic Novel: An Introduction*. New York: Cambridge University Press, 2014.

Baker, Kyle. *Nat Turner*. New York: Abrams, 2008.

Bilal [Enki], and [Pierre] Christin. *The Hunting Party*. New York: Catalan Communications, 1990.

The Ranks of the Black Order. New York: Catalan Communications, 1989.

Brooks, Max, and Caanan White. *The Harlem Hellfighters*. New York: Broadway Books, 2014.

Brown, Chester. *Louis Riel* (2003). Montreal: Drawn & Quarterly, 2013.

Burns, Charles. *The Hive*. New York: Pantheon Books, 2012.

Sugar Skull. New York: Pantheon Books, 2014.

X'ed Out. New York: Pantheon Books, 2010.

Cooke, Darwyn, and Richard Stark. *Parker: The Hunter*. San Diego, CA: IDW Publishing, 2009.

Crumb, Robert. "Patton." *Zap Comix* 11 (1985), republished in Robert Crumb, *The Complete Crumb Comics* 15. Seattle, WA: Fantagraphics Books, 2011, 104–15.

R. Crumb's Heroes of Blues, Jazz and Country. New York: Abrams, 2006.

Deitch, Kim. *Alias the Cat!* New York: Pantheon Books, 2007.

The Search for Smilin' Ed! Seattle, WA: Fantagraphics Books, 2010.

Eisner, Will. *A Contract with God*. New York: W. W. Norton, 2006.

Ennis, Garth, and Goran Parlov. *Max Fury: My War Gone By*. New York: Marvel, 2014.

Frey, Hugo. "History and Memory in Franco-Belgian *Bande Dessinée*." *Rethinking History: Journal of Theory and Practice* 6, no. 3 (2002): 293–304.

Gaiman, Neil, and Andy Kubert. *Marvel 1602*. New York: Marvel, 2010.

Gardner, Jared. *Projections: Comics and the History of Twenty-First Century Storytelling*. Stanford University Press, 2012.

Guthrie, Woody. *Bound for Glory*. New York: E. P. Dutton, 1943.

Jaxon [Jack Jackson]. *Comanche Moon*. San Francisco, CA: Rip Off Press, 1979.

Los Tejanos and Lost Cause. Seattle, WA: Fantagraphics Books, 2012.

Katchor, Ben. *The Jew of New York*. New York: Pantheon Books, 1998.

Kubert, Joe. *Jew Gangster*. New York: DC Comics, 2005.

Sgt Rock: The Prophesy. New York: DC Comics, 2007.

Marcus, Greil. *Invisible Republic: Bob Dylan's Basement Tapes*. London: Picador, 1997.

Mignola, Mike, and John Byrne. *Hellboy: Seed of Destruction*. Milwaukie, OR: Dark Horse Books, 1994.

Miller, Frank, and David Mazzucchelli. *Batman Year One*. New York: DC Comics Deluxe Edition, 2007.

Moore, Alan, and Eddie Campbell. *From Hell*. London: Knockabout Comics, 2000.

Moore, Alan, and Kevin O'Neill. *The League of Extraordinary Gentlemen*, Vol. 1. New York: Wildstorm/DC Comics, 1999.

Pak, Greg, and Carmine Di Giandomenico. *X-Men: Magneto Testament*. New York: Marvel, 2009.

Pratt, Hugo. *Corto Maltese: Ballad of the Salt Sea*. London: Harvill, 1996.
   Corto Maltese: The Celts. London: Harvill, 1996.
Rakoff, David, and Seth. *Love, Dishonor, Marry, Die, Cherish, Perish: A Novel*. New
   York: Pantheon Books, 2013.
Reyns-Chikuma, Chris. "Economie et identité dans la BD belge francophone:
   L'Exemple des *Maîtres de l'orge* de Jean Van Hamme." *The French Review* 84,
   no. 2 (Dec. 2010): 342–55.
Sacco, Joe. *The Great War*. New York: W. W. Norton, 2013.
Sontag, Susan. "Fascinating Fascism," in *Under the Sign of Saturn*. London: Vintage,
   1996, 73–105.
Spiegelman, Art. *In the Shadow of No Towers*. New York: Pantheon Books, 2004.
Stassen [J. P.] *Deogratias: A Tale of Rwanda*. New York: First Second, 2006.
Sturm, James. *James Sturm's America: God, Gold, and Golems*. Montreal: Drawn &
   Quarterly, 2007.
Sturm, James, and Rich Tommaso. *Satchel Paige: Striking Out Jim Crow*. New York:
   Jump at the Sun, 2007.
Tabachnick, Stephen E. *The Quest for Jewish Belief and Identity in the Graphic
   Novel*. Tuscaloosa, AL: University of Alabama Press, 2014.
Talbot, Bryan. *The Adventures of Luther Arkwright*. Milwaukie, OR: Dark Horse
   Books, 2007.
Tardi, Jacques. *Adele and the Beast*. New York: NBM, 1990.
Tardi, Jacques, and Jean-Patrick Manchette. *West Coast Blues*. Seattle, WA: Fanta-
   graphics Books, 2009.
Vance, James, and Dan Burr. *Kings in Disguise*. Princeton, NJ: Kitchen Sink Press,
   1990.
Walker, George A. *Written in Wood: Three Wordless Graphic Narratives*. Richmond
   Hill, ON: Firefly Books, 2014.
Young, Frank M., and David Lasky. *The Carter Family: Don't Forget this Song*. New
   York: Abrams, 2012.

NOTES

1 Greil Marcus, *Invisible Republic: Bob Dylan's Basement Tapes* (London:
   Picador, 1997), 272.
2 Robert Crumb, "Patton," *Zap Comix* 11 (1985), republished in Robert Crumb,
   The Complete Crumb Comics, Vol. 15 (Seattle, WA: Fantagraphics Books, 2011),
   104–15; Robert Crumb, *R. Crumb's Heroes of Blues, Jazz and Country* (New
   York: Abrams, 2006).
3 See Will Eisner, *A Contract with God* (New York: W. W. Norton, 2006); James
   Vance and Dan Burr, *Kings in Disguise* (Princeton, NJ: Kitchen Sink Press, 1990);
   James Sturm, *James Sturm's America: God, Gold, and Golems* (Montreal: Drawn
   & Quarterly, 2007); James Sturm and Rich Tommaso, *Satchel Paige: Striking Out
   Jim Crow* (New York: Jump at the Sun, 2007); Joe Kubert, *Jew Gangster* (New
   York: DC Comics, 2005); Jaxon, *Comanche Moon* (San Francisco, CA: Rip Off
   Press, 1979); and Jaxon, *Los Tejanos and Lost Cause* (Seattle, WA: Fantagraphics
   Books, 2012).
4 Susan Sontag, "Fascinating Fascism," in *Under the Sign of Saturn* (London:
   Vintage, 1996), 105.

5 Art Spiegelman, *In the Shadow of No Towers* (New York: Pantheon Books, 2004), 11.

6 See Stephen E. Tabachnick, *The Quest for Jewish Belief and Identity in the Graphic Novel* (Tuscaloosa, AL: University of Alabama Press, 2014). Of course not all works fit this model, as the author discusses very openly.

7 [J. P.] Stassen, *Deogratias: A Tale of Rwanda* (New York: First Second, 2006).

8 See Jan Baetens and Hugo Frey, *The Graphic Novel: An Introduction* (New York: Cambridge University Press, 2014), 134–36.

9 Woody Guthrie, *Bound for Glory* (New York: E. P. Dutton, 1943).

10 Chester Brown, *Louis Riel* (2003; Montreal: Drawn & Quarterly, 2013).

11 David Rakoff and Seth, *Love, Dishonor, Marry, Die, Cherish, Perish: A Novel* (New York: Pantheon Books, 2013).

12 Kyle Baker, *Nat Turner* (New York: Abrams, 2008).

13 George A. Walker, *Written in Wood: Three Wordless Graphic Narratives* (Richmond Hill, ON: Firefly Books, 2014).

14 Tom Thomson (1877–1917). Thomson is credited as a key Canadian painter whose works greatly influence "The Group of Seven" – he is a national hero also known because of his tragic death aged forty, the full causes of which are shrouded in mystery and mythology.

15 Frank M. Young and David Lasky, *The Carter Family: Don't Forget this Song* (New York: Abrams, 2012).

16 The series began as a comic in the late 1970s. It is collected in Bryan Talbot, *The Adventures of Luther Arkwright* (Milwaukie, OR: Dark Horse Books, 2007).

17 Mike Mignola and John Byrne, *Hellboy: Seed of Destruction* (Milwaukie, OR: Dark Horse Books, 1994).

18 Frank Miller and David Mazzucchelli, *Batman Year One* (New York: DC Comics Deluxe Edition, 2007).

19 Brian Augustyn and Mike Mignola, *Batman: Gotham by Gaslight* (New York: DC Comics, 2013); Garth Ennis and Goran Parlov, *Max Fury: My War Gone By* (New York: Marvel, 2014); Neil Gaiman and Andy Kubert, *Marvel 1602* (New York: Marvel, 2010).

20 Greg Pak and Carmine Di Giandomenico, *X-Men: Magneto Testament* (New York: Marvel, 2009); Joe Kubert, *Sgt Rock: The Prophesy* (New York: DC Comics, 2007).

21 Jake and Dinos Chapman, *The Sum of All Evil* (2012–13).

22 Alan Moore and Eddie Campbell, *From Hell* (London: Knockabout Comics, 2000).

23 Numerous titles have now been published under "The League of Extraordinary Gentlemen" concept. The first work of the series was Alan Moore and Kevin O'Neill's *The League of Extraordinary Gentlemen*, Vol. 1 (New York: Wildstorm/DC Comics, 1999).

24 See Jacques Tardi and Jean-Patrick Manchette, *West Coast Blues* (Seattle, WA: Fantagraphics Books, 2009).

25 See, for example, Darwyn Cooke and Richard Stark, *Parker: The Hunter* (San Diego, CA: IDW Publishing, 2009).

26 Kim Deitch, *Alias the Cat!* (New York: Pantheon Books, 2007); *The Search for Smilin' Ed!* (Seattle, WA: Fantagraphics Books, 2010).

27 Deitch cited from the non-paginated final panel of the final page of *Alias the Cat!*

28 Charles Burns, *X'ed Out* (New York: Panthon, 2010); *The Hive* (New York: Pantheon Books, 2012); *Sugar Skull* (New York: Pantheon Books, 2014).

29 Ben Katchor, *The Jew of New York* (New York: Pantheon Books, 1998).

30 See, for example, Joe Sacco, *The Great War* (New York: W. W. Norton, 2013); and Max Brooks and Caanan White, *The Harlem Hellfighters* (New York: Broadway Books, 2014).

31 See, for example, Enki Bilal and Pierre Christin, *The Ranks of the Black Order* (New York: Catalan Communications, 1989); Bilal and Christin, *The Hunting Party* (New York: Catalan Communications, 1990); and Jacques Tardi, *Adele and the Beast* (New York: NBM, 1990). Some of the earliest French titles to feature in English translation were historical "Westerns" in the *Blueberry* series created by Jean-Michel Charlier and Jean Giraud ("Moebius"). Titles were published by Egmont/Methuen in the later 1970s and by Epic in the later 1980s and early 1990s: Hugo Pratt, *Corto Maltese: Ballad of the Salt Sea* (London: Harvill, 1996); Hugo Pratt, *Corto Maltese: The Celts* (London: Harvill, 1996). For a general context of representations of history in French comics and graphic novels, see Hugo Frey, "History and Memory in Franco-Belgian *Bande Dessinée*," *Rethinking History: Journal of Theory and Practice* 6, no. 3 (2002): 293–304. Recent works of historical fiction are also helpfully analyzed in Chris Reyns-Chikuma, "Economie et identité dans la BD belge francophone: L'Exemple des *Maîtres de l'orge* de Jean Van Hamme," *The French Review* 84, no. 2 (Dec. 2010): 342–55.

6

DARREN HARRIS-FAIN

Revisionist Superheroes, Fantasy, and Science Fiction

Introduction

Revision, as writing instructors often tell their students, means "re-vision," to see again, to look at afresh. Revision, in genres as in writing, takes what is already there and changes it according to one's purpose. Writers revise to strengthen their arguments, add supporting detail, and improve organization and clarity. Genre revisionists, however, take existing genre materials and alter them for other purposes, taking familiar character types and situations in different directions, rendering cruder generic materials more realistically or in a more sophisticated fashion, satirizing or critiquing genre conventions, or simply playing with someone else's characters. But no matter the reason, genre revisionism involves re-vision, looking again at something familiar and seeing it with new eyes.

Literary revisionism, and revisionist works in other arts, is not unique to genre fiction. Major authors such as Geoffrey Chaucer, William Shakespeare, and John Milton drew heavily on existing literary sources; nor is such revisionism limited to earlier authors, as demonstrated by Geraldine Brooks' *March* (2005), which reimagines Louisa May Alcott's *Little Women* (1868–69) from the father's point of view. Not only did James Joyce structure his novel *Ulysses* (1922) on Homer's *Odyssey*, but *Ulysses* also revises the very form of the novel, eschewing traditional narrative conventions in favor of fragmentation, experimentation, and polyphonic points of view. Revisionist tendencies are even more pronounced in genre fiction. For instance, the hard-boiled school of American detective fiction of the 1920s and 1930s is a revision of the more genteel detective stories that preceded it, and the recent proliferation of female detectives is a revision of a previously male-dominated genre. Romance fiction, science fiction, and the western have also evolved, mostly in content but occasionally in technique also. Another type of genre revisionism reworks established materials, returning to older narratives and presenting them in a new way. Sometimes this is done professionally, as with

Gregory Maguire's Oz-based novels, and sometimes through reams of fan fiction about characters from popular franchises. Often fan fiction reflects fans' desires to write about favorite characters and worlds, and sometimes fan writing places familiar characters into unfamiliar (and unauthorized) romantic or erotic scenarios.

Given the abundance of revisionism in genre fiction, it is unsurprising that similar tendencies can be found in graphic fiction. One of the most common types of revisionism involves new takes on established characters – something that is a given in the history of long-standing comics characters but that has escalated as comics and graphic novels have matured. A second type concerns the content of graphic narratives, especially revisions presenting familiar materials in more sophisticated ways. The desire to deal with genres more maturely relates to a third type, where the very conventions of a given genre are challenged and critiqued.

Revising Characters

In most fiction, characters' lives are limited to the individual work. Readers may disagree on the characteristics and traits of fictional figures, and in drama there is room for different interpretations of characters. However, it is less common for characters in literary fiction to reappear in subsequent works than in genre fiction, where series featuring the same central characters are common. This is even more pronounced in comics, which are typically serialized in newspaper strips or comic books. Thus characters introduced in the 1930s, like Superman and Batman, may still enjoy new adventures decades later. During these characters' long histories, they change in various ways for a variety of reasons. If a character is created by a single author, like Sherlock Holmes, the character's core traits may change little from story to story, but readers learn more about him with each successive story. On the other hand, if characters are the work of several hands over decades, they may change considerably.

Consider Batman, introduced in 1939. In his earliest adventures he was ruthless, remorselessly dispatching criminals. His persona became much lighter in the early 1940s, especially after Robin's introduction in 1940. Batman became an officially deputized member of the police, and his 1950s adventures tended toward the bright and fantastic. This version of Batman persisted into the 1960s, shaping the campy television program starring Adam West. But while Batmania swept the nation, younger writers and artists sought to restore Batman's darker roots. Since the 1970s, the comic book Batman has almost always maintained this approach, with occasionally lighter depictions such as the nostalgic *Batman '66* (2013) and *The Lego Batman Movie* (2017).

Any superhero with longevity is the product of continuous revisions. A major factor motivating these revisions is that superheroes are "redeveloped by regularly changing writers and illustrators (in ways that are sometimes slight and sometimes dramatic)," which frustrates the efforts of fans who desire continuity "to identify various strands of superhero revisions as canonical and non-canonical."[1] Terrence R. Wandtke claims that, because of changes introduced in the comics and other media, superheroes are constantly under revision, and concurrent versions of a character might even be contradictory. Fans tend to privilege current versions over earlier ones, he says, but the shadows of earlier versions linger over the contemporary. In a 1981 interview, Dwight Decker asked Frank Miller, "Can a group of writers and artists maintain the same character over 20 years and have it be the same character? It seems like you're lopping off the bottom of the series' continuity as you're adding to the top." Miller replied, "Characters have to be reinterpreted over time. The ones that aren't die."[2]

Among the characters subject to revision in genre graphic novels, superheroes are perhaps the most prone to this process because of their long histories and because they commonly reflect contemporary issues. As noted in many histories of superheroes, these characters have been potent barometers of shifting trends in American culture since their inception, and thus revisions in superhero characterization may easily point to changes in American society.[3]

In his introduction to *The Amazing Transforming Superhero!* Wandtke describes four types of superhero revisionism: 1. additive, "seemingly minor additions that can be read as the logical outgrowth of the basic premise established within a superhero narrative" (15–16); 2. fundamental revision, "major changes which signal a departure from what has been presented before in a specific superhero narrative" (17) and that deviate from the character's initial premise; 3. conceptual, rewriting "the basic ideas not of a superhero but of the superhero as a general idea with wide-ranging social impact" (19); and 4. critical revisions, defined as changes made in response to critical positions taken by critics, fans, and others (22). Thus defined, superhero revisionism has occurred with most if not all superheroes, including in multiple graphic novels.

One example exhibiting Wandtke's ideas about fundamental, conceptual, and critical revisionism is *Demon in a Bottle* (2006), which collects the story arc about Tony Stark's alcoholism in *Iron Man*, nos. 120–28 (1979). This graphic novel presents a fundamental revision of Iron Man's characterization with the introduction of his alcoholism; a conceptual revision in the suggestion that even a superhero could struggle with addiction; and a critical revision through the ongoing role of Stark's alcoholism in subsequent comics as well as the presentation of the character in twenty-first-century cinema, including the casting of an actor, Robert Downey Jr., who has also struggled with addiction.

Examples of fundamental revisionism can also be found in the various narrative and marketing strategies employed by DC and Marvel regarding their respective universes. One example is *Crisis on Infinite Earths* (1985–86), which simplified DC's complicated continuity while introducing certain radical character changes. Related to this is the phenomenon known by fans as the "retcon," short for "retroactive continuity," in which previous events in a superhero's career are reinterpreted to explain a contemporary plot development – as happened, for example, with the way in which DC's 2011 relaunch, the New 52, reversed the paralysis of Batgirl introduced in Alan Moore's 1988 graphic novel *Batman: The Killing Joke*, which also reimagined the Joker's origin.

While graphic novels like *Crisis on Infinite Earths* and *The Killing Joke* played with established continuities, others introduced further revisions. Some presented alternate versions of established superheroes in radically different ways, playing with the canon in a way similar to how science fiction's alternate histories change established history. DC's Elseworlds imprint cast established characters in unfamiliar settings and situations. Examples include *Batman: Gotham by Gaslight* (1989), which places Batman in Victorian London pursuing Jack the Ripper; *Kingdom Come* (1996), depicting a DC universe in which older superheroes conflict with each other and with younger costumed vigilantes; and *Superman: Red Son* (2003), where Kal-El lands in the Ukraine rather than Kansas and becomes a Soviet hero rather than the champion of truth, justice, and the American way. Similarly, Neil Gaiman's *Marvel 1602* (2004) transposes familiar Marvel characters to the early seventeenth century.

The two most commonly discussed examples of superhero revisionism are Frank Miller's *Batman: The Dark Knight Returns* (1986) and Alan Moore's *Watchmen* (1986–87). The latter began as a revision of Charlton Comics' superheroes that DC had purchased, and thus in its conception exemplifies character revisionism, as does *The Dark Knight Returns*. As Geoff Klock argues, *The Dark Knight Returns* is "a radical move in the history of the superhero narrative" because, instead of simply offering another variant on Batman or adding to his mythology, it combines multiple and seemingly contradictory elements from Batman's long history into a coherent whole.[4] Thus, Klock says, Miller offers a "misreading" of comic book history that aligns with Harold Bloom's ideas about revision as rewriting and correction

(28). According to Klock, "Miller's writing is very conscious of this process and actively strives to participate in comic book tradition, invoking various recognizable aspects in such a way as to recast readers' understanding of what they have seen before" (31). In this sense, Miller's revision of Batman truly is an example of re-vision, of seeing again but in a new way.

A more radical revision of an established character can be found in Gaiman's *The Sandman*. Published as seventy-five issues between 1989 and 1996, *The Sandman* comprises both stand-alone stories and longer narrative arcs that, in their collected format, work as graphic novels. Initially conceived as a revision of a character created by Joe Simon and Jack Kirby in the 1970s, Gaiman's *Sandman* instead introduced an entirely new character: Morpheus (also known as Dream and Oneiros), a supernatural being who controls the realm of dreams. Although it occasionally intersects with the DC universe, *The Sandman* inhabits much broader worlds, ranging from contemporary America to Shakespeare's England, from medieval Baghdad to Greek mythology (see fig. 6.1). Essentially a fantasy series, *The Sandman* is revisionist not just in how its title character deviates from his inspiration, but also in how Gaiman's characterization departs from the title's superhero roots. "The Sandman violates all the rules about what makes a character popular in the super-hero-dominated comics industry," writes Hy Bender:

> Rather than being muscular, cheery, and colorful, he's thin, humorless, and perpetually dressed in black. In lieu of maintaining a secret identity to fit in with normal people, he prefers to avoid people...And instead of battling for his life against monsters and mad scientists, he seldom encounters situations that place him in any physical jeopardy...because his powers rival those of gods.[5]

The history of superheroes also shaped another graphic novel series offering substantial revisions of established characters: Alan Moore's *The League of Extraordinary Gentlemen*. His premise – that the heroes and villains of late Victorian tales of adventure and the fantastic are active in an alternate England – not only presents familiar characters such as Allan Quatermain, Captain Nemo, Dr. Jekyll (and his alter ego, Mr. Hyde), the Invisible Man, and Mina Murray from Bram Stoker's *Dracula* (1897) in a new story, but does so following the familiar pattern of the superhero team. Their new adventures thus expand upon their previous histories as characters, and mostly their characterizations resemble their fictional foundations. According to Brad Ricca, in these books and *Lost Girls* (2006), Moore "appropriates and adapts a wide range of canonical and non-canonical works, revisiting well-known characters, extending or re-examining popular stories,

Fig. 6.1 Revising Shakespeare, revising fantasy. From *The Sandman: Dream Country* ©1990 DC Comics. Written by Neil Gaiman and illustrated by Kelley Jones, Charles Vess, Colleen Doran, Malcolm Jones III, Dave McKean, Robbie Busch, and Steve Oliff. Courtesy of DC Comics.

exploring and forging new intertextual connections and celebrating latent or repressed elements from his source material."[6]

Perhaps the most radical character revision in *The League of Extraordinary Gentlemen*, especially in the first two volumes of the series, is Mina Murray, who at the conclusion of *Dracula* has married Jonathan Harker. In Moore's graphic novels, however, she is a divorced, fiercely independent woman who effectively becomes the leader of the League. As Laura Hilton notes, "Mina's leadership presents one of the central divergences from Stoker's Mina through the opposition of the 'patriarchal hierarchy' of

Dracula due to her position as 'a ruling woman' in the League."[7] Although Stoker's Mina marries due to the conventions of her period and of Gothic fiction, Hilton says, "Moore's Mina instead embraces independence and autonomy in reflection of the New Woman ... whilst only occasionally adhering to the limitations of conventional Victorian conservatism and the traditional Gothic heroine" (204). Thus Moore is able to revise Mina as "a progressive female character who is often capable of thriving in a patriarchal society" while still remaining true to the graphic novel's setting, rather than simply imposing contemporary feminism on a Victorian character.[8]

Revising Genre Content

The graphic novels in *The League of Extraordinary Gentlemen* series are also revisionist texts in content. As noted above, the books unite characters from disparate fictional sources into a steampunk England threatened by forces themselves derived from different fictional sources. Not only does *The League of Extraordinary Gentlemen* present the further adventures of familiar characters, but it does so within a shared universe, much like superheroes initially appeared in their own comics but were soon revealed to inhabit the same fictional space.

In addition to adding to these characters' fictional histories and juxtaposing those histories, in *The League of Extraordinary Gentlemen* Moore and his artist Kevin O'Neill go beyond their source material regarding both violence and sex. Although the original sources have their share of violence, none of it was described in explicit detail, and much was left to readers' imaginations. In contrast, *The League of Extraordinary Gentlemen* is extraordinarily violent, and there is often nothing gentlemanly about the conduct of either the book's heroes or their villains. Moreover, given the nature of graphic narrative and O'Neill's unflinching depictions of violent scenes, *The League of Extraordinary Gentlemen* often puts the "graphic" in graphic novel.

The sex in the series is equally graphic – at times practically pornographic. In part, this reflects Moore's project of unifying different fictional strands. In Victorian England, popular entertainments such as the novels of H. Rider Haggard, Robert Louis Stevenson, Bram Stoker, and H. G. Wells were bound by the conventions and legal restrictions of the day, when even a novel teeming with sexuality like *Dracula* could only go so far; but the stereotypically straight-laced Victorian age also produced an abundance of pornography, some of which – such as the clandestinely published magazine *The Pearl* – is alluded to in the books. In *The League of Extraordinary Gentlemen*, these two fictional streams come together, and the visual aspect of the graphic novels makes their sexual content all the more explicit.

But as sexually graphic as *The League of Extraordinary Gentlemen* can be, it pales compared to Moore's highly pornographic *Lost Girls*. A three-volume graphic novel whose format evokes the nineteenth-century triple-decker, *Lost Girls* too presents familiar figures from fantastic fiction in the same narrative – specifically, Lewis Carroll's Alice, Wendy from J. M. Barrie's *Peter Pan* (1904), and Dorothy from L. Frank Baum's Oz books – but does so in a way that alters not only their characterizations but also the content of their respective stories. All three are depicted as grown women who meet at an Austrian hotel just before the First World War. Moore revises their characterizations in two ways: first, by extending their stories beyond their fictional sources, and second, by denuding their stories of their fantastic elements. There is a strong sense of unreality in *Lost Girls*, but at the same time the narrative is strictly realistic, with the women's sexual stories and fantasies evoking their familiar fantastic versions while simultaneously presenting their lives and the horrors of the coming war as all too real.

In taking his sources' youthful protagonists into (very) adult territory and recasting his fantastic sources into a realistic mold, Moore substantially revises core genre texts, and Annalisa Di Liddo argues that Moore's revisionism extends beyond the source material into these books' extra-textual associations in popular culture. *Lost Girls*, she says, "is underpinned not only by a trio of noteworthy source works, but also by the complex stratification of subtexts and already 'adult' by-meanings that arise from the massive amount of rewrites their protagonists have been subjected to, and which to great degree have become rooted in the collective imagination."[9] In this sense, *Lost Girls* is not simply a revision of existing sources but also of previous revisions of these frequently rewritten texts.

For much of his career, Moore has revised other writers' works, whether these are the Charlton superheroes in *Watchmen* or the weird mythologies of H. P. Lovecraft, as in *Neonomicon* (2010). Moore's revisionism has transcended mere tributes or sexual depictions of favorite characters, as in much fan fiction. Rather, his revisions often subvert their source material. According to Julie Sanders, "as the notion of hostile takeover present in a term such as 'appropriation' implies, adaptation can also be oppositional, even subversive. There are as many opportunities for divergence as adherence, for assault as well as homage."[10] Although Moore's graphic novels avoid didacticism, one nevertheless senses his values in how he treats familiar characters and situations – values that occasionally are at odds with those of the writers whose work he appropriates and revises, as in his disturbing *Neonomicon*.[11]

Given Moore's propensity to play in other creators' sandboxes, it is perhaps ironic that he strongly opposed DC Comics' announcement of *Before Watchmen*, a set of prequels (later collected as graphic novellas) drawn from the world and characters of *Watchmen*. Understandably, part of his hostility stemmed from longstanding bitterness about his contract with DC and subsequent treatment by the company, but he may also have worried that the quality of these titles would be lower than the original, which after all received a Hugo Award from the World Science Fiction Society and was named in both *Time*'s "Top 10 Graphic Novels" list and its "All-*Time* 100 Greatest Novels" list. Additionally, he may have been concerned about having his own work revised by others.

But if the multitude of genre-based graphic novel revisions demonstrates anything, it is the appeal of compelling characters and scenarios – and in fantastic fiction, one of the most frequently revised bodies of material is fairy tales. Retellings and revisions of popular fairy tales abound, in film and television as well as fiction and works such as Bill Willingham's *Fables*, a comic book whose collections and spinoffs have resulted in several graphic novels.[12] Here well-known characters from fairy tales and folklore have been transplanted into contemporary New York City, forming a secret community. Although the fantastic permeates the series, the major characters lead mundane lives, even if they frequently get into various scrapes. Consequently, the assorted *Fables* books constitute a substantial revision of fairy-tale content – not just in the stories they tell, but in the way they expand the generic boundaries of the fairy-tale form. For instance, one familiar character, the Big Bad Wolf from "The Three Little Pigs," is recast in human form as Bigby Wolf, a trench-coated, chain-smoking detective straight out of hard-boiled crime fiction. Nor is noir the only genre Willingham fuses with fairy tales. As Cristina Bacchilega notes, *Fables* also dips into fantasy, mystery, and romance.[13] Willingham's *Fables* thus upends the entire notion of a fairy-tale "genre" to encompass other kinds of genre as well.

Revising Genre Conventions

It is unsurprising that in revisionist genre graphic novels, one finds both revisions of established characters and narrative content and works that challenge genre conventions. Sometimes such challenges are technical – for instance, Moore's use of supplementary prose texts in *Watchmen* and *The League of Extraordinary Gentlemen*, Miller's use of television screens in *The Dark Knight Returns*, or Chris Ware's deconstructions of graphic narrative conventions in *Jimmy Corrigan: The Smartest Kid on Earth* (2000) and *Building Stories* (2012). As Julian Darius has noted, *Watchmen* and *The*

Dark Knight Returns were also revolutionary in employing narrative techniques such as flashbacks, juxtapositions, and multiple points of view, as well as their allusions and symbolic motifs.[14] Though such experiments are aesthetically interesting, challenges to a genre's conventions and formulas are primarily the focus of most readers regarding key revisionist texts.

Genres are categories of narrative sharing certain central elements. In westerns, for example, a key element is setting, a particular time and place. But westerns often share other elements, such as the characterization of the hero or the nature of his antagonists. Thus genres typically develop conventions and formulas governing their content, but these may change over time or be challenged by creators wishing to reinvigorate a stale genre or shape genre materials to contemporary concerns, as seen in John Cawelti's explanation of how convention and invention possess different cultural functions:

> Conventions represent familiar shared images and meanings and they assert an ongoing community of values; inventions confront us with a new perception or meaning that we have not realized before...Conventions help maintain a culture's stability while inventions help it respond to changing circumstances and provide new information about the world.[15]

Authors who "try to undercut existing formulas" often do so "in response to changing cultural values," and in genre fiction "the writers that we most value are those who make their own distinctive uses of the formula or formulas in question."[16] It is little wonder, then, that three of the most widely read graphic novelists – Neil Gaiman, Frank Miller, and Alan Moore – are also genre revisionists, regarding characters and content as well as genre conventions.

Marvel's superhero comics of the 1960s revised earlier depictions of the superhero,[17] and DC's silver age heroes revised their golden age counterparts. In the 1980s, as comic book audiences shifted further away from children and young teens toward older teens and young adults, "adult themes were regularly introduced to the fantasy world of superhero narratives."[18] Such stories introduced greater psychological realism, as well as a more realistic depiction of sex and violence. By far, none were as successful as Miller's *The Dark Knight Returns* and Moore's *Watchmen*. Such texts, which Wandtke labels as "conceptual revisionism," "view the superhero seriously and playfully at the same time, earnestly embracing the conventions of superhero narratives while foregrounding those conventions in a way that indicates skeptical detachment" (19).

Critics often note that one of the most revisionist aspects of *Watchmen* is its realism.[19] Because it shows superheroes not simply as psychologically complex, flawed human beings, but perhaps morally questionable as well,

Watchmen undermines the veneration typically granted to superheroes by readers and forces them to question the entire concept of the superhero.[20] As Di Liddo observes, in *Watchmen* "the narrative potential of the cracks surfacing on the mask of the superhero is brought to its extreme consequences in Moore's production."[21] In doing so, she says, Moore critiques the ideologies associated with the figure of the superhero, in particular "the legitimization of the ethics of vigilantism" (47–48). Similarly, Klock argues that Moore draws on established superhero archetypes but that "*Watchmen*'s revisionary referencing is used to ask questions about the history it absorbs."[22] In asking what superheroes would be like if they actually existed and how the world might change as a result, Moore provides us with a rereading of the superhero amounting to a deconstruction of its essential premises.

The Dark Knight Returns is often compared to *Watchmen* as a revisionist superhero text, but as Wandtke says, Miller's treatment "was much more sentimental and affectionate while Moore's was much more ironic and bitter."[23] Miller's project began as a way of inserting a greater degree of realism (as well as new life) into superhero comics. In a 1985 interview, Miller said, "Superheroes have lost their human context. That's precisely why the comics have gotten so weak, and the stories seem so pointless and so irrelevant."[24] Having already re-energized Daredevil by making him grittier and more realistic, in the mid-1980s Miller turned his attention to Batman. Although Batman in his earliest adventures was also a grim figure, Miller's Batman differs in both his tortured psyche and his brutality. Also, while Klock acknowledges that many things about Miller's Batman are not so much reinventions as reintroductions, he adds that some elements of *The Dark Knight Returns* are truly new, such as a female Robin and the creation of a homoerotic aspect in the Batman–Joker relationship.[25]

Just as Miller has revised certain superhero conventions, so some argue that his *Sin City* novels are revisionist noir texts. Scott McCloud suggests that the extreme violence in *Sin City* and its depictions of women should not be taken seriously because the series is "a tongue-in-cheek, over-the-top hyper-noir send-up."[26] Yet when asked if *Sin City* is meant to be taken straightforwardly or instead as satire or tribute, Miller replied that "the ones I'm proudest of are the ones that are sincere attempts to replicate, or better, re-interpret. I do have some jolly fun with its conventions and quirks now and then, and confess that in a job or two, it's run away from me. But the series as a whole is not intended as parody."[27] Miller's intentions aside, one could safely say that *Sin City* is as much a revision of the hardboiled crime story as Roman Polanski's *Chinatown* (1974) or James Ellroy's *L.A. Confidential* (1990). Like *The Dark Knight Returns*, *Sin City* challenges the conventions of Miller's chosen genre by pushing those conventions to such an extreme that readers may question the underpinnings of the genre itself.

Conclusion

The reasons behind revisionist genre graphic novels are many and varied. Often, authors simply desire to work with someone else's characters and settings. Popular stories by definition enjoy broad appeal, and sometimes graphic novelists just want to play in a particular universe. Such excursions are rooted in respect for the originals, but any extensions beyond those originals constitute a form of revisionism. Likewise, sometimes authors want to create new stories in established genres because of those genres' appeal. They might not intend to alter the genre, but genres change over time with each new contribution, even if the addition is not meant to transform the genre.

But genres are also consciously revised. Perhaps an author enjoys a genre but believes its conventions have become stale or predictable. The author may thus decide to play with established formulas, resulting in a work that effectively revises the genre's established patterns. Such revision may also occur with characters, especially characters who endure for decades. Frequently these kinds of revision are not meant to be radical, but rather to expand the possibilities for a certain character or type of story. Another rationale for such revisionism is to update older story styles or characters for a new time; thus alterations in setting or characterization may lead to departures from the familiar.

Revisionism might also be used to comment on contemporary concerns. Literary works sometimes address current issues, but genre fiction has a stronger tradition of reflecting contemporary culture – sometimes directly, sometimes obliquely. Both *The Dark Knight Returns* and *Watchmen*, for example, are Cold War texts, and *A Game of You*, volume five of *The Sandman*, includes a character whose life touches on contemporary conversations about transgender individuals.

In addition to offering social, cultural, or political critiques, revisionist graphic novels may also critique the genre materials they revise. Some claim that genres pass through predictable cycles of origin, classicism, revisionism, and parody, with the latter two allowing authors to look at what has preceded them critically. Such criticism may be directed at unrealistic tropes or characters and take the form of a greater level of believability. It may also question the very premises that underlie the genre, questioning not just the plausibility of the source materials but also the values that permeate them.

Whatever the reason, revisionist genre works have transformed the graphic novel landscape. They have brought increased attention to graphic novels when they have altered familiar genres and inspired film adaptations; they have been written about by outsiders struck by their innovations; and they have challenged comics readers to expand their ideas about what their favorite genres and characters can be. Despite their basis in earlier stories or genres, they are often among the most original of graphic novels, and the graphic novel canon would be diminished without their presence.

Works Cited

Augustyn, Brian, and Mike Mignola. *Batman: Gotham by Gaslight*. New York: DC Comics, 2006.

Bacchilega, Cristina. *Fairy Tales Transformed? Twenty-First-Century Adaptations and the Politics of Wonder*. Detroit, MI: Wayne State University Press, 2013.

Bender, Hy. *The Sandman Companion*. New York: Vertigo/DC Comics, 1999.

Brayshaw, Christopher. "Interview Four," in *The Comics Journal Library*, Vol. 2: *Frank Miller*. Seattle, WA: Fantagraphics Books, 2003, 65–87.

Cawelti, John G. "The Concept of Formula in the Study of Popular Culture," in *Mystery, Violence, and Popular Culture*. Madison, WI: University of Wisconsin Popular Press, 2004, 3–12.

"Formulas and Genres Reconsidered Once Again," in *Mystery, Violence, and Popular Culture*. Madison, WI: University of Wisconsin Popular Press, 2004, 130–38.

Comic Book Superheroes Unmasked. Dir. Steve Kroopnick. A&E Home Video, 2005. Film.

Coogan, Peter. *Superhero: The Secret Origin of a Genre*. Austin, TX: MonkeyBrain, 2006.

Darius, Julian. "58 Varieties: Watchmen and Revisionism," in Richard Bensam, ed., *Minutes to Midnight: Twelve Essays on Watchmen*. Edwardsville, IL: Sequart Research and Literacy Organization, 2010, 97–108.

Decker, Dwight. "Interview One," in *The Comics Journal Library*, Vol. 2: *Frank Miller*. Seattle, WA: Fantagraphics Books, 2003, 15–31.

Di Liddo, Annalisa. *Alan Moore: Comics as Performance, Fiction as Scalpel*. Jackson, MS: University Press of Mississippi, 2009.

Gaiman, Neil, Andy Kubert, et al. *Marvel 1602*. New York: Marvel, 2010.

Gaiman, Neil, et al. *The Sandman*. 10 vols. New York: DC Comics, 2012.

Green, Matthew J. A. "A Darker Magic: Heterocosms and Bricolage in Moore's Recent Reworkings of Lovecraft," in Matthew J. A. Green, ed., *Alan Moore and the Gothic Tradition*. Manchester University Press, 2013, 253–75.

Hilton, Laura. "Reincarnating Mina Murray: Subverting the Gothic Heroine?," in Matthew J. A. Green, ed., *Alan Moore and the Gothic Tradition*. Manchester University Press, 2013, 195–212.

Hoberek, Andrew. *Considering Watchmen: Poetics, Property, Politics*. New Brunswick, NJ: Rutgers University Press, 2014.

Jones, Gerard, and Will Jacobs. *The Comic Book Heroes*. Rev. ed. Rocklin, CA: Prima, 1997.

Klock, Geoff. *How to Read Superhero Comics and Why*. New York: Continuum, 2002.

Maslon, Laurence, and Michael Kantor. *Superheroes! Capes, Cowls, and the Creation of Comic Book Culture*. New York: Crown Publishing, 2013.

McCloud, Scott. *Reinventing Comics*. New York: HarperCollins, 2000.

Michelinie, David, Bob Layton, John Romita Jr., Carmine Infantino, et al. *Iron Man: Demon in a Bottle*. New York: Marvel, 2008.

Millar, Mark, Dave Johnson, and Kilian Plunkett. *Superman: Red Son*. New York: DC Comics, 2004.

Miller, Frank. *Sin City*. 7 vols. Milwaukie, OR: Dark Horse Comics, 2010.

Miller, Frank, et al. *Batman: The Dark Knight Returns*. New York: DC Comics, 1986.

Moore, Alan, Brian Bolland, et al. *Batman: The Killing Joke*. New York: DC Comics, Deluxe edition, 2008.

Moore, Alan, and Kevin O'Neill. *The League of Extraordinary Gentlemen*, Vols. 1 and 2. La Jolla, CA: America's Best Comics, 1: 2000, 2: 2003.

Moore, Alan, Melinda Gebbie, et al. *Lost Girls*. 3 vols. Atlanta, GA: Top Shelf, 2006.

Moore, Alan, Jacen Burrows, et al. *Neonomicon*. Rantoul, IL: Avatar, 2011.

Moore, Alan, Dave Gibbons, et al. *Watchmen*. New York: DC Comics, 1987.

Ricca, Brad. "'I fashioned a prison that you could not leave': The Gothic Imperative in *The Castle of Otranto* and 'For the Man Who Has Everything',," in Matthew J. A. Green, ed., *Alan Moore and the Gothic Tradition*. Manchester University Press, 2013, 159–78.

Sanders, Julie. *Adaptation and Appropriation*. London: Routledge, 2006.

Superheroes: A Never-Ending Battle. Dir. Michael Kantor. Public Broadcasting System, 2013. Film.

Thompson, Kim. "Interview Two," in *The Comics Journal Library*, Vol. 2: *Frank Miller*. Seattle, WA: Fantagraphics Books, 2003, 33–49.

Waid, Mark, Alex Ross, and Todd Klein. *Kingdom Come*. New York: DC Comics, 1997.

Wandtke, Terrence R. "Frank Miller Strikes Again and Batman Becomes a Postmodern Anti-Hero: The Tragi(Comic) Reformulation of the Dark Knight," in Terrence R. Wandtke, ed., *The Amazing Transforming Superhero! Essays on the Revision of Characters in Comic Books, Film and Television*. Jefferson, NC: McFarland, 2007, 87–111.

"Introduction: Once upon a Time Once Again," in Terrence R. Wandtke, ed., *The Amazing Transforming Superhero! Essays on the Revision of Characters in Comic Books, Film and Television*. Jefferson, NC: McFarland, 2007, 5–32.

Ware, Chris. *Building Stories*. New York: Pantheon Books, 2012.

Jimmy Corrigan: The Smartest Kid on Earth (2000). New York: Pantheon Books, 2003.

Willingham, Bill, et al. *Fables*. 21 vols. New York: DC Comics/Vertigo, 2003–15.

Wolfman, Marv, George Pérez, et al. *Crisis on Infinite Earths*. New York: DC Comics, 1998.

NOTES

1 Terrence R. Wandtke, "Introduction: Once upon a Time Once Again," in Wandtke, ed., *The Amazing Transforming Superhero! Essays on the Revision*

of Characters in Comic Books, Film and Television, (Jefferson, NC: McFarland, 2007), 5.

2 Dwight Decker, "Interview One," in The Comics Journal Library, Vol. 2: Frank Miller (Seattle, WA: Fantagraphics Books, 2003), 25.

3 See, for example, Comic Book Superheroes Unmasked, dir. Steve Kroopnick (A&E Home Video, 2003); Peter Coogan, Superhero: The Secret Origin of a Genre (Austin, TX: MonkeyBrain, 2006); Gerard Jones and Will Jacobs, The Comic Book Heroes, rev. edn (Rocklin, CA: Prima, 1997); Laurence Maslon and Michael Kantor, Superheroes! Capes, Cowls, and the Creation of Comic Book Culture (New York: Crown Publishing, 2013); and Superheroes: A Never-Ending Battle, dir. Michael Kantor (Public Broadcasting System, 2012).

4 Geoff Klock, How to Read Superhero Comics and Why (New York: Continuum, 2002), 28.

5 Hy Bender, The Sandman Companion (New York: Vertigo/DC Comics, 1999), xi–xii.

6 Brad Ricca, "'I fashioned a prison that you could not leave': The Gothic Imperative in The Castle of Otranto and 'For the Man Who Has Everything'," in Matthew J. A. Green, ed., Alan Moore and the Gothic Tradition (Manchester University Press, 2013), 159.

7 Laura Hilton, "Reincarnating Mina Murray: Subverting the Gothic Heroine?," in Green, ed., Alan Moore and the Gothic Tradition, 202.

8 Ibid., 204.

9 Annalisa Di Liddo, Alan Moore: Comics as Performance, Fiction as Scalpel (Jackson, MS: University Press of Mississippi, 2009), 139.

10 Julie Sanders, Adaptation and Appropriation (London: Routledge, 2006), 9.

11 Matthew J. A. Green, "A Darker Magic: Heterocosms and Bricolage in Moore's Recent Reworkings of Lovecraft," in Green, ed., Alan Moore and the Gothic Tradition, 269.

12 Bill Willingham, et al., Fables, 21 vols. (New York: DC Comics/Vertigo, 2003–15).

13 Cristina Bacchilega, Fairy Tales Transformed? Twenty-First-Century Adaptations and the Politics of Wonder (Detroit, MI: Wayne State University Press, 2013), 157.

14 Julian Darius, "58 Varieties: Watchmen and Revisionism," in Richard Bensam, ed., Minutes to Midnight: Twelve Essays on Watchmen (Edwardsville, IL: Sequart Research and Literacy Organization, 2010), 101.

15 John G. Cawelti, "The Concept of Formula in the Study of Popular Culture," in Mystery, Violence, and Popular Culture (Madison, WI: University of Wisconsin Popular Press, 2004), 7.

16 John G. Cawelti, "Formulas and Genres Reconsidered Once Again," in Mystery, Violence, and Popular Culture, 134, 131.

17 Di Liddo, Alan Moore, 47.

18 Wandtke, "Introduction," 29.

19 Darius, "58 Varieties," 102–4; Andrew Hoberek, Considering Watchmen: Poetics, Property, Politics (New Brunswick, NJ: Rutgers University Press, 2014), 39; Wandtke, "Introduction," 20–21.

20 Wandtke, "Introduction," 21.

21 Di Liddo, Alan Moore, 47.

22 Klock, How to Read Superhero Comics, 66.

23 Terrence R. Wandtke, "Frank Miller Strikes Again and Batman Becomes a Post-modern Anti-Hero: The Tragi(Comic) Reformulation of the Dark Knight," in Wandtke, ed., *Amazing Transforming Superhero!*, 91.

24 Kim Thompson, "Interview Two," in *The Comics Journal Library*, Vol. 2: *Frank Miller* (Seattle, WA: Fantagraphics Books, 2003), 34.

25 Klock, *How to Read Superhero Comics*, 34–35.

26 Scott McCloud, *Reinventing Comics* (New York: HarperCollins, 2000), 81.

27 Christopher Brayshaw, "Interview Four," in *The Comics Journal Library*, Vol. 2: *Frank Miller* (Seattle, WA: Fantagraphics Books, 2003), 82.

7

MARTHA KUHLMAN

The Autobiographical and Biographical Graphic Novel

In Philippe Lejeune's classic work *On Autobiography*, he defines the genre as "a retrospective prose narrative that someone writes concerning his own existence."[1] Lejeune argues that when the author, narrator, and protagonist are the same, an autobiographical pact is established between author and reader, which ensures that the name on the cover "is linked, by a social convention, to the pledge of responsibility of a real person" (11). Lejeune later expands this definition beyond prose narrative, recognizing that "the evolution of new media" might encompass different relationships as in the case of film, where a screenwriter and a director can create an autobiographical narrative even if they are separate individuals (193). In principle, this paves the way to a consideration of graphic narrative, given that the writer and the cartoonist could be the same person (as in the case of Art Spiegelman's *Maus*, Alison Bechdel's *Fun Home*, and Marjane Satrapi's *Persepolis*) or could be two or more individuals collaborating on a life story told in comics form (Harvey Pekar's *American Splendor*, and *March*, the memoir of John Lewis, are two examples). Thus, Lejeune's invocation of new media anticipates the autobiographical comics narrative, which has come to be recognized as the most analyzed subfield within comics studies.[2]

The reason for this fascination with autobiographical comics lies in the unique intersection between autobiographical narrative and the particularities of the text/image combination in comics, raising intriguing questions about authorship, authenticity, and the representation of trauma. These autobiographical graphic narratives, or "autographics," a term suggested by Gillian Whitlock, have the unique potential to exploit the possibilities of comics form to express an evolving sense of identity.[3] Autographics can be self-reflexive in their depictions of the narrator/protagonist and include the moment of drawing and/or writing; image and text do not necessarily always correspond, calling into question claims of authenticity or ironically reinforcing them; and the cartoonist can foreground the manipulation of several time frames to stitch the narrative together. To signal the author's subjectivity and participation in the narrative, sometimes the author's hand will be included in the drawing on the page, as is the case with Spiegelman's *Maus* in the "Prisoner from Hell Planet" chapter, or in the revelatory two-page spread found in the middle of Bechdel's *Fun Home*. The visual representation of the protagonist-author in the narrative, sometimes called an "avatar," can switch between versions of this character at different points in their lives, creating contrasts between younger and more mature incarnations of the same person. Similar complications arise in biographical comics when the writer and/or cartoonist represent people other than themselves, frequently concentrating on the lives of historical figures, an instance to which I will return at the conclusion. Given the wide variety of autobiographical comics, this essay will address a few salient themes, bearing in mind that there can be significant overlap among them: confessional, historical, confronting illness, and travel.

Confessional Comics

In the American context, the autobiographical impulse originated in the underground comix movement, whose leading figure was Robert Crumb, concentrated in San Francisco in the late 1960s and early 1970s. Seeking an alternative to the commercial comics produced under the repressive Comics Code Authority of 1954, these artists went in the opposite direction, creating work that was deliberately provocative and breaking taboos against depicting subjects that were considered "private" in mainstream society, especially drug use and sexuality.[4] Justin Green's *Binky Brown Meets the Holy Virgin Mary* (1972), considered the first autobiographical comic of its kind, depicts Green's struggles with obsessive-compulsive disorder, the Catholic religion, and his own sexual insecurities. Beginning with "A Confession to my Readers," Green explains how he wants to "purge" himself of his neurosis on the one hand, and to connect with fellow-sufferers, on the other.[5] His melodramatic opening depicts the cartoonist bound and hanging from the ceiling as he draws his comic with a pen clenched in his teeth, thus enacting the autobiographical pact in visual form. Within the underground community, Green's confessional style was tremendously influential and inspired Art Spiegelman to pursue his own testimonial form of graphic narrative in *Maus*.[6]

Confessional autographics represent the ordinary lives of people, their most private frustrations and obsessions, and in some instances their traumatic experiences. Contemporaneous with Crumb and Green, Harvey Pekar, a humble file clerk in Cleveland, began publishing his serial *American Splendor* in 1976. These stories were more like anecdotes from the daily life of a working-class guy than wrenching accounts of personal angst, and differ from Green's and Spiegelman's works in that Pekar enlisted the help of cartoonist friends to draw these stories, including Crumb. A trip to the grocery store, a conversation with a friend, or a walk through Cleveland provide ample material for Harvey to elaborate upon his existence as an everyday anti-hero. Harvey's example gave rise to the second generation of autobiographical comics artists in the 1990s, including a group of cartoonist friends in Toronto: Chester Brown, Seth, and Joe Matt.[7] This later iteration of autographics was decidedly more high-pitched, focusing on abjection, shame, and guilt; Matt and Brown in particular represented awkward interactions and sexual frustrations.

Despite the fact that the field of alternative comics is generally male-dominated, a number of women have produced significant and daring work in the arena of autobiographical comics. Inspired by the brutal honesty and self-deprecating humor in *Binky Brown*, Aline Kominsky created her alter ego "Goldie" in *Wimmen's Comix* (1972) to explore her insecurities about her body image and sexuality. She also pursued these subjects in the collaborative comics she created with her husband, R. Crumb, under the title *Dirty Laundry* (1974–78). Cartoonists such as Julie Doucet, Mary Fleener, Debbie Drechsler, Lynda Barry, Alison Bechdel, and Phoebe Gloeckner have ventured into similar territory in their frank and intimate personal comics, with Gloeckner's work representing the most disturbing images of childhood sexual abuse in *A Child's Life and Other Stories* (1998) and *The Diary of a Teenage Girl* (2002). Lynda Barry, by contrast, adopts a more indirect approach to childhood trauma and the discrimination she experienced as a Filipino mixed-race child through her colorful scrapbook style of collage in *One Hundred Demons* (2002). Her introduction to this book places the problem of authenticity at the core of her endeavor: "Is it autobiography if parts of it are not true? Is it fiction if parts of it are?" (7).[8]

Historical/Autobiographical Comics

Authenticity and veracity become even more urgent when autographics are represented in the context of significant historical crisis, upheaval, or change. Without a doubt, Art Spiegelman's *Maus* (*Maus I*, 1986; *Maus II*, 1991), the story of his father Vladek's survival of Auschwitz, is the most significant and influential text for both cartoonists and scholars. The problem of truth claims was immediately apparent when Spiegelman objected to the fact that *The New York Times Book Review* categorized his work as "fiction," since such a designation would inadvertently play into the arguments of Holocaust deniers.[9] What makes *Maus* so central to autobiographical comics, in addition to the gravity of the subject matter, is that Spiegelman represents not just his father's story, but a historiography that acknowledges his own imperfect role as the mediator of his father's story, thus revealing moments of doubt, self-reflection, and gaps in memory. This is evident from the beginning of *Maus I*, when Spiegelman includes an unflattering account of his father's affair with Lucia, an attractive but poor young woman, before he married Spiegelman's mother, Anja. Despite the fact that Vladek requests that this episode be omitted from the book because it is not "proper," his son includes the story and their conversation about it.[10] By depicting his conflicts with his father and exposing the limits of their knowledge and memory, Spiegelman achieves what Hatfield terms "ironic authentication," which renders the account more believable since it acknowledges its imperfections.[11]

Although Spiegelman seeks to represent Vladek's experiences as accurately as possible within the context of the Holocaust, sometimes his research conflicts with Vladek's memory of the wartime period.[12] Moreover, Spiegelman represents his own guilt and feelings of inadequacy compared to his father, most famously drawing himself hunched over a drafting table in a room littered with corpses at the beginning of *Maus II* to express his despair over his father's death and his own paradoxical commercial success. Through this potent visual metaphor, in combination with the general extended metaphor of mice, cats, pigs, and dogs (and their masks) representing different nationalities, Spiegelman continually challenges the reader's assumptions. With the publication of *MetaMaus* (2011), Spiegelman further exposes his process of assembling his graphic biography/autobiography: readers have access to preliminary sketches, documentary materials, and recordings of Vladek, in addition to recordings and footage of Spiegelman himself – an archive that deepens one's insight into this groundbreaking work. Spiegelman's *In The Shadow of No Towers* (2004) is more fully autobiographical and focuses on his reactions to the destruction of the World Trade Center in the 9/11 attacks, using a combination of comics in color, photos, digital effects, and early New York newspaper comics.[13]

Following Spiegelman's example, artists worldwide realized the potential of comics to tell a compelling personal story within a historical framework. Marjane Satrapi, an Iranian-French artist with the French independent publisher L'Association, seized upon this combination in her autobiography *Persepolis* (2004), which recounts her experience of growing up in Iran in the 1970s.[14] Satrapi's coming-of-age story unfolds simultaneously as Iran transitions from the relatively secular regime of the Shah to Islamic rule. Her autobiography is split into two voices: captions are narrated by the adult Satrapi reflecting upon her experiences, and her younger self or avatar, "Marji," who participates directly in the story dialogues. This artifice and doubling is fore-grounded when Marji directly addresses the reader (4), and when she gazes into the mirror in moments of doubt or self-recognition. Moments of self-reflexivity appear when she contemplates her reflection at the end of Book I before her departure (151), and again when she puts on her hijab in front of a mirror as she prepares to return home after studying at an Austrian school (245). In the end, Iran's restrictive laws, particularly with regard to the limited rights of women, convince Satrapi to leave Iran for France. From her introduction, it is clear that her narrative is directed at a Western audi-ence in an effort to debunk stereotypes about Iran as a nation of terrorists or extremists, and she is careful to distinguish governmental policy from the attitudes of more progressive Iranians such as herself.

In Aleksandar Zograf's graphic memoir, *Regards from Serbia: A Cartoon-ist's Diary* (2007), Zograf faces a similar dilemma as he tries to disentangle himself from Serbian nationalists and convey his perspective on the civil wars in the former Yugoslavia to a Western audience. He speaks as a cartoonist, not a politician, and thus his artistic vision is not "strictly documentary," rather, "it is some kind of fantastic magic realism" in the tradition of Rus-sian literature.[15] His page layouts are often jagged or distorted, and include imaginary monsters and apparitions alongside people he encounters in his daily life, intermingling dream and reality. When a friend of his, depicted with a bird's head, asks him why he is creating comics about his suffer-ing, he replies, "We are experiencing a unique moment in history. Maybe there's some deeper meaning in just watching all of this happening" (49). But the graphic narrative diary never succeeds in divulging whether that deeper meaning might justify the violence and absurdity of the war raging around him. Instead, Zograf appears in a constant state of crisis as his town is rav-aged by conflict and eventually bombed by NATO.

Throughout this cartoon diary, Zograf calls attention to the formal prop-erties of comics, and attempts to engage his audience by exposing the arti-fice of the panel frame. At one point he directly addresses the reader, "Hey! Anybody there? Listen...Try to imagine what it would be like if you were born as Aleksandr Zograf! I could be you and you could be me!" (35). In "All Against Each Other and God Against All," Zograf speaks as some-one who will explain the civil wars in Yugoslavia to those outside. With a pen poised above his head as if he has just finished drawing his body, he states, "I will show myself as a hero of this very comic strip...I have some messages to jabber in your face" (38) (fig. 7.1). As the war esca-lates to include Bosnia, the violence and confusion increases with Serbs, Croats, and Muslims fighting each other. Zograf's own confusion is visible in his own anguished self-representations and in the disorienting sequence

Fig. 7.1 Zograf draws himself representing the conflict in Serbia through a jagged page layout that portrays national leaders as a monstrous beast. © 2007 Aleksandar Zograf, *Regards From Serbia*, by permission Top Shelf Books.

of panels, which leads counter-intuitively from right to left according to the arrows between the gutters. An ominous, gigantic white figure representing "national leaders" gathers a crowd in its outstretched arms and murmurs, "We will protect you...But first put your uniforms on...You sweet little things" (38). In this exemplary page, Zograf depicts his bewilderment and despair in visual metaphors to show how people are manipulated by their leaders. In the end, he does not provide a reassuring sense of closure, but rather turns American readers' gaze back upon their own nationalistic reactions following the 9/11 attacks.

Another significant work that offers a personal memoir against the backdrop of history is Keiji Nakazawa's *Barefoot Gen: A Cartoon Story of Hiroshima*, originally published in 1972 but brought to the attention of a wider audience when it was translated into English in 2004. Spiegelman read Nakazawa's manga-style graphic narrative after he had already started work on *Maus*, and was deeply affected by its horrific images, which were based on Nakazawa's own boyhood memories of the bombing. Autographics in other countries have started to appear as the form gains in popularity, including Nikolai Maslov's *Siberia* (2006), his brutal account of growing up in Soviet Russia, and Marzena Sowa's *Marzi* (2011), which tells of her childhood experiences in Poland under martial law in the 1980s. Historical/autobiographical graphic narratives have also taken hold in the American context, with GB Tran's *Vietnamerica* (2011), a visually striking color graphic narrative about coming to terms with his family's history in the war as a second-generation child of refugees, and John Lewis' memoir *March* (2013), the result of his collaboration with writer Andrew Aydin and artist Nate Powell, which begins with President Obama's inauguration and then tells Lewis' remarkable journey from sharecropper, to Civil Rights Leader, to Congressman.

Facing Illness

Another variant on the confessional narrative comic deals with the anguish and dark humor of facing debilitating illnesses. Lines drawn by hand register the state of mind of the cartoonist, and thus represent the subjective nature of one's changing sense of self in the grip of illness.[16] Irony and self-reflexivity present in autographics become tinged with an added poignancy since the narrative is connected to the mortality of a real person. Most often, graphic narratives of illness will reward the readers' expectations for a happy ending in which the patient overcomes hardships and survives.[17] However, for authors who are recording their experiences (or the experience of friends or family) as they are living them, readers must adjust their perspective and realize that the story is improvised and the ending is indeterminate.

Already well known for his comics about everyday life, Harvey Pekar, with writer and activist Joyce Brabner and artist Frank Stack, collaborated on *Our Cancer Year* (1994) which concerns Brabner's peace activism, the beginning of the first Gulf War, and, most importantly, his struggle with lymphoma. This unflinching and sometimes harrowing account represents the indignities and messiness of dealing with cancer and chemotherapy, and was an important reference point for others who later pursued this subject.[18] Stack's black pen strokes are loose and vary in style to represent Harvey's changing states of mind in the fog of chemotherapy. One of the most cited sections of the book shows Harvey waking up and struggling to grasp who he is: "I'm sleeping. Who am I?" Then, turning to Joyce, he asks, "Tell me the truth. Am I some guy who writes about himself in a comic book called *American Splendor*? Or am I just a character in that book?" Panels on the page from Harvey's perspective are uneven and lack borders, while Joyce's view is delimited by crisper lines, reflecting their contrasting subjective states (fig. 7.2). We see Harvey through the circular frame of her glasses as he stands before her, uncertain and naked, his vulnerability represented as literal and figurative simultaneously. Ultimately his cancer goes into remission after he endures an aggressive regimen of chemotherapy.

Other works that address cancer specifically include *Mom's Cancer* (2006) by Brian Fies, Miriam Engleberg's *Cancer Made Me a Shallower Person* (2006), *Cancer Vixen* (2006) by Marisa Acocella Marchetto, David Small's *Stitches* (2009), and *Probably Nothing* (2014) by Matilda Tristram.[19] Acocella Marchetto's brightly colored *Cancer Vixen*, the title alone defying the notion of "cancer victim," takes an audacious approach to the topic by asking what happens when "a shoe-crazy, lipstick-obsessed, wine-swilling, pasta slurping, fashion-fanatic, single-forever, about-to-get married big-city cartoonist with a fabulous life finds a lump in her breast?"[20] At the beginning of each chemotherapy session, the self-described "narcissistic fashionista" boasts a new over-the-top Italian shoe (159, 163, 167). With characteristic dark humor, she sports her "cancer card" to get out of social obligations (107). But there are sober moments as well; she tells us that women without health insurance (like herself) "have a 49% greater risk of dying from breast cancer" (94). At the other end of the spectrum, in *Mom's Cancer*, which originally appeared as a black-and-white web comic, Fies represents how his mother's mind and body are compromised by the progression of the disease and the shock of chemotherapy.[21] In one example, he draws parts of his mother's body – clenched face, straining limbs – fragmented against a black background to show how she feels broken into pieces by her treatment (72).

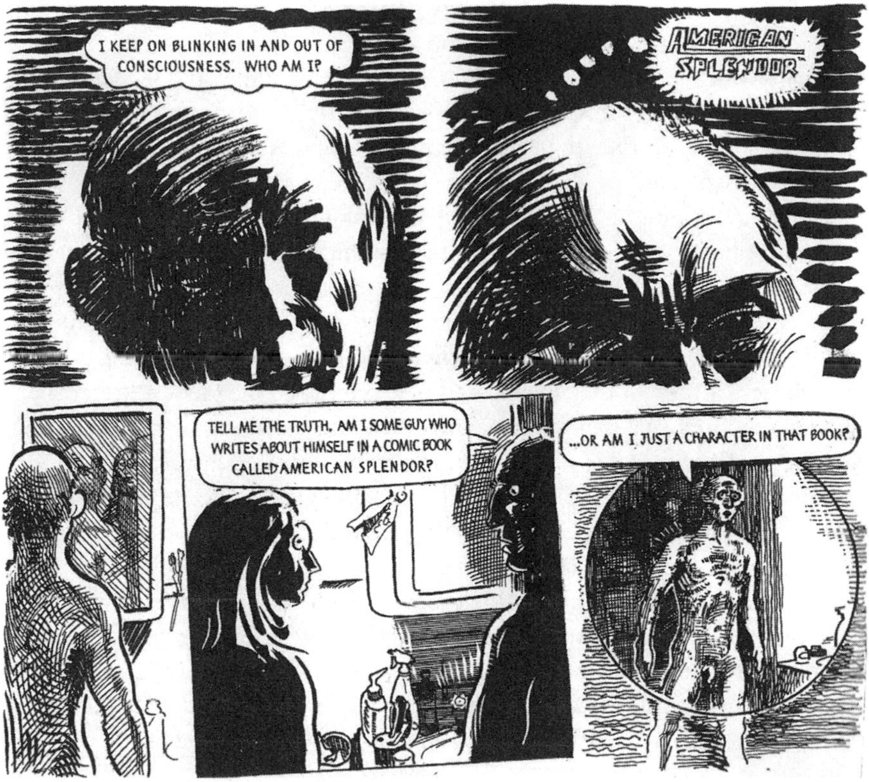
I KEEP ON BLINKING IN AND OUT OF CONSCIOUSNESS. WHO AM I?
AMERICAN SPLENDOR
TELL ME THE TRUTH. AM I SOME GUY WHO WRITES ABOUT HIMSELF IN A COMIC BOOK CALLED AMERICAN SPLENDOR?
...OR AM I JUST A CHARACTER IN THAT BOOK?

Fig. 7.2 In his weakened state due to chemotherapy, Harvey Pekar struggles to remember who he is. © 1994 *Our Cancer Year*, Harvey Pekar and Joyce Brabner. By permission of Running Press, a member of the Perseus Books Group.

Ironically, just as the book version of her ordeal of overcoming cancer was about to go to press, she passed away due to complications related to her treatment – a reminder that these narrative endings are necessarily fragile and provisional.

In an international context, David Beauchard's *Epileptic* (1996–2003), a long-form graphic narrative of over 300 pages, is a groundbreaking example of graphic narratives on illness. Beauchard, part of the Parisian collective L'Association, recounts his family's efforts to help his epileptic brother, Jean-Christophe, through a bewildering maze of medical treatments and alternative medicine in search of a cure. In the beginning, he represents his child-self alongside his older brother enthusiastically drawing intricate battles with rampaging Mongol warriors. But as Jean-Christophe's affliction takes hold, young David's war drawings are redirected against this new enemy and become metaphors for their struggle with his disease.[22] Eventually David's fascination with war is tempered by real stories told by his family and his own investigations into books to find out about the First World War, the Algerian War, the Vietnam War, and the Second World War. He changes his name to David in order to "stake out a position" on the side of the victims – the Jews – rather than the Nazi oppressors who Jean-Christophe, in his powerlessness, finds so appealing.[23]

Beauchard populates his black-and-white memoir with monstrous creatures and ghosts of dead relatives, intermingling dream, fantasy, and reality at the same time that he experiments with the comics form. In his personal invented mythology, Jean-Christophe's epilepsy is rendered as an inexorable black dragon that entangles its victim, sometimes even encircling a scene as a panel border (112). Beauchard also includes the dissenting or conflicting accounts of his family members, calling attention to the artifice of autobiography when his mother objects to his representation of her great-grandmother (94). Like Spiegelman, he uses the graphic memoir as a means of working through the trauma of his brother's illness, even as he realizes that the quest for a cure is futile. His epilogue is an imagined conversation with Jean-Christophe as they ride horses through a landscape that is the history of their relationship, concluding with a quote from the poet Fernando Pessoa: "Sit under the sun, abdicate, and be your own king" (361). Although the meaning of this phrase appears obscure, it can be understood as sign of Beauchard's final acceptance of himself and his brother as he is.[24]

Travel

Graphic narratives of travel constitute a subgenre of comics autobiography that place the author's identity in relation to a foreign other such that differences in culture, gender, politics, and religion become relevant points of comparison and analysis. Inevitably, these comics pose questions about the representation of national and ethnic stereotypes. This variant of autobiographical graphic narrative, which significantly overlaps with comics journalism more generally, is best exemplified by the works of Joe Sacco and Guy Delisle. Sacco's style, heavily influenced by Crumb and the underground tradition, is characterized by fine line drawings of people and landscapes. Delisle, who got his start with L'Association, has a more understated, simplified style enhanced by pen-and-ink washes. Both artists represent themselves in unfamiliar landscapes and political contexts that they struggle to understand.

Sacco's early comics from the 1980s were autobiographical – about relationships, living in Berlin, and rock music – but his work took on a more serious tone when he recognized the power of entwining personal stories with greater historical events. With his degree in journalism from the University of Oregon, Sacco decided to combine his talent for cartooning and his reporting perspective to cover some of the most contentious political situations of his time: the civil wars in the former Yugoslavia (*Safe Area Goražde*, 2000; *War's End: Profiles from Bosnia*, 2005; *The Fixer and Other Stories*, 2009) and the Israeli-Palestinian conflict (*Palestine*, 1996; *Footnotes in Gaza*, 2009). Sacco does not claim to be an "objective journalist;" instead, he makes an effort to hear both sides of the story and does not lose sight of himself as a subjective, mediating presence in the conflicts he represents. He depicts himself as a slight, vulnerable figure in glasses who is eager to find the real stories of ordinary people, but also anxious and frighteningly dependent on his sources. In *The Fixer*, he offers a self-deprecating portrait of himself as a naive acolyte, "a little enthralled, a little infatuated," of the formidable Neven, his fixer in Sarajevo.[25] Most often, however, he allows the individuals he interviews to take center stage, using the expressive possibilities of comics to engage the reader in their stories. In *Palestine*, for instance, Sacco explains how he dramatized the severity of one Palestinian prisoner's torments while in an Israeli prison by decreasing the panel size to create a claustrophobic effect, and then opening the page layout with larger panels when he was released.[26] Sacco's landscapes, which feature meticulous renderings of the daily lives of individuals scraping together a living in conflict zones, have been compared to Breughel's in scope and detail. To avoid the kind of stereotyping that is common in caricature, Sacco takes care to show the particular features of each individual, even in a crowd scene.

Details of ordinary life are emphasized in Delisle's work as well, but from a more bemused, distanced perspective. His narratives come from his observations traveling on business for various animation assignments (*Pyongyang*, 2005; *Shenzhen*, 2006), and his experience taking care of the children while his wife is on assignment for Doctors Without Borders (*Burma Chronicles*, 2008; *Jerusalem: Chronicles from the Holy City*, 2012). Delisle observes that under the veneer of incessant cheery propaganda in Pyongyang, electricity shortages, out-of-order elevators, and staggeringly ostentatious unfinished building projects are daily occurrences. His reappearing visual metaphor of a wind-up toy man succinctly captures the atmosphere of manipulation and fear that he perceives, but cannot break through due to cultural and linguistic limitations.[27] Rather than bridging cultural divides, irony and humor seem to sharpen them, such as the moments when Delisle sings some lines from Bob Marley ("Get up, stand up, Stand up for your Rights!") to his co-workers, and gives a copy of Orwell's *1984* to one of his Korean hosts (71, 40). In *Burma Chronicles*, his wife and child add a domestic element to his travels, which now involve trips to the grocery store and play dates. It's harder for him to find any political insights first hand and he can't quite hold his own in discussions with other NGO workers. At one point, he purposely guides his son in a stroller toward political dissident Aung San Suu Kyi's house, only to be foiled by some irate guards.[28] Overall, Delisle's work takes a gentle, self-deprecating view; his graphic narratives are as much about him as they are about the foreign cultures he encounters.

Biography

In graphic narrative biographies, the constructed nature of a life story is openly acknowledged in the separation between the writer and the life of the person who is depicted. As proof of an authentic effort to represent the truth about a person's biography, the author will frequently take pains to include notes, appendixes, forewords, and epilogues. While it is not possible to do justice to all graphic narrative biographies, a discussion of three exemplary cases – *Louis Riel: A Comic Strip Biography* (2003), *Alan's War: The Memories of G.I. Alan Cope* (2008), and *Logicomix* (2009) – illustrate some of the possibilities of this form.

Chester Brown, known for his autobiographical comics in the confessional mode, undertakes a challenging political narrative in *Louis Riel*.[29] In this first comic book project to receive funding from the Canadian Council for the Arts, Brown employs an understated, six-panel framework to tell the story of Louis Riel, leader of the Métis (half-white, half-native population), and his disputes with the Canadian leadership over the governance and ownership of lands to the west of Quebec. His foreword openly acknowledges simplifications and distortions made in the service of telling a coherent story, listing several reference works for anyone who wants to read further, in addition to a handwritten index. Riel is represented in a positive, heroic light, although the question of whether he was mentally ill is left unanswered. Nonetheless, the ending – which includes a detailed replay of his trial and execution – seems to affirm his status as a martyr.

Alan's War: The Memories of G.I. Alan Cope is the result of the friendship between L'Association artist Emmanuel Guibert and American veteran Alan Cope, whom he had meet by chance on an island off the coast of France. Amazed by his prodigious memory and his eye for detail, Guibert recorded Cope's recollections and personal stories from the Second World War. The biography is not, however, primarily about the war – as Guibert puts it, "ours wasn't the work of historians" – instead, it becomes an intimate account of Cope's life through his first-person narrative as visually interpreted in Guibert's evocative pen-and-ink drawings. Cope was in many ways atypical for a soldier, and describes himself as not being "the military type" but rather "a dreamer."[30] His story revolves around friendships lost and found over a period of some fifty years, and the kinds of realizations he comes to as an older man looking back on his younger self. What is most striking in Guibert's drawings are the "blank spaces and elliptical portrayals" that leave room for the reader's imagination. This collaborative project, which continued through Cope's declining health, was a way of bringing meaning and value to this older man who "came to the conclusion that [he] hadn't lived his own life" (281). The book, however, is an eloquent testimony to the fact that the opposite is true; we appreciate his unique perspective, curiosity about other languages and countries, and loyalty to his friends. His story is extended in a second volume Guibert composed after Cope's death, *How the World Was* (2014), which is a lyrical portrait of his childhood in California.

Of the three biographies, *Logicomix* by Apostolos Doxiadis and Christos H. Papadimitriou with art by Alecos Papadatos and Annie Di Donna, goes the furthest in exposing its own process of composition. Using Bertrand Russell's *Autobiography* as a source, the graphic novel explores the philosopher's ideas about logic and mathematics in light of his own story and personal struggles. The role of the writers and the artists in shaping the narrative is exposed throughout in extended self-referential asides, since they appear as characters in the book. At the beginning of Part II, for example, when they discuss how they are developing the "logic and madness" theme, Papadimitriou interjects that they have omitted Russell's brother. But Doxiadis argues that they had to leave this out because it complicated the plot and digressed from their main project.[31] Emotion and passion are opposed to reason and logic in both Russell's narrative and in the framing narrative of the writers and artists, but ultimately the book demonstrates that this is a false dichotomy. Cleverly foregrounding the interplay between form and content, this biography argues that passion and reason cannot be separated but must work in concert with each other to achieve a balanced worldview.

Whether we consider autobiography or biography, the term "graphic novel" does not seem apposite. Although some simplification or alteration is necessary to fit the messy business of life into a coherent form, to call these examples "novels" misses the urgency and authenticity of their stories. The intimacy of the connection to a life is palpable in the individual variations of line and the idiosyncratic styles of cartoonists, as we have seen in the works of Spiegelman, Crumb, Bechdel, Marchetto, Sacco, and Satrapi. An idea is translated through the medium of the hand and graphically rendered as an expression of a lived experience in a way that cannot be conveyed by prose alone. Even when the writer, the artist, and the subject of the story are separate individuals, the form of comics – the quality of the line, the sequence of panels, the page layout – introduces elements of interpretation and reception that are markedly different from prose. "Graphic narrative," however, is a broad enough term to encompass both the truth claims and the fictional aspects of these stories. And as this brief tour of the genre has shown, graphic narrative brings a vibrant and provocative form of expression to the study of autobiography and biography writ large.

Works Cited

Aune, M. G. "Teaching the Graphic Travel Narrative," in Stephen E. Tabachnick, ed., *Teaching the Graphic Novel*. New York: Modern Language Association, 2009, 223–27.

Acocella Marchetto, Marisa. *Cancer Vixen*. New York: Knopf, 2006.

Barry, Lynda. *One Hundred Demons*. Seattle, WA: Sasquatch Books, 2002.

Beaty, Bart. "Selective Mutual Reinforcement in the Comics of Chester Brown, Joe Matt, and Seth," in Michael A. Chaney, ed., *Graphic Subjects: Critical Essays on Autobiography and Graphic Novels*. Madison, WI: University of Wisconsin Press, 2011, 247–59.

B.[eauchard], David. *Epileptic*. Trans. Kim Thompson. New York: Pantheon Books, 2005.

Bechdel, Alison. *Fun Home: A Family Tragicomic*. New York: Houghton Mifflin, 2006.

Brown, Chester. *Louis Riel: A Comic Strip Biography*. Montreal: Drawn & Quarterly, 2003.

Chaney, Michael, ed. *Graphic Subjects: Critical Essays on Autobiography and Graphic Novels*. Madison, WI: University of Wisconsin Press, 2011.

Chute, Hillary L. *Graphic Women: Life Narrative and Contemporary Comics*. New York: Columbia University Press, 2010.

Delisle, Guy. *Burma Chronicles*. Trans. Helge Dascher. Montreal: Drawn & Quarterly, 2008.

Jerusalem: Chronicles from the Holy City. Trans. Helge Dascher. Montreal: Drawn & Quarterly, 2012.

Pyongyang: A Journey in North Korea. Trans. Helge Dascher. Montreal: Drawn & Quarterly, 2005.

Shenzhen: A Travelogue from China. Trans. Helge Dascher. Montreal: Drawn & Quarterly, 2006.

Doxiadis, Apostolos, Christos H. Papadimitriou, Alecos Papadatos, and Annie Di Donna. *Logicomix: An Epic Search for Truth*. New York: Bloomsbury, 2009.

Engleberg, Miriam. *Cancer Made Me a Shallower Person: A Memoir in Comics*. New York: HarperCollins, 2006.

Eubanks, Adelheid. "Logicomix: From Text to Image/From Logic to Story." *The Comparatist* 35 (2011): 182–97.

Fies, Brian. *Mom's Cancer*. New York: Abrams Comicarts, 2006.

Gardner, Jared. "Autobiography's Biography, 1972–2007." *Biography* 31, no. 1 (Winter 2008): 1–25.

Gloeckner, Phoebe. *A Child's Life and Other Stories*. Berkeley, CA: Frog, 1998.

The Diary of a Teenage Girl. Berkeley, CA: Frog, 2002.

Green, Justin. *Binky Brown Meets the Holy Virgin Mary*. Introduction by Art Spiegelman. New York: McSweeney's, 2009.

Guibert, Emmanuel. *Alan's War: The Memories of G.I. Alan Cope*. Trans. Kathryn Pulver. New York: First Second, 2008.

How the World Was: A California Childhood. Trans. Kathryn Pulver. New York: First Second, 2014.

Hatfield, Charles. *Alternative Comics: An Emerging Literature*. Jackson, MS: University Press of Mississippi, 2005.

Kirtley, Susan E. *Lynda Barry: Girlhood Through the Looking Glass*. Jackson, MS: University Press of Mississippi, 2012.

Kominsky-Crumb, Aline. *The Complete Dirty Laundry Comics*. San Franciso, CA: Last Gasp, 1993.

Lejeune, Philippe. *On Autobiography*. Trans. Katherine Leary. Minneapolis, MN: University of Minnesota Press, 1989.

Lewis, John, Andrew Aydin, and Nate Powell. *March: Book One*. Portland, OR: Top Shelf, 2013.

Maslov, Nikolai. *Siberia*. Trans. Blake Ferris. Brooklyn, NY: Soft Skull Press, 2006.

Nakazawa, Keiji. *Barefoot Gen: A Cartoon Story of Hiroshima*, Vol. 1. Introduction by Art Spiegelman. Trans. Project Gen. San Franciso, CA: Last Gasp, 2004.

O'Brien, Sharon. "Showing the Voice of the Body: Brian Fies's *Mom's Cancer*, the Graphic Illness Memoir, and the Narrative of Hope," in Jane Tolmie, ed., *Drawing from Life: Memory and Subjectivity in Comic Art*. Jackson, MS: University Press of Mississippi, 2013, 264–88.

Pekar, Harvey. *Best of American Splendor*. New York: Ballantine Books, 2005.

Pekar, Harvey, and Joyce Brabner. *Our Cancer Year*. New York: Thunder's Mouth Press, 1994.

Porcellino, John. *The Hospital Suite*. Montreal: Drawn & Quarterly, 2014.

Rosenkranz, Patrick. *Rebel Visions: The Underground Comix Revolution, 1963–1975*. Seattle, WA: Fantagraphics Books, 2008.

Sacco, Joe. *The Fixer and Other Stories*. Montreal: Drawn & Quarterly, 2009.

Footnotes in Gaza. New York: Metropolitan Books, 2009.

Palestine. Seattle, WA: Fantagraphics Books, 1996.

Safe Area Goražde. Seattle, WA: Fantagraphics Books, 2001.

War's End: Profiles from Bosnia, 1995–96. Montreal: Drawn & Quarterly, 2005.

Satrapi, Marjane. *The Complete Persepolis*. New York: Pantheon Books, 2004.

Small, David. *Stitches: A Memoir*. New York: W. W. Norton, 2010.

Sowa, Marzena, and Sylvain Savoia. *Marzi: A Memoir*. New York: Vertigo, 2011.

Spiegelman, Art. *Comix, Essays, Graphics and Scrap*. New York: Raw Books, 1999.

The Complete Maus. New York: Pantheon Books, 1991.

In the Shadow of No Towers. New York: Pantheon Books, 2004.

MetaMaus. New York: Pantheon Books, 2011.

Stoddard Holmes, Martha. "Cancer Comics: Narrating Cancer through Sequential Art." *Tulsa Studies in Women's Literature* 32, no. 2 (Fall 2013/Spring 2014): 147–62.

Tabachnick, Stephen E. "Autobiography as Discovery in *Epileptic*," in Michael A. Chaney, ed., *Graphic Subjects: Critical Essays on Autobiography and Graphic Novels*. Madison, WI: University of Wisconsin Press, 2011, 101–16.

Tolmie, Jane, ed. *Drawing From Life: Memory and Subjectivity in Comic Art*. Jackson, MS: University Press of Mississippi, 2013.

Tran, GB. *Vietnamerica: A Family's Journey*. New York: Villard Books, 2011.

Tristram, Matilda. *Probably Nothing: A Diary of Not-Your-Average Nine Months*. New York: Penguin, 2014.

Whitlock, Gillian. "Autographics: The Seeing 'I' of Comics." *Modern Fiction Studies* 52, no. 4 (Winter 2006): 965–79.

Zograf, Aleksandar. *Regards From Serbia: A Cartoonist's Diary of a Crisis in Serbia*. Foreword by Chris Ware. Portland, GA: Top Shelf, 2007.

NOTES

1 Philippe Lejeune, *On Autobiography*, trans. Katherine Leary (Minneapolis, MN: University of Minnesota Press, 1989), 4.

2 See Michael Chaney's edited collection, *Graphic Subjects: Critical Essays on Autobiography and Graphic Novels* (Madison, WI: University of Wisconsin Press, 2011); Charles Hatfield's *Alternative Comics: An Emerging Literature* (Jackson, MS: University Press of Mississippi, 2005), which devotes two chapters to this topic; Hillary L. Chute's *Graphic Women: Life Narrative and Contemporary Comics* (New York: Columbia University Press, 2010); and Jane Tolmie's edited collection, *Drawing From Life: Memory and Subjectivity in Comic Art* (Jackson, MS: University Press of Mississippi, 2013).

3 Gillian Whitlock, "Autographics: The Seeing 'I' of Comics," *Modern Fiction Studies* 52, no. 4 (Winter 2006): 965–79.

4 See Patrick Rosenkranz, *Rebel Visions: The Underground Comix Revolution, 1963–1975* (Seattle, WA: Fantagraphics Books, 2008).

5 See Jared Gardner, "Autography's Biography, 1972–2007," *Biography* 31, no. 1 (Winter 2008): 1–25.

6 In fact, the first pages of the story that would later be revised to become *Maus* were published in a comic book titled *Funny Aminals* [sic] edited by Green in 1972. See Chute, *Graphic Women*, 16–18.

7 For more on this group, see Bart Beaty, "Selective Mutual Reinforcement in the Comics of Chester Brown, Joe Matt, and Seth," in Chaney, ed., *Graphic Subjects*, 247–59.

8 See Susan E. Kirtley, *Lynda Barry: Girlhood Through the Looking Glass* (Jackson, MS: University Press of Mississippi, 2012).

9 Art Spiegelman, "Letter to the New York Times Book Review," in *Comix, Essays, Graphics and Scraps* (New York: Raw Books, 1998), 16.

10 Art Spiegelman, *The Complete Maus* (New York: Pantheon Books, 1991), 25.

11 Hatfield, *Alternative Comics*, 126.

12 This happens when Spiegelman has documentation that there was an orchestra in Auschwitz, but Vladek cannot recall this. Spiegelman compromises by drawing the orchestra obscured behind a crowd (see Hatfield, *Alternative Comics*, 141).

13 See Martha Kuhlman, "The Traumatic Temporality of Art Spiegelman's *In the Shadow of No Towers*," *Journal of Popular Culture* 40, no. 5 (2007): 849–66.

14 Marjane Satrapi, *The Complete Persepolis* (New York: Pantheon Books, 2004).

15 Aleksandar Zograf, *Regards From Serbia: A Cartoonist's Diary of a Crisis in Serbia*, foreword by Chris Ware (Atlanta, GA: Top Shelf, 2007), 54.

16 Martha Stoddard Holmes suggests that "graphic body studies" could designate a field that analyzes "graphic representations of embodied experiences and social identities, drawing on the work of disability studies and other body studies theories but attending to the specific attributes of a hybrid genre that writes words and draws pictures." See her "Cancer Comics: Narrating Cancer through Sequential Art," *Tulsa Studies in Women's Literature* 32, no. 2 (Fall 2013/Spring 2014): 147.

17 Sharon O'Brien notes how the narrative of recovery "echoes the American ideology of upward mobility incarnated in Horatio Alger stories." "Such a story," she notes, "may be comforting to some, but it can be oppressive to the many people with chronic illnesses that cannot be 'cured'." See "Showing the Voice of the Body: Brian Fies's *Mom's Cancer*, the Graphic Illness Memoir, and the Narrative of Hope," in Tolmie, ed., *Drawing From Life*, 284.

18 John Porcellino mentions Pekar's book in his own memoir, *The Hospital Suite* (Montreal: Drawn & Quarterly, 2014).

19 See Stoddard Holmes, "Cancer Comics," for a discussion of the works by Fies, Engleberg, and Acocella Marchetto.

20 Marisa Acocella Marchetto, *Cancer Vixen* (New York: Knopf, 2006).

21 Brian Fies, *Mom's Cancer* (New York: Abrams Comicarts, 2006).

22 See Stephen E. Tabachnick's "Autobiography as Discovery in *Epileptic*," in Chaney, ed., *Graphic Subjects*, 101–15.

23 David B.[eauchard], *Epileptic*, trans. Kim Thompson (New York: Pantheon Books, 2005), 172.

24 Tabachnick, "Autobiography," 114–15.

25 Joe Sacco, *The Fixer and Other Stories* (Montreal: Drawn & Quarterly, 2009), 24.

26 Joe Sacco, *Palestine* (Seattle, WA: Fantagraphics Books, 1996), 102–13. A transcript of Sacco's presentation at the 2003 University of Florida comics conference is available here: www.english.ufl.edu/imagetext/archives/v1_1/sacco/

27 Guy Delisle, *Pyongyang: A Journey in North Korea*, trans. Helge Dascher (Montreal: Drawn & Quarterly, 2005), 59, 75.

28 Guy Delisle, *Burma Chronicles*, trans. Helge Dascher (Montreal: Drawn & Quarterly, 2008), 32.

29 Chester Brown, *Louis Riel: A Comic Strip Biography* (Montreal: Drawn & Quarterly, 2003).

30 Emmanuel Guibert, *Alan's War: The Memories of G.I. Alan Cope*, trans. Kathryn Pulver (New York: First Second, 2008), 63.

31 Apostolos Doxiadis, Christos H Papadimitriou, Alecos Papadatos, and Annie Di Donna, *Logicomix: An Epic Search for Truth* (New York: Bloomsbury, 2009), 77, 78. For an in-depth discussion of how the artists use maps and mapping, see Adelheid Eubanks, "Logicomix: From Text to Image/From Logic to Story," *The Comparatist* 35 (2011): 182–97.

8

JAN BAETENS*

Other Non-Fiction

There are many good reasons why non-fictional works have become so prominent in contemporary graphic novel production. Some of them are related to the transformations of the graphic novel itself. Others have to do with shifting ideas of what non-fiction actually means and how the boundaries between fiction and non-fiction are currently being redefined, both inside and outside of the field of the graphic novel. Before discussing some key works and authors as well as analyzing the essential stakes and issues of non-fictional graphic novels, it is necessary to have a closer look at the reasons for the very presence of this particular form of visual narrative today. For clarity's sake, I will stick here to a corpus of narrative works, thus leaving aside certain types of graphic non-fiction whose goal is not primarily narrative, such as, for instance, textbooks (Scott McCloud's *Understanding Comics* of 1993 is a modern classic of the genre) or the many scrapbooks, sketchbooks, cover art collections, and other visual diaries that can be seen as more or less commercial side effects of the success of the modern graphic novel.

Why Are There Non-Fictional Graphic Novels Today?

First of all, it should be stressed that the graphic novel, like any other medium, is permanently subject to change, at least in the strongly multimedial and highly competitive mediascape of which it is a part. In order to survive, media have to adapt and their adjustments result from creative interaction with other media. For many years, the graphic novel has been able to shape and explore its own form, content, and environment by distinguishing itself from mainstream comics, which were, in the period of the graphic novel's coming of age, superhero comics.[1] To a certain extent, this opposition still holds today, but it can no longer suffice to describe what a graphic novel really is – or has become since the late 1960s and early 1970s. The graphic novel is no longer limited to the black-and-white drawings of the

Xerox-years, just as it no longer adheres only to the formerly new content matter of biography, autobiography, and historical counter-documentary, as brilliantly illustrated in the work of a regrettably half-forgotten pioneer, Jaxon, pen-name of Jack Jackson and author of *Comanche Moon*.[2]

An important factor in the progressive opening of the graphic novel to other forms and content has been the rediscovery of the many comics classics, thanks to the facsimile republishing policy of several niche and trade publishers. It is now easy for the general public as well as beginning authors to have access to series that until some decades ago were difficult to find, from *Little Nemo in Slumberland* to *Krazy Kat*, from *Terry and the Pirates* to *Gasoline Alley*, from *Dick Tracy* to *Little Orphan Annie*, and many others. Thanks to the impact of the graphic novel, which raised new interest in non-superhero comics, all of this material has now become available once again, but its very availability has had a huge impact on the graphic novel itself. The broad editorial commitment to this type of work, often actively supported by key contemporary graphic novelists such as Chris Ware, has modified our stereotyped view of comics so radically that it has forced the graphic novel to redefine and reinvent itself, replacing the now rather hollow dichotomy between comics and graphic novel by a more innovative approach to what the graphic novel might be after the rediscovery of so many comics classics (which appeared to have done in various regards what the graphic novel had been claiming to do all by itself). The rise of the non-fictional graphic novel, I would like to claim, is a direct consequence of this sharper awareness of what comics used to be in the past, before their reduction to superheroes for children.

Medium change is not only the consequence of an internal makeover, however. Given the growing interweaving of media in our "convergence culture," one must also take into account relationships between media, in this case between the graphic novel and non-comics media.[3] The most striking impact on the graphic novel in this regard is undoubtedly represented by the shift from fiction to docu-fiction as well as documentary and non-fiction in film and television, two media whose social hegemony, although challenged today by video-game culture and other forms of digital culture on the internet, are much stronger than that of the graphic novel, which is still a niche product catering to relatively small audiences. One can plausibly suppose that the ubiquity of docu-fiction and non-fiction in Hollywood and in many television production houses has had an influence on the remarkable progress of non-fictional graphic novels.

No less important than these changes in medium structure and use are, however, our changing ideas concerning non-fiction and similar notions of objectivity and representation of the real. They represent the second aspect that explains the contemporary interest in the non-fictional graphic novel.

Two major stereotypes, inextricably linked one to another, continue to dominate our thinking about objectivity. On the one hand, there is the conviction that the most objective way of representing data is to replicate or *reproduce* it. On the other hand, there is also the belief that the most objective way of reproducing data is to picture it, to make a *photograph* of it with the help of a purely mechanical device, deprived of any human agency or intervention. Both principles have been under fierce attack, first in scientific circles, and then in larger social debates about issues of objectivity and representation. The limits of photography as a tool of absolute and transparent reproduction are now widely acknowledged, while the ideal of data reproduction has been supplanted by that of what Lorraine Daston and Peter Galison, authors of a respected study of the history of the notion of objectivity, as well as other philosophers and historians of science and media (see, for instance, Gitelman) call "trained judgment," the learned capacity to make a meaningful interpretation of constructed data.[4]

The relevance of these larger discussions for the non-fictional graphic novel is vital. The distrust of photography as well as the doubt directed toward unmediated reproduction have cleared the ground for this new form of serious storytelling at two levels. First, they make room for the graphic novel in general, for it is now accepted that fiction may play a positive, that is knowledge-enhancing role in our approach to the world, which is not just the world as a mass of empirical data but also the world as we experience and experiment with it. In other words, the fact that a graphic novel goes beyond the mere reproduction of visible and verbal data is no longer seen as incompatible with ideas of truth and realism, which are no longer separated from the idea of interpretation. Second, they encourage the inclusion of non-fictional topics and stances in the graphic novel, since the preference given to drawings rather than to photographs is no longer discarded as a subjective – and therefore no longer reliable – twisting and misinterpretation of allegedly objective images. Drawn images, in other words, can now be accepted as valuable representations of the world itself. An even more compelling motivation is the actual lack of other visual material, which may force the journalist to choose drawings if he or she wants to present the story in a graphic way, as is done in Gladstone and Neufeld's critical report on mass media and politics, *The Influencing Machine* (2011). This book takes great pains to emphasize the authenticity of its text. In the credits page of the book, we see the cartoonish representation of the journalist Brooke Gladstone and a speech balloon stating: "Most of the words spoken herein by actual people are drawn from historical documents, transcripts, or interviews. Ellipses are used to indicate both pauses and internal edits....Great care was taken to ensure that no remark was taken out of context."[5] However, no remark whatsoever can be found that explains, justifies, or motivates the visual representation technique and style that were used for the graphic dimension of the book. This significant lacuna testifies to the now commonly accepted journalistic value of (in this case rather cartoonish) drawings, as brilliantly illustrated in the French *La Revue dessinée* (*The Drawn Journal*, founded in 2013), a trimonthly exclusively devoted to drawn investigative journalism.

If the first key word in this debate on truth and fiction in journalism is agency, and the growing awareness and acceptance of human agency in the representation of the world, the second one, at least in the context of the graphic novel as a narrative structure as opposed to non-narrative uses of drawn material, is undoubtedly story or storytelling. As convincingly demonstrated by Martha A. Sandweiss in her book on the visual representation of the discovery of the West, suspicion of photography is not a new phenomenon at all.[6] For many decades after the invention of photography, the nineteenth-century publishing industry continued to juxtapose etchings based on photographs with the photographs themselves, not only for reasons of sharpness and clarity (photographs show too much, and they highlight details as much as essential information), but also and perhaps more importantly because of issues of narrative (photographs may tell a story, true, but etchings tell it better since they are not condemned to the evocation of just one slice of time).

Story, however, is an umbrella term, which it is useful to unpack. First of all, the narrative transformation of data involves the foregrounding – which is a matter of recording as well as inventing – of something which may not always be immediately visible in reality itself: a storyline, with a causally related beginning, middle, and end. This storyline also has characters, with their own agency and motivation. Second, narrative implies not only an abstract storyline, but also very concrete forms and techniques of storytelling, which inevitably hint at the active presence and intervention of a verbal and visual narrator whose agency affects the material he or she is representing to the reader and viewer. The willingness to admit storylines and storytelling techniques in modes of representation that claim to address the real is an important factor that helps us understand the appearance of the non-fictional graphic novel.

How It Started

It is commonly accepted that the form of the emerging graphic novel of the 1970s leaned heavily toward non-fiction. Some graphic novel formats were definitely new, such as the autobiographical graphic novel. Other forms were adaptations of existing practices in the broader comics field, where a well-established tradition of didactic and historical works existed. The change brought forward by the graphic novel in this field was twofold. On the one hand, non-fiction in the graphic novel had a different target audience than the comics. Graphic novels were geared toward adults rather than children. On the other hand, the graphic novel had a strong counter-cultural dimension which was very different from the often patriotic and propagandistic tone of non-fiction in comics. The critical dimension of the first non-fictional re-adaptations of historical material in graphic novel form was not necessarily visible at the level of the style of these works, which was far from revolutionary. Jaxon, the key representative of this first generation, relied on a very traditional drawing style, strongly marked by the habits of book illustration and dedicated to the meticulous reproduction of historical details. But the counter-cultural dimension was ubiquitous as far as their content was concerned. The first non-fictional graphic novels displayed a strong interest in the history of those who do not write history (the heroes of these graphic novels were outsiders, losers, nobodies, or public enemies) and in everyday history (the major storylines of these graphic novels center on the small stories or non-stories of ordinary people).

In the evolution from these historical examples of the genre to its contemporary forms, it is difficult to overestimate the impact of the French author Jacques Tardi, who works in the continental *bande dessinée* tradition. Although not always immediately translated in the United States, his work was closely followed by all progressive readers and authors in the field, who had discovered him in *RAW*, the avant-garde magazine edited by Art Spiegelman and Françoise Mouly between 1980 and 1991. Often focusing on the personal and collective traumas of the First World War and highly critical of all kinds of patriotic historiography, Tardi crossed the frontier between fiction and non-fiction in *It Was the War of the Trenches* (originally published and immediately very widely circulated in 1984 and 1993).[7] Tardi's work has indeed been decisive in the shift from official history to ordinary history and from patriotic historiography to critical historiography. However, the most crucial contribution of Tardi to the non-fictional graphic novel lies less with the introduction of new content matter than with the efficient use of storytelling techniques. Most pivotal in this regard has been the combination of three storytelling devices. First, the use of a sober drawing technique, an expressive update of Hergé's black-and-white clear line technique, which contrasted very efficiently with the horror and the "sublime," that is, the non-representable nature of the war experience of common soldiers. Second, the emphasis of the first-hand witness narrative. Third and last, the systematic repetition of a special page design made of three horizontal tiers, which fit perfectly the form of trenches as well as the surrounding battlefield.[8] The tremendous contribution of Tardi to the non-fictional graphic novel has been this combination of a theme, a voice, and a visual style, and to a large extent all major later graphic novelists have borrowed from his practice, even if Tardi's main theme, his clear line style, or his narrative modes, have been replaced by competing options, which concentrate more closely on contemporary history (the focus is on today's war zones, not on the First World War trenches), on the invention of a more individual style (a distinctive feature of the graphic novel in general, where the visible presence of the maker's "hand" is greatly appreciated), and the commitment to a personal, eye-witness testimony of the graphic novelist himself or herself (although all authors continue to pay great attention to the voices and ideas of the witnesses, usually the victims, they encounter).

A supplementary characteristic of the graphic novel that explains its success in portraying non-fictional, more particularly historical, subject matter has been put forward by Hillary Chute, who praises the medium's ability to inscribe the context of the story told:

> Graphic narrative accomplishes this work with its manifest handling of its own artifice, its attention to its seams. Its formal grammar rejects transparency and renders textualization conspicuous, inscribing the context in its graphic presentation.[9]

Safe Area Goražde: A Turning Point in Graphic Journalism

Joe Sacco's work will help exemplify the shift from historical non-fiction to graphic journalism, which will prove to be a very special type of journalism. Graphic journalism is a great challenge – a danger as well an opportunity – to more established forms of journalism, not only because of the drawings, supposedly less objective and therefore less reliable than photographs, but also because of the very process of its making, which contrasts sharply with most currently accepted rules.

The difficulties raised by drawn journalism – and drawn non-fiction in general – are twofold. On the one hand, there is of course the threat of an imbalance between the verbal and the visual, as happens in the 2009 graphic adaptation of *The Origin of Species* by Michael Keller and Nicolle Rager Fuller, where the images are actually reduced to a completely ancillary role. Yet it is also possible for a text to be relegated to the mere role of captioning, or, as Roland Barthes once provocatively declared, of paradoxically "illustrating the image":

The image no longer *illustrates* the words; it is now the words which, structurally, are parasitic on the image. The reversal is at a cost: in the traditional modes of illustration the image functioned as an episodic return to denotation from a principal message (the text) which was experienced as connoted since, precisely, it needed an illustration; in the relationship that now holds, it is not the image which comes to elucidate or "realize" the text, but the latter which comes to sublimate, patheticize or rationalize the image.[10]

The priority given to the image at the expense of the text is a feature of pop journalism and may come as a surprise when authors, as is the case in nonfictional graphic novels, want to turn to more serious forms of investigative journalism.

On the other hand, there is also the peril of an excessively cartoonish style. In themselves drawings are not anathema to the objective and the real, as well-demonstrated in many scientific disciplines that continue to rely on hand-made drawings (archeology may be a fitting example), but they lose their credibility as soon as their style is too heavily marked by the personal touch of their maker. Besides, there is also the problem of the temporal gap between the observation of an event and its graphic reproduction. In the case of photography, this gap is by definition non-existent: one can only picture what is actually happening "now" in front of the camera, even if later manipulations always remain possible. In the case of drawings, however, even the fastest sketcher can never catch things as they move in front of his or her eyes. In a zeitgeist obsessed with the idea of instantaneous recording and circulation of visual data, this gap at the very least raises questions about the status and nature of the journalist's work.

In *Safe Area Goražde* (2000), which set a new standard for graphic journalism, Joe Sacco manages to provide a satisfying solution to most of these difficulties.[11] In that sense, the book is also a great breakthrough in comparison with previous books, most particularly *Palestine* (2001, but initially published in smaller installments in 1993).[12] *Safe Area Goražde* is the report of Sacco's several short-term stays in Goražde, one of the Bosnian enclaves in Serbian territory that were under (fragile!) United Nations protection during the civil war in former Yugoslavia. While staying in Sarajevo, as most Western reporters did in those days, Sacco used a UN convoy to sneak into Goražde, where he eventually returned three times. The book is a series of direct testimonies of what Sacco saw and heard in the no longer besieged city, alternating with the reconstruction of the inhabitants' experiences at the outbreak of the war (both strands of the book, one in the present, one in the past, are clearly separated).

Safe Area Goražde is a tremendous achievement in graphic novel journalism thanks to a number of explicit authorial decisions, which all highlight the specific force of this kind of documentary, both in comparison to non-graphic novel journalism (newspapers, magazines, television) and to previous forms of graphic novel journalism. This accomplishment is not the result of the author's political commitment alone, which was similar to that of most embedded journalists. Sacco was certainly not the only reporter who openly criticized Serbian nationalism (for most journalists, this was even a kind of default option during the war). Nor did the novelty of his book result from the seriousness with which the author dared question his own initial convictions: *Safe Area Goražde* is not an anti-Serbian witch-hunt, and while the story unfolds Sacco becomes increasingly irritated with the city versus country antagonism as fueled by the "cosmopolitan" inhabitants of Sarajevo, who were often unwilling to sympathize with the "peasants" of Goražde.

What makes *Safe Area Goražde* such a poignant work are less the human qualities of the reporter, however admirable these may be, than the thoughtful editorial and compositional techniques which Sacco applies in a very systematic way. The most important of these, although not necessarily the most discernable one since its effects appear so utterly "natural," is of course Sacco's interpretation of what is considered the very basis of an authentic documentary since the pioneering work of John Grierson: "the creative treatment of actuality."[13] By definition, such a treatment involves a great deal of distance, which in turn makes room for reflection and understanding, without which no real journalism can ever be possible. Yet this distance from the obsession of the day goes much further than just temporal distance. It also demands a rearrangement of the material, in this case field material (a diary, field notes, taped conversations, pictures), along narrative lines, or, more precisely, in the characters' stories that function as the recurring stepping stones of the reportage. In the long interview with Gary Groth which was originally published in the *Comics Journal* in 2002 and which concludes the 2011 special edition of *Safe Area Goražde*, Sacco states:

Well, Palestine was pretty organic. What happened, happened and I laid it out almost chronologically.... With the Goražde book, I realized I had certain types of information and I wondered how I was going to organize it. You begin to think, "What does the reader need?" Most of the readers are going to come into this book with very little understanding of what happened in Yugoslavia. So I have to tell the story of Yugoslavia even though I'm just trying to tell the story of one town. Then I realized, as much as possible I'll try to tell the story of Yugoslavia through the one town. But you do need basic information in there.... How was I going to do that? I realized I had two tracks. There was the historical track that took the reader chronologically through the major incidents of the war. And there was the atmospheric track that was basically my impressions of the people I was meeting....The question was how do I interweave those two tracks?...I realized, to make it more powerful it's better to introduce the characters. Let them grow on the reader, as they grew on me, and as you get to know the characters through the atmospheric track, the historic track is building up.[14]

Next to this organizational principle at story level, Sacco relies on two other storytelling techniques, the first already tested in *Palestine*, the second a major change in his work. The first technique concerns the word and image interaction in the hybrid medium of the graphic novel. The overall strategy followed by Sacco is to pursue as strong a balance as possible. Most conspicuous in this regard is the scattered pattern of the speech balloons and narrative captions (fig. 8.1), which Sacco presents as inspired by the style of Louis-Ferdinand Céline, the French author of the 1932 novel *Journey to the End of the Night*. *Journey to the End of the Night* was famously illustrated by Jacques Tardi in the years he himself was working on his First World War graphic novels. In the already mentioned interview with Gary Groth, we read:

GROTH: As far as I can remember, you're the only cartoonist I know who uses this Sacco-patented technique of floating captions that run throughout panels or over panels. They're fragmented captions. Why did you develop that technique? I have my own theories but...

SACCO: I'll tell you, because I know exactly why. Because some years ago I was reading a lot of Ferdinand Céline. I was very taken, very taken with the way he'd set off dramatic phrases by ellipses. He would pile up these redundant phrases that would make me howl with laughter. I loved these clipped statements. I thought they were very effective. I just wanted to figure out a way to incorporate these in comics somehow. I was very influenced by his writing. That was what I came up with. I realized, "Well, all I have to do is just basically separate the words." It's very easy to do in comics. You just separate the words. And I could use these little phrases in their fragmented captions to lead the eye of the reader around the page, and sometimes the placement of a caption corresponds very specifically to something going on visually under it, often to dramatic effect, let me say. The other useful thing about this technique is that it can emphasize a scattered feeling, that all sorts of things are going on at once.

Surprising though his reference to Céline may be, for stylistic as well as ideological reasons, the point that Sacco makes in the interview is very clear: when one invents new forms of graphic journalism, one also needs new forms of word and image interaction.

Fig. 8.1 Joe Sacco, *Safe Area Goražde*, page 59. © Fantagraphics Books. Reproduced with kind permission of the publisher.

If this visual dispatching of the verbal information had already been explored in *Palestine*, the other main storytelling device of *Safe Area Goražde* initiates an important twist in Sacco's work: the relative withdrawal of the narrator. The narrator is both less present in the story itself, which now revolves around the characters, and in the drawing style, which is much less cartoonish than in *Palestine*, where the influence of Robert Crumb was still profoundly perceptible.

Beyond the Pictures and Drawings Divide

I have not yet emphasized what many readers may identify as the most salient feature of the non-fictional graphic novel, namely the visual reshaping and reinterpretation of actuality by means of the inherent mechanisms of selecting, foregrounding, and combining, if not inventing, of elements that are nevertheless claimed to be "true." Sacco of course heavily utilizes these techniques too, most emphatically in the sequences where he reconstructs the witnesses' past stories:

> I feel I can take liberties. I thought of this when I was watching the movie *Barry Lyndon*. You see *Barry Lyndon* and the viewer suspends disbelief and suddenly they are there in the 1700s.... I'll give you some real specifics if you want them.... The first attack – the scene where people are crawling through the orchard and being fired upon. I walked through that apple orchard and I took pictures. I took pictures across the main road. Now often, I would take pictures when someone said, "We crawled across the main road." I'd think, OK, I have to take a picture of the main road and what it looks like and give myself an impression. I did ask specifically, "How were you crouching? What were you wearing?" Or were you wearing this as opposed to that. There are a lot of characters. I can't ask everyone. I don't even think it's that important in some cases, but I try to bring as much realism as I can do.... Basically, I put together as much of this – this all went through my head and that's what came out of my hand. To me, maybe not accurately describing it details for details, but as much as possible I tried to bring something to it that reflected reality.[15]

However, it is another work of graphic novel reportage, the second landmark publication in the genre, that puts a crucial emphasis on this part of the creative treatment of actuality: *The Photographer* by Emmanuel Guibert and Didier Lefèvre, a book on war-torn Afghanistan during the rebellion against the Soviet invasion in the 1980s.[16] The photographer in question is Lefèvre. He documented the humanitarian mission of a Doctors Without Borders team and his pictures were converted into a graphic novel by his friend and comics artist Emmanuel Guibert. The distinctive feature of this book is the merging of graphic novel and photographic source material. Normally the latter is either made invisible or confined to the margins of the book, where it is mentioned or quoted as proof of the graphic novel's authenticity (such is the case in the anniversary edition of *Safe Area Goražde*, in which Sacco shows lengthy excerpts from the visual archive of his text).

The merging of photographs and drawings in the comics or graphic novel format is not necessarily common, but far from exceptional (a small but highly significant example of this mix may be found in Spiegelman's *Maus* [1996] for example). *The Photographer*'s use of this form of hybridity goes beyond the standard role that pictures play in non-fictional graphic novels, however. Usually, the first aim of pictures is to prove the legitimacy of a graphic novel's content matter. What the drawings tell must be true, since they show the same events, places, and figures as the pictures that go alongside them. In the case of Guibert and Lefèvre, however, the drawings definitely do *not* show the same content as the pictures. The authors do not reduplicate the drawings as is usually done when the narrative is followed or preceded by commentaries detailing the makeover of the pictures by the drawings as well as the careful and deontologically acceptable way in which this makeover took place. Instead, Guibert and Lefèvre *alternate* both media. Between pictures and drawings there is no overlap, but a system of relay that reinforces the rhetorical power of the story, which moves ahead straightforwardly while never losing the double warrant of photography's truthfulness and drawing's expressivity. Moreover, and this is a key difference with previous practices as well, *The Photographer* exploits not only the information content of both photographs and drawings, it also displays the many layout possibilities of these media. The book establishes an almost seamless match between the traditional grid structure of the graphic novel and the no less regular segmentation of photographic contact sheets. This way, the transition from one medium to another becomes much more organic, opening possibilities for experiments with pictures that are stock mechanisms in the graphic novel, but that are normally excluded from the field of documentary photography, a domain often reduced to the binary opposition of the archival contact sheet and the one picture to make it into print. In *The Photographer* there is a very subtle play with the basic grid, that can be shaped into other compositional patterns each time a special emphasis is needed in the drawings as well as in the pictures.

Non-Fiction in the Graphic Novel is Here to Stay

As this essay has tried to demonstrate, non-fictional graphic novels are not only prominent in contemporary graphic novel production, but there are good reasons to think that this will also be the case in the future. This is first of all because the graphic novel is part of a shifting mediascape, which forces it to stay competitive in comparison with other forms and media: since our idea of comics is less naive than it used to be, the graphic novel will have to continue to enlarge its scope, style, and types of narrative, and this will inevitably profit the elaboration of new forms of non-fictional graphic novels; and second, since the graphic novel is more and more part of our modern convergence culture, it will have to establish a creative dialogue with other media in which the part of non-fiction is also growing. Of course this does not mean that the graphic novel is just following a number of larger cultural tendencies. As shown by the examples of *Safe Area Goražde* as well as *The Photographer*, graphic novelists have the possibility to pioneer new forms of word and image hybridization and to explore new frontiers in journalism, for instance via their innovative use of subjectivity and page layout.

Works Cited

Baetens, Jan, and Hugo Frey. *The Graphic Novel: An Introduction*. New York: Cambridge University Press, 2014.

Barthes, Roland. "The Photographic Message," in *Image, Music, Text*. London: Fontana, 1977, 191–99.

Chute, Hillary. "Comics as Literature? Reading Graphic Narrative." *PMLA* 123, no. 2 (2008): 452–65.

Daston, Lorraine, and Peter Galison. *Objectivity*. New York: Zone Books, 2007.

Gitelman, Lisa. *"Raw Data" is an Oxymoron*. Cambridge, MA: MIT Press, 2013.

Gladstone, Brooke, and Josh Neufeld. *The Influencing Machine*. New York: W. W. Norton, 2011.

Guibert, Emmanuel, Didier Lefèvre, and Frédéric Lemercier. *The Photographer*. New York: First Second, 2009.

Jenkins, Henry. *Convergence Culture: Where Old and New Media Collide*. New York University Press, 2006.

Keller, Michael, and Nicolle Rager Fuller. *Charles Darwin's On the Origin of Species: A Graphic Adaptation*. New York: Rodale, 2009.

McCloud, Scott. *Understanding Comics*. Northampton, MA: Kitchen Sink Press, 1993.

Jaxon [Jack Jackson]. *Comanche Moon*. San Francisco, CA: Rip Off Press, 1979.

Sacco, Joe. *Palestine*. Seattle, WA: Fantagraphics Books, 2001.

  Safe Area Goražde: The Special Edition (2000). Seattle, WA: Fantagraphics Books, 2011.

Sandweiss, Martha A. *Print the Legend: Photography and the American West*. New Haven, CT: Yale University Press, 2002.

Spiegelman, Art. *The Complete Maus*. New York: Pantheon, 1996.

Tardi, Jacques. *It Was the War of the Trenches*. Seattle, WA: Fantagraphics Books, 2010.

Winston, Brian. *Claiming the Real: The Griersonian Documentary and its Limitations* (1985). London: BFI Publishing, 2008.

Witek, Joseph. *Comic Books as History: The Narrative Art of Jack Jackson, Art Spiegelman, and Harvey Pekar*. Jackson, MS: University Press of Mississippi, 1989.

NOTES

* My most sincere thanks to Dr. Charlotte Pylyser for her help with the stylistic editing of this text.
1 Jan Baetens and Hugo Frey, *The Graphic Novel: An Introduction* (New York: Cambridge University Press, 2014).
2 On the historiographical work by Jaxon, see Joseph Witek, *Comic Books as History: The Narrative Art of Jack Jackson, Art Spiegelman, and Harvey Pekar* (Jackson, MS: University Press of Mississippi, 1989), 58–95.
3 Henry Jenkins, *Convergence Culture: Where Old and New Media Collide* (New York University Press, 2006).
4 Lorraine Daston and Peter Galison, *Objectivity* (New York: Zone Books, 2007); Lisa Gitelman, *"Raw Data" is an Oxymoron* (Cambridge, MA: MIT Press, 2013).
5 Brooke Gladstone and Josh Neufeld, *The Influencing Machine* (New York: W. W. Norton, 2011).
6 Martha Sandweiss, *Print the Legend: Photography and the American West* (New Haven, CT: Yale University Press, 2002).
7 Jacques Tardi, *It Was the War of the Trenches*, trans. Kim Thompson (Seattle, WA: Fantagraphics Books, 2010).
8 Historically speaking, this particular constraint may have been inspired by the Italian "striscia," a small horizontal publishing format that was typical of certain forms of popular literature (comics, but also photo novels) in Italy and France during the 1960s and 1970s and whose content was often war-related. An indirect supplementary proof of this hypothesis is perhaps the fact that one finds the same technique in the famous legendary biography of Ché Guevara by Alberto and Enrique Breccia, script by Héctor Oesterheld, *La Vida del Ché* (1968; Vitoria-Gasteiz: Ikusager, 1987). The book was originally published in Argentina, a country strongly influenced by the Italian tradition.
9 Hillary Chute, "Comics as Literature? Reading Graphic Narrative," *PMLA* 123, no. 2 (2008): 457.
10 Roland Barthes, "The Photographic Message," in *Image, Music, Text* (London: Fontana, 1977), 25.
11 Joe Sacco, *Safe Area Goražde* (2000; Seattle, WA: Fantagraphics Books, 2011).
12 Joe Sacco, *Palestine* (Seattle, WA: Fantagraphics Books, 2001).
13 Brian Winston, *Claiming the Real: The Griersonian Documentary and its Limitations* (1985; London: BFI Publishing, 2008).
14 Sacco, *Safe area Goražde*, 236–37.
15 Ibid., 240–41.
16 Emmanuel Guibert, Didier Lefèvre, and Frédéric Lemercier, *The Photographer* (New York: First Second, 2009).

9

ESTHER BENDIT SALTZMAN

Novel to Graphic Novel

"I work as far as the eye is concerned," Cam Kennedy says of his work on adaptations; "It's down to me to open up the text so that people will say: 'This looks interesting'. That has to be done through the drawings."[1] Indeed, the application of comics format to literary classics can excite both popular and academic interest. Since literary scholarship historically deals with opening up texts for understanding and meaning, the interest generated by the study of graphic novel adaptations can facilitate and stimulate new discussion of literary classics, increasing academic interest through interdisciplinary studies.

This chapter argues that the interpretive choices made by graphic novel adapters and artists inspire interest by establishing a dialogic relationship between them, the author of the adapted text, and the readers of both.[2] Specifically, the transcoding of textual components into the comics medium adds the voice of the adapter and/or artist to the transmission of narrative; this can encourage scholars and students to investigate detailed aspects of a source text, explore implications of alternate readings, and question the adapter/artist's verbal, artistic, and technical choices.[3] This in turn encourages a re-examination, or possible re-evaluation, of the adapted text through close reading, facilitating analytical engagement and thereby enhancing literary studies.

This study will concentrate on the adaptation of the novel into its graphic novel counterpart by focusing on the following four classics: H. G. Wells' *The Invisible Man*, Richard Stark's *Parker: The Hunter*, Robert Louis Stevenson's *The Strange Case of Dr. Jekyll and Mr. Hyde,* and Jonathan Swift's *Gulliver's Travels*. The chosen adaptations represent a range of adherence to their adapted texts, a variety of artistic styles, and an array of visual techniques. To investigate the contributions of these adaptations to academic conversation, this chapter examines techniques used in producing them and explores their potential effects on readers.

Traditionally, literary scholarship has been based on verbal textuality. Until recently, most work on literary adaptations was associated with film. In *A Theory of Adaptation*, Linda Hutcheon calls for a comprehensive theory of adaptation inclusive of multiple media, including video games, theme parks, and, of course, graphic novels.[4] Jørgen Bruhn, Anne Gjelsvik, and Eirik Frisvold Hanssen identify five areas of academic trends in adaptation studies: fidelity issues; the inclusion of multiple types of media adaptations; the study of "multilevel," or multiple, adaptations concurrently; adaptation as a dialogic process; and the use of "global theoretic frameworks such as intermediality or genetic criticism."[5] These trends demonstrate the multidimensional ways that adaptations and their inspirations can be studied, and that this chapter aims to address.

Many scholars agree that evaluation based on fidelity is restrictive.[6] In *Novel to Film*, Brian McFarlane explains, "Fidelity criticism depends on a notion of the text as having and rendering up to the (intelligent) reader a single, correct 'meaning' which the filmmaker has either adhered to or in some sense violated or tampered with."[7] Therefore, strict adherence to a source text might limit alternative readings. Visual images and departures from the source text, though, increase possibilities for interpretation. Since comics are "characterized by a plurality of messages," they offer unique opportunities for academic investigation.[8] Examining the similarities and differences between adapted text and adaptation can illuminate important aspects of an adapted text. The adapter may embrace much of a source text or adopt a "what if" approach exploring possibilities for departure. Both approaches have the potential to engage the imagination and direct the reader back to the adapted text.

As a hybrid medium, graphic novel adaptations share elements with other visual media, but their medium-specific characteristics make them exceptionally helpful in literary analysis. Graphic novel artists/adapters may apply cinematic techniques or techniques historically attributed to illustration and/or fine art. Specifically, comics employs the use of framed, stationary, and sequential images, and the varied styles of cartoon art. Thus, readers can analyze visuals within or bleeding from the frames, the frame sequence, and the page design (or *mise-en-page*). Graphic novels allow readers time to examine each aspect; readers can compare images from earlier or later pages or the work as a whole. Will Eisner explains that visual messages are instrumental in evoking empathy.[9] An empathetic reader may be more inclined to go back to a source text for resolution of discrepancies.

The Importance of Choices and Applications

The adapter, whether scriptwriter or artist, makes choices involving both adapted text and adaptation, including which chapters, scenes, or characters to include in the interests of time, space, purpose, and message. Important aspects of content include themes and motifs, tone, style, and narration. The adapter also decides which elements of the verbal text to include or alter, and what to include in visual form. These choices are manifested through applications of wording and visual techniques.

Scott McCloud identifies five areas of choice in the production of comics: "choice of moment," "choice of frame," "choice of image," "choice of word," and "choice of flow."[10] Comics share some choices, like choice of image, with other visual media, but there are also choices specific to comics. For example, a painter will choose a moment, and although there can be multiple moments in one painting, comics provide direction through the flow of panels. Film and comics share the use of angles and perspective, directing the viewer's eye through sequential images. Film, though, shows images in rapid succession. In comics, the reader can see different "camera" angles simultaneously and take time to analyze each frame. McCloud also describes six transition choices used in producing comics: "moment to moment," "action to action," "subject to subject," "scene to scene," "aspect to aspect," and "non-sequitur" (no established order).[11] In contrast to film, comics can visualize multiple transitions simultaneously in varied numbers of panels and on one or more pages. The variety and application of adapter/artist choices affect reader response and provide opportunities for the re-examination of source texts.

The Invisible Man: Artistic Style as a Study in Genre

Two graphic novel adaptations of H. G. Wells' *The Invisible Man* exhibit contrasting approaches while both adhere to Wells' storyline. The first is Rick Geary's adaptation for Classics Illustrated; the second is adapted by Sean Taylor with illustrations by Bhupendra Ahluwalia for Campfire. The examination of these texts in tandem with Wells' illustrates a multilevel approach to graphic novel scholarship. Wells' text, a work of science fiction with tonal elements that include comedy and horror, challenges readers to label it with an identity. Some characters are depicted with Dickensian sketch-like humor.[12] Landlady Mrs. Hall's inquisitive and naive nature is treated with disdain by Griffin, the Invisible Man, but with comedic tenderness by Wells. Mr. Thomas Marvel, "a person of copious, flexible visage, a nose of cylindrical protrusion, a liquorish, ample, fluctuating mouth, and a beard of bristling eccentricity," provides comic relief as a vagrant whom Griffin forces into servitude.[13] As Wells' text progresses, Griffin becomes more terrifying as he reveals his story. Geary captures more lightness and humor, while Ahluwalia and Taylor capture aspects of horror.

Geary's style is whimsical, colorful, and truly cartoon-like. His bandaged Griffin is round in stature, and more comical than frightening. About using his style to treat Gothic subjects, Geary explains:

> I tend to avoid the direct representations of gore and violence. Not that I'm squeamish about such stuff, but my sense of the humor has always leaned toward the indirect and incidental. Plus the Victorian era was long enough ago to provide the detachment that makes a whimsical approach possible. The first stories I did in this vein were looked upon with doubt by some publishers. I'm not sure that my style was "perfect" for them, but it's that kind of narrative I was drawn to.[14]

Interestingly, Wells' inspiration for the story was "The Perils of Invisibility," by W. S. Gilbert.[15] The humorous poem addresses a man's negative experience with invisibility; as Wells' inspiration, it makes Geary's style a reasonable approach.

In contrast, Ahluwalia's art is more realistic and highly detailed with illustrations closer to paintings than traditional cartoon art; it accents the horror in Wells' text. Griffin's bandages look like those of a burn patient. As Griffin admits causing his father's suicide, the close-up of his bandaged face increases reader discomfort as he seems to be smiling underneath. The graphic novel's dark palette adds Gothic overtones, and even the comic characters appear serious or angry.

Additional artistic and verbal choices secure the tone of each adaptation. Reinforcing his lighter tone, Geary visualizes terrified townspeople falling over one another after Griffin removes his bandages, and he maintains the townspeople's country vernacular speech. Favoring a serious tone, Ahluwalia and Taylor's townspeople speak in academic English, and scenes with tumbling townspeople are not visualized. Geary's style, though, becomes less comic as Griffin relates his increasingly chilling story to Kemp. Geary relates Griffin's history in a series of framed flashback images; a seemingly empty robe narrates the events from the only unframed image (see fig. 9.1). The green coloring of the flashback panels differentiates them as past events. Geary's chosen images foreshadow the impending "perils" that Griffin will face when invisible. In the middle right panel Griffin appears nude and exposed; in each escape he will need to face nature unclothed to avoid detection. In the bottom right frame, only Griffin's skull remains, warning of the final peril, his death.

Fig. 9.1 Griffin transforms into the Invisible Man. From *The Invisible Man* by Rick Geary. By permission of First Classics, Inc.

Both graphic novels, then, focus attention on select aspects of Wells' text. Studying them together provides a more comprehensive study illuminating Wells' text in new and exciting ways.

Intentional Translation in Cooke's Adaptation of *The Hunter*

Darwyn Cooke's treatment of *The Hunter*, a crime novel in the hard-boiled subgenre of detective fiction, translates the novel into the comics medium. The original novel was written by Richard Stark, a pseudonym for Donald Westlake, and is set in 1962. The novel follows thief extraordinaire Parker as he systematically reverses a double-cross and proceeds to recover his money. The 1960s setting comes through Cooke's visuals. The matte pages have a yellowish tint as if they are typed pages yellowed with time. Cooke varies the image/word balance for effective translation. Both Westlake's and Cooke's versions begin with Parker rejecting the offer of a ride. In Stark's novel, the interaction occurs in the first paragraph. Cooke devotes the entire first page to it; the caption, describing the "fresh-faced" driver, is complemented by Parker's answer telling him to "go to hell."[16] This blunt interaction introduces us to Parker with immediate clarity, but Cooke's decision magnifies the scene with emphatic immediacy. Cooke's next series of pages contain no dialogue as visual storytelling depicts him illegally obtaining money and fake identification. We then find out that he has escaped from prison. Once he is in his estranged wife's apartment, full dialogue is instituted, changing the rhythm and slowly revealing the facts behind their tumultuous relationship.

Cooke's adaptation is the only one in this study that involved aspects of collaboration with the original author. Interviewed by Tom Spurgeon for *The Comics Reporter*, Cooke describes his admiration for Westlake and his intention to faithfully translate Westlake's novel; he had told Westlake, "this is not going to be an attempt to interpret your words with my words as much as bringing this whole story into another medium." He also asked for Westlake's "insight," concerned about the author's reaction to his work. Cooke explains that Westlake's characterization provided a challenge because Parker is defined by actions, not emotions; Westlake had written him "that the whole point of the series was an exercise at the beginning to see if he could write a character who's completely internal."[17]

The illusiveness of Parker's inner state is integral to Westlake's novel; readers of either version would find him mysterious and be looking for clues – and Cooke visually provides them. Westlake's description of Parker's "chipped chunk of concrete" face and hard physical features are translated into his rectangular face and shoulders and square jaw. His treatment of others is expressed in the faces of those who interact with him.

According to Cooke, a rare glimpse of Parker's inner feelings comes in relation to his wife's memory.[18] Cooke discusses his use of horizontal panels, each the width of the page, to bring attention to Stark's line, "He was afraid of her."[19] In each panel Parker is getting up from a couch; a silhouette of his wife crawls on top of him in the fourth. The diagonally stroked blue wash and coffin-like appearance of the panels give the reader a feeling of discomfort while slowing down the narrative rhythm and highlighting Parker's fear. Cooke explains that he was

> looking for a compact way in four panels to get across the fact that she haunts his sleep or his dreams. And it's funny because the prose on that page...there are maybe eight lines in the entire series of books that would give you any indication of what's going on in this guy's heart. And that's a big one.[20]

Ed Brubaker, present during Spurgeon's interview, said of the sequence, "It made me pick up the book" to see if a dream sequence was there (which it wasn't). Cooke's adaptation, then, directed him back to Westlake's text.

The adaptation also changes some narrative order for effective translation into the comics medium. In both versions, Parker waits until dark to bury his dead wife. Westlake narrates Parker's thoughts about her. Cooke moves this narration to a scene on a subway, juxtaposing it with close-ups of a happy couple on a vacation poster.[21] The disparity between poster images and verbal narration amplifies Parker's anger and resentment. Both scenes are equally effective; Cooke's successful translation maintains the essence of Westlake's text.

Degrees of Departure: Adaptations of *Dr. Jekyll and Mr. Hyde*

The two versions of *Dr. Jekyll and Mr. Hyde* approach Stevenson's text with different degrees of adherence, contributing to literary studies in correspondingly different ways. The first is by Alan Grant, a comics writer, and Cam Kennedy, a comics artist, and was produced for the UNESCO City of Literature Trust.[22] In an interview, Grant expresses reverence for Stevenson's text:

> My brief was to be as faithful to Stevenson's original as I possibly could, so I didn't want to muck around with it by shifting the order of the scenes. I tried to use Stevenson's words as far as possible – I'd say 99% of the words in both *Kidnapped* and *Jekyll and Hyde* are the author's own.[23]

Grant includes a good deal of representative text, and Kennedy replicates layering of concepts through his visual art. Images are in vivid color and carry out Stevenson's story and themes. The depiction of Hyde visualizes Stevenson's verbal references to Hyde's ape-like appearance. This adaptation's greatest contribution to analysis is the visualization of the double. Utterson and Enfield are often paired and of like stature, and page design consistently incorporates double images or the symmetrical use of frames. On page 13, Kennedy depicts Jekyll's shadow as a silhouette of Hyde, visually communicating to the reader that Hyde's characteristics remain part of Jekyll whether visible or not.

A complex demonstration of visual image and textual translation occurs on page 67 of the graphic novel as Utterson and Enfield notice Jekyll sitting in his window. Bars on the window reference Stevenson's prison motif, conveying Jekyll's confinement in Victorian society. Utterson and Enfield get their first view of Jekyll's secret, and Jekyll displays his inability to control his two sides.

To emphasize the scene's importance, Kennedy breaks with the comics format of sequential panels. Four images appear on a white page; each corner is bracketed, making the page into a single panel. In the upper left corner is only Jekyll's head; a narration caption using Stevenson's words describes Jekyll's "abject terror and despair."[24] Rather than terrified, Jekyll's face appears intensely brooding and almost angry, his head tilted forward with eyes peering intensely under his "darkened brow."[25] The discrepancy between the caption and image allows for interpretive readings of Jekyll's psyche. The image might be highlighting Jekyll's despair or nodding to Stevenson's allusions to addiction. Regardless, the image visually freezes Jekyll in transition to his darker side.[26]

The image to its right contains Utterson and Enfield looking back at the empty window. This image is framed as if to separate Hyde from the two gentlemen; they remain part of constrictive Victorian society as the caption states, "the window was instantly thrust down." The last image at the bottom of the page displays the gentlemen's horrified reactions. Stevenson's effect in the scene is to narrate Jekyll's critical moment of change and the friends' moment of recognition. Grant and Kennedy's departure from sequential framing gives cohesiveness to the images, essentially slowing the moment down for effect and emphasis.

Lorenzo Mattotti and Jerry Kramsky depart from Stevenson's text to dramatically probe Hyde's psyche. Aptly described on the back cover as a "psychological thriller," the graphic novel conveys the depths of Jekyll's dark side with graphic visualizations that evoke reader discomfort. With Jekyll's ending letter from Stevenson's text providing the framework, the graphic novel reframes the narrative from his perspective. A key passage toward the end of the letter is crucial to the analysis of the team's approach:

> With Jekyll, it was a thing of vital instinct. He had now seen the full deformity of that creature that shared with him some of the phenomena of consciousness, and was co-heir with him to death...This was the shocking thing; that the slime of the pit seemed to utter cries and voices; that the amorphous dust gesticulated and sinned; that what was dead, and had no shape, should usurp the offices of life. And this again, that that insurgent horror was knit to him closer than a wife, closer than an eye; lay caged in his flesh, where he heard it mutter and felt it struggle to be born; and at every hour of weakness, and in the confidence of slumber, prevailed against him, and deposed him out of life.[27]

The graphic novel sets the tone with the first captions, as Mattotti and Kramsky blend Stevenson's words with their own: "I feel nothing but horror...," "...Horror towards those links of community...with that kind of an animal. He will be our downfall...We are just like wild beasts, wandering through ever wider labyrinths."[28] The corresponding frames show Hyde as a shadow winding around city buildings. Subsequent depictions of Hyde will be shadowed or inhumanly pale with swirled facial features. Using distorted images and an intense color palette of primarily reds, yellows, dark blues, and black, the artwork is expressionistic, and works to give an impression of Jekyll's inner turmoil and Hyde's dark character.[29]

Mattotti and Kramsky adopt some of Stevenson's text, but they significantly alter or add text to emphasize Hyde's psyche. They also highlight Stevenson's allusions to addiction; Jekyll injects himself with a drug rather than drinking a potion.[30] Stevenson's Poole overhears Jekyll "weeping like a woman or a lost soul."[31] In the adaptation, he "has been crying night and day for some sort of medicine and cannot get it to his mind."[32] The depiction of Jekyll's first transformation even looks like an acid trip; as he transforms, the art transforms, taking on a surrealistic character as Jekyll distorts. His brain and a fetus appear on opposite sides of what looks like a cage door, signaling expulsion from the prison of his conscience.[33] Body parts separate, and on page 17 Hyde emerges (see fig. 9.2).

The page's second panel, captioned "In ambiguous shadows," depicts Hyde as an animal, its disproportionately large head resembling a uterus. The uterine image morphs into a close-up of Hyde's mouth in the central frame. This center image, working with the caption "Tortured," conveys a painful birthing process and intensifies Stevenson's theme of birth and death. Following the close-up of Hyde's crooked, claw-like hands, the art returns to its previous style, but Hyde is in a contorted position. This is comics at its

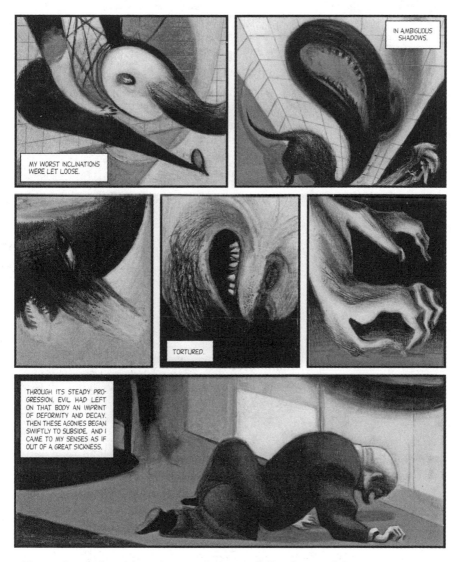

The panels contain the following captions: "MY WORST INCLINATIONS WERE LET LOOSE." / "IN AMBIGUOUS SHADOWS." / "TORTURED." / "THROUGH ITS STEADY PROGRESSION, EVIL HAD LEFT ON THAT BODY AN IMPRINT OF DEFORMITY AND DECAY. THEN THESE AGONIES BEGAN SWIFTLY TO SUBSIDE, AND I CAME TO MY SENSES AS IF OUT OF A GREAT SICKNESS."

Fig. 9.2 Dr. Jekyll transforms into Mr. Hyde. *Dr. Jekyll and Mr. Hyde* by Lorenzo Mattotti and Jerry Kramsky, page 17. By permission © CASTERMAN S.A.

best; the horror of Hyde's emergence is depicted in the sequential images of a distorted birth.

Mattotti and Kramsky add scenes for further impact. In Stevenson's text, Jekyll's letter states, "the pleasures which I made haste to seek in my disguise were, as I have said, undignified; I would scarce use a harder term. But in the hands of Edward Hyde, they soon began to turn monstrous."[34] Mattotti and Kramsky create and depict these deeds, adding additional murders and scenes depicting Hyde's sexual appetite. Hyde's behaviors progress from seeking prostitutes, to acts of sado-masochism, and finally to the vampiric or werewolf-like mauling of his last victim; at this point he is even depicted as a wolf. The graphic nature of this version is extremely effective in terms of contemporary culture. Stevenson's text is enjoyed by contemporary readers, but it no longer shocks them. The treatment of his narrative with an almost underground comics approach links the texts through the idea of counter-culture. Hyde entered a culture counter to that of the Victorians. Similarly, underground comics began as a rebellion against the establishment during the 1960s;[35] thus, Mattotti's and Kramsky's approach connects Victorian Britain to the generations that follow.

Political Satire in Rowson's *Gulliver's Travels*

Martin Rowson's *Gulliver's Travels* revisits Swift's text by having its protagonist, now a descendent of Gulliver, revisit the lands that his ancestor visited in the 1700s. A political cartoonist, Rowson chooses key concepts from Swift's narrative to satirize Britain's New Labour Party and its leaders. Using Swift's work as a springboard, Rowson links readers to the original both visually and ideologically while at the same time departing from it.

As Rowson's Gulliver discovers his ancestor's history, we see differences in each location that can be traced back to his ancestor. Rowson effectively uses different artistic styles for each of the four books, as he explains in an interview with Craig Naples. His use of a cross-hatch method for Lilliput connects his political cartooning to William Hogarth's eighteenth-century art. He uses a "spatter" style for Brobdingnag to highlight "bodily functions" prevalent there, a war-cartoon style for Blefuscu, and a combination for the Land of the Houyhnhnm, which has an unusually large number of square frames per page "because it's the land of pure rationality."[36]

Much of Rowson's effectiveness also comes from his variation in the number and use of panels and use of detail. Rather than use a storyboard, Rowson approached each page separately, creating emphasis, interest, and movement.[37]

Reminiscent of Hogarth, Rowson uses detail to add aspects of commentary. On his tour of Lilliput Gulliver looks for "glimpses of the passing manifestations of culture, commerce, and religion," but the reader sees a street lined with statues of a soccer player, a rock star, and a crucified Elvis Presley; through word and image we "read" that Lilliput has been corrupted.[38] Similarly, as the tour progresses his guide says in the speech balloon, "Man mountain! As you see from our faces, we Lilliputians are a happy people, are we not?" The visual component, however, depicts Lilliputians loitering, two of them stomping on a third, and another vomiting; and all are wearing happy-face masks. Rowson uses conflicting word and image to emphasize the Lilliputians' unhappiness.

Detail is also an important communicator in Rowson's depiction of the floating island of Laputa, "World Heritage Site and now permanent host to the global diplomatic perpetual plenary summit." The island almost looks like a floating cruise ship; each layer (or deck) progresses from non-industrialization on the bottom to the contemporary period at the top; we even see a nuclear dome in melt-down. A small cross, perched on the ruins of a Greek temple, is tilted over as if broken. The wording of the island's name as a "permanent" summit, in combination with Rowson's image, conveys the idea that government, like the island, doesn't get anywhere.

Adapting Swift's use of scatological satire, Rowson uses verbal and visual images of excrement strategically. In Lilliput, the Blumflum Dome is "the fount of all Lilliput's Prosperity." The dome rises above an eighteenth-century ship in a nod to the century's shipbuilding economy. In the dome, Swift's rope dancers have become Rowson's blindfolded tightrope walkers appearing at all levels of the dome. Swift's rope dancers perform to advance in service of the King. Rowson's tightrope walkers advance in economic control, and convey the inability of different governmental departments to see what others are doing. Further, their purpose is to produce "plapplip," which we later find out is excrement, and what the government will feed the people. As Rowson explains, the purpose of satire is to "even up the score between the powerful and the powerless."[39] Rowson's application of political cartooning is caustically effective in producing a graphic novel as political commentary.

Conclusions

Graphic novel adaptations can provide sophisticated opportunities for interpretation and analysis. They stimulate imagination, speculation, and critical thinking by instituting minor and major changes from their adapted texts; these translations or changes encourage a return to those texts for further analysis. Adaptations that adhere to their inspirations' storylines, such as Grant and Kennedy's *Dr Jekyll and Mr Hyde* and the different treatments of *The Invisible Man* by Geary and by Taylor and Ahluwalia, adjust or highlight elements that can engage readers in the intertexual analysis of both adaptation and adapted text. Examining more than one treatment of the same text provides another level of analysis. The two versions of *The*

Invisible Man emphasize alternative elements of Wells' text through their visual and verbal choices. The two versions of *Dr Jekyll and Mr Hyde* facilitate analysis based on differences in adherence to storyline.

Graphic novels that differ from their adapted texts offer additional benefits. Dramatic departures in graphic novels such as Mattotti and Kramsky's *Dr. Jekyll and Mr. Hyde* and Rowson's *Gulliver's Travels* can expand on allusions, provide alternate readings, and probe or develop characterizations. By focusing on themes and issues rather than storylines, they forge a bridge between generations. Mattotti and Kramsky help us question the nature of evil, and Rowson challenges the actions of the powerful. Whether they adhere to or depart from their source texts, graphic novel adaptations use word and image to communicate. The humanities help us to explore the human condition; graphic novels facilitate that exploration through academic dialogue by providing new voices, new ways to communicate our beloved narratives, and, consequently, new ways for readers to respond to them.

Works Cited

Aragão, Octavio. "A Victorian Mindset: Interview with Rick Geary." *Intempol*. Octavio Aragão, May 17, 2011. http://intemblog.blogspot.co.uk/2011/05/vitorian-mindset-interview-with-rick.html.

Bruhn, Jørgen. "Dialogizing Adaptation Studies: From One-Way Transport to a Dialogic Two-Way Process," in Jørgen Bruhn, Anne Gjelsvik, and Eirik Frisvold Hanssen, eds., *Adaptation Studies: New Challenges, New Directions*. London: Bloomsbury, 2013, 69–88.

Bruhn, Jørgen, Anne Gjelsvik, and Eirik Frisvold Hanssen. "'There and Back Again': New Challenges and New Directions in Adaptation Studies," in Jørgen Bruhn, Anne Gjelsvik, and Eirik Frisvold Hanssen, eds., *Adaptation Studies: New Challenges, New Directions*. London: Bloomsbury, 2013, 1–16.

Cooke, Darwyn. "Dr. Jekyll and Mr. Hyde – Interview with Alan Grant and Cam Kennedy." *The List*. The List, Ltd., February 14, 2008. www.list.co.uk/article/6362-dr-jekyll-and-mr-hyde-interview-with-alan-grant-and-cam-kennedy/ Feb. 15, 2015.

Richard Stark's Parker: The Hunter. San Diego, CA: IDW Publishing, 2012.

Eisner, Will. *Graphic Storytelling and Visual Narrative*. Tamarac, FL: Poorhouse Press, 1996.

Geary, Rick, and H. G. Wells. *The Invisible Man*. New York: Papercutz, 1991.

Grant, Alan, and Cam Kennedy. *Robert Louis Stevenson's Strange Case of Dr Jekyll and Mr Hyde*. Glasgow: Waverley Books, 2008.

Hatfield, Charles. "An Art of Tensions," in Jeet Heer and Kent Worcester, eds., *A Comics Studies Reader*. Jackson, MS: University of Mississippi Press, 2009, 132–48.

Hutcheon, Linda. *A Theory of Adaptation*. New York: Routledge, 2006.

Little, Stephen. *Isms: Understanding Art*. New York: Universe, 2004.

Mattotti, Lorenzo, Jerry Kramsky, and Robert Louis Stevenson. *Dr. Jekyll and Mr. Hyde*. New York: ComicsLit/NBM Publishing, 2002.

McCloud, Scott. *Making Comics: Storytelling Secrets of Comics, Manga and Graphic Novels*. New York: HarperCollins, 2006.

  Understanding Comics: The Invisible Art. New York: HarperCollins, 1994.

McFarlane, Brian. *Novel to Film: An Introduction to the Theory of Adaptation*. Oxford: Clarendon Press, 1996.

Naples, Craig. "An Interview with Martin Rowson, Gentleman." *Writer Pictures*. EIBF Chapter XI, Appendix i, August 28, 2013.

Priest, Christopher. Introduction, in H. G. Wells, *The Invisible Man*. London: Penguin, 2005, xiii–xxv.

Rowson, Martin, *Gulliver's Travels*. London: Atlantic Books, 2012.

Sabin, Roger. *Adult Comics: An Introduction*. London and New York: Routledge, 1993.

Sanders, Julie. Introduction, in *Adaptation and Appropriation*. London: Routledge, 2006.

Spurgeon, Tom. "CR Sunday Interview: A Talk with Darwyn Cooke and Special Guest Ed Brubaker about *The Hunter*." *The Comics Reporter*, May 10, 2009. Interview date May 4.

Stark, Richard. *The Hunter*. University of Chicago Press, 1962.

Stevenson, Robert Louis. *The Strange Case of Dr. Jekyll and Mr. Hyde*, in Stephen Greenblatt and M. H. Abrams, eds., *The Norton Anthology of English Literature*, Vol. E: *The Victorian Age*. New York: W. W. Norton, 2006, 1645–1685.

Taylor, Sean, Bhupendra Ahluwalia, H. G. Wells, et al. *The Invisible Man*. New Delhi: Campfire, 2010.

Wells, H. G. *The Invisible Man*, ed. Patrick Parrinder. London: Penguin, 2005.

NOTES

1 Darwyn Cooke, "Dr Jekyll and Mr Hyde – Interview with Alan Grant and Cam Kennedy," *The List*, The List, Ltd., Feb. 14, 2008; www.list.co.uk/article/6362-dr-jekyll-and-mr-hyde-interview-with-alan-grant-and-cam-kennedy/ Feb. 15, 2015.

2 Hutcheon uses "adapted text" for the texts that inspire adaptations. For a discussion of intertextuality and the production of meaning, see, for instance, Julie Sanders' introduction to her *Adaptation and Appropriation* (London: Routledge, 2006), 1–3.

3 For information on transcoding and codes of signification see, for instance, Linda Hutcheon, *A Theory of Adaptation* (New York: Routledge, 2006), 7–8, 16–18, and Charles Hatfield, "An Art of Tensions," in Jeet Heer and Kent Worcester, eds., *A Comics Studies Reader* (Jackson, MS: University of Mississippi Press, 2009), 133–34, respectively.

4 Hutcheon, *A Theory of Adaptation*.

5 Jørgen Bruhn, Anne Gjelsvik, and Eirik Frisvold Hanssen, "'There and Back Again': New Challenges and New Directions in Adaptation Studies," in Bruhn, Gjelsvik, and Frisvold Hanssen, eds., *Adaptation Studies: New Challenges, New Directions* (London: Bloomsbury, 2013), 4–5.

6 For further discussion of fidelity and fidelity criticism see, for instance, Hutcheon, *A Theory of Adaptation*, 6–7, response continuum 171–72; Sanders' *Adaptation and Appropriation*, definitions of adaptation and appropriation (chapters 1 and 2); and Jørgan Bruhn, "Dialogizing Adaptation Studies: From One-Way Transport to a Dialogic Two-Way Process," in Bruhn, Gjelsvik, and Frisvold Hanssen, eds., *Adaptation Studies*, 5–6.

7 Brian McFarlane, *Novel to Film: An Introduction to the Theory of Adaptation* (Oxford: Clarendon Press, 1996), 8.

8 Hatfield, "Art of Tensions," 132.

9 Will Eisner, *Graphic Storytelling and Visual Narrative* (Tamarac, FL: Poorhouse Press, 1996), 47.

10 Scott McCloud, *Making Comics: Storytelling Secrets of Comics, Manga and Graphic Novels* (New York: HarperCollins, 2006), 10.

11 Scott McCloud, *Understanding Comics: The Invisible Art* (New York: Harper-Collins, 1994), 70–72, and McCloud, *Making Comics*, 37.

12 Christopher Priest, in his introduction to *The Invisible Man* (London: Penguin, 2005), notes Wells' admiration of Dickens.

13 H. G. Wells, *The Invisible Man*, ed. Patrick Parrinder (London: Penguin, 2005), 43.

14 Octavio Aragão, "A Victorian Mindset: Interview with Rick Geary," *Intempol*, Octavio Aragão, May 17, 2011, http://intemblog.blogspot.co.uk/2011/05/vitorian-mindset-interview-with-rick.html.

15 Priest, Introduction, xvii–xviii.

16 Darwyn Cooke, *Richard Stark's Parker: The Hunger* (San Diego, CA: IDW Publishing, 2012), 9.

17 Tom Spurgeon, "CR Sunday Interview: A Talk with Darwyn Cooke and Special Guest Ed Brubaker about *The Hunter*," *The Comics Reporter*, May 10, 2009 (interview date May 4).

18 Ibid.

19 Cooke, *Richard Stark's Parker*, 19.

20 Spurgeon, "Talk with Darwyn Cooke."

21 Cooke, *Richard Stark's Parker*, 46.

22 Alan Grant and Cam Kennedy, *Robert Louis Stevenson's Strange Case of Dr Jekyll and Mr Hyde* (Glasgow: Waverley Books, 2008).

23 Cooke, "Dr Jekyll and Mr Hyde."

24 Grant and Kennedy, *Dr Jekyll and Mr Hyde*, 27; Robert Louis Stevenson, *The Strange Case of Dr Jekyll and Mr Hyde*, in Stephen Greenblatt and M. H. Abrams, eds., *The Norton Anthology of English Lterature*, Vol. E: *The Victorian Age* (New York: W. W. Norton, 2006), 1663.

25 Stevenson, *Dr Jekyll and Mr Hyde*, ed. Greenblatt and Abrams, 1680.

26 Ibid., 1681.

27 Ibid., 1684.

28 Lorenzo Mattotti, Jerry Kramsky, and Robert Louis Stevenson, *Dr. Jekyll and Mr. Hyde* (New York: ComicsLit/NBM Publishing, 2002), 3.

29 For explanations of Expressionism and of Surrealism, see, for instance, Stephen Little, *Isms: Understanding Art* (New York: Universe, 2004), 104–5, and 118–19, respectively.

30 Mattotti, Kramsky, and Stevenson, *Dr. Jekyll and Mr. Hyde*, 15, 21, 27, 32, and 49.
31 Stevenson, *Dr Jekyll and Mr Hyde*, ed. Greenblatt and Abrams, 1668.
32 Mattotti, Kramsky, and Stevenson, *Dr. Jekyll and Mr. Hyde*, 9.
33 Ibid., 16.
34 Stevenson, *Dr Jekyll and Mr Hyde*, ed. Greenblatt and Abrams, 1679.
35 Roger Sabin, *Adult Comics: An Introduction* (London and New York: Routledge, 1993), 36–37.
36 Craig Naples, "An Interview with Martin Rowson, Gentleman," *Writer Pictures*, EIBF Chapter XI, Appendix I, Aug. 28, 2013.
37 Ibid.
38 Martin Rowson, *Gulliver's Travels* (London: Atlantic Books, 2012). Rowson's graphic novel is not paginated, so no page numbers will be given.
39 Ibid.

10

M. KEITH BOOKER

Graphic Novel into Film

The rise of the graphic novel as a cultural form has been one of the most interesting phenomena in the print culture of the past three decades. Now a widely acknowledged and even critically respected form, the graphic novel nevertheless remains a bit difficult to define or even characterize, partly because the exigencies of the comics publishing industry often blur the boundary between the graphic novel and conventional comics. Thus, Alan Moore and Dave Gibbons' *Watchmen*, typically described as a graphic novel and in fact most widely read as a single-volume publication, was actually originally published in a limited series of twelve issues that appeared from September 1986 through October 1987. That said, it is also the case that the rise of the graphic novel as an identifiable format in comics publishing has been inextricably intertwined in recent years with what has been easily the most important *commercial* development in comics publishing during that period: the rise of comic book film adaptations as perhaps the single most lucrative phenomenon in the entire American film industry, especially with the spectacular box-office success of the Marvel Cinematic Universe in recent years. Whether published originally as a single volume or republished as a single volume after initial serial publication, the most distinctive feature of the graphic novel as opposed to conventional serial comics is that it involves a single self-contained plot line of the kind needed to tell coherent stories within the time frame of a single commercial film. Thus, graphic novels are much better suited for adaptation to film than are serial comics, which might be strong on concept or audience recognition, but which typically involve massive, ongoing narrative structures that are far too unwieldy to be adapted to film in their entirety, thus typically forcing filmmakers to develop their own original stories based on the characters and scenarios of the comics.

   Two recent critical volumes (one written by myself and the other edited by Ian Gordon and others) have been devoted to the topic of the adaptation of comics to film, indicating the growing importance of such adaptations as a cultural phenomenon.[1] Meanwhile, graphic novels in particular are so well suited to film adaptation that one might argue that one of the most important functions (for better or worse) of the graphic novel nowadays is to serve as a sort of experimental cultural laboratory for the film industry, allowing for the exploration of new ideas and styles in the relatively inexpensive graphic novel format before major investments are made in the development of films based on these ideas and styles.

While it is still the case that the most prominent "comic book films" have relied primarily on the name recognition of major comics characters, such as Superman, Batman, or Spider-Man, often developing original plots that only vaguely resemble those of any stories that actually appeared in the comics, graphic novel adaptations are much more like the adaptations of conventional novels in that they usually supply the principal plot points for the film version, as well as the major characters and basic scenario. In addition, because of their self-contained nature, graphic novels often have more consistent and easily identifiable visual styles than do serial comics, which might feature artwork by a number of different artists over a period of years. Thus, it is generally much more feasible to at least consider attempting to replicate the visual style of a graphic novel in its film adaptation, as opposed to adapting the visual style of a serial comic to film.

Superhero films, which have dominated the box-office success of comic book film adaptations, depend particularly strongly on their characters and scenarios (as opposed to specific plots) in comparison with most films, and so have been less limited to graphic novel adaptations than have many other kinds of comics adaptations. Granted, superhero adaptations such as Zack Snyder's 2009 adaptation of *Watchmen* have sometimes been based on what are typically considered to be graphic novels. However, the most interesting graphic novel adaptations may well be those that have appeared outside the superhero subgenre, and in point of fact film adaptations of graphic novels have covered very much the same ground as graphic novels themselves, which is to say the same ground as the novel itself, though with more emphasis on "genre" narratives, such as horror, science fiction, and superhero narratives. Indeed, in many ways, the adaptation of graphic novels into film is not fundamentally different from the cinematic adaptation of conventional novels. Again, though, graphic novel adaptations do at least potentially involve the important additional element that the original novel already has a visual style of its own, while this style might or might not be reflected in the visual style of the film adaptation.

Some of the best early adaptations of graphic novels, however, were live-action adaptations that relied very little on the artistic styles of the graphic novels on which they were based. On the other hand, film has other resources (such as sound and music), and films such as Terry Zwigoff's *Ghost World* (2001) have captured some of the spirit of the graphic novels that provided their source material through the inventive use of these resources rather than through the direct replication of the aesthetics of the original comic. For example, the quirkiness of Daniel Clowes' original graphic novel is nicely captured in the opening sequence of *Ghost World*, which opens with a dance/musical scene from the 1965 Bollywood film *Gumnaam*. This scene includes a highly kinetic performance (itself mimicking the style of a 1960s American dance band) of a Hindi dance tune entitled "Jaan Pehechan Ho," featuring vocals by Mohammed Rafi, a Bollywood legend who (like the rest of the band) wears semi-formal Western dress and a Zorro-style mask. The dancers who accompany the performance are similarly dressed as they gyrate joyously to the music, led by the frenetic dancing of Laxmi Chhaya, another Bollywood star. Meanwhile, this seemingly extraordinary performance is intercut with shots of a row of identical, extremely ordinary suburban homes, marked by the flicker of television light through the windows. Through the windows we can see that the little boxes of houses that all look just the same are inhabited by bored, almost robotic individuals who similarly resemble one another, until we finally see a shot of a teenage girl, Enid (Thora Birch), who turns out to be watching the Indian film on videotape in her bedroom, dancing frenetically along with the dancers on her television. Presumably, Enid is attempting thereby to declare some sort of distinctive identity for herself that might set her apart from the excruciatingly banal sameness of her neighbors.

Enid's attempt, however, is highly ironic. Convinced that her own postmodern culture produces nothing but banal clichés and spiritless copies, Enid seems to have turned to the Indian film in search of something more authentic, much in the way that the hippies a generation before her often turned to India to seek more authentic mystical experiences. The joke, of course, is that *Gumnaam* itself is a quick-and-dirty rip-off of the then-recent Western film *Ten Little Indians* (1965), recycled for an Eastern audience. *Gumnaam* is thus an attempt to mimic the very Western culture that Enid so despises for its lack of originality, thus suggesting the difficulty of escaping the gravitational pull of Western culture in the postmodern era of globalization. All in all, this entire first scene has a somewhat eerie quality of cultural dissonance, a quality that is maintained through the rest of the film, thereby echoing the radical alienation of the young, eye-rolling protagonists (Enid and her friend Rebecca, played by Scarlett Johansson) from the society that they are preparing to enter as adults, but whose values they still staunchly resist. The film thus captures the spirit of Clowes' graphic novel quite well, no doubt at least partly because Clowes himself wrote the screenplay.

Zwigoff followed with another Clowes adaptation, *Art School Confidential* (2006), based on a feature in Clowes' anthology series *Eightball*. This film also reflects the offbeat tone of its original graphic source, but moves somewhat away from the whimsical charm of *Ghost World* into darker and more cynical territory. The film focuses on aspiring artist Jerome Platz (Max Minghella), who attends the Strathmore Academy to further his goal of becoming the greatest artist of the twenty-first century. Unfortunately, Platz has both bad luck and questionable talent, not to mention highly suspect judgment. He is frustrated at every turn in efforts to produce his own art, so he eventually turns to the expedient of presenting the paintings of another painter as his own work. The plan backfires, though, when the paintings appear to contain evidence that leads to Platz's arrest for a series of murders, the real painter meanwhile having been killed in a fire. Given that this fire was apparently caused by Platz's careless disposal of a cigarette, Platz feels that there might be some justice in his arrest. Meanwhile, he refuses the attempts of his family's lawyer to free him from jail on bail because he is assured by an opportunistic art gallery owner that his incarceration makes his paintings much more marketable. *Art School Confidential* is a satire that thoroughly skewers the hypocrisy and pretense of art schools and the art business as a whole, though its rather misanthropic vision ultimately extends to the entire human endeavor, suggesting that the art world may merely be a microcosm of the corrupt world at large, echoing the argument by Fredric Jameson that in our contemporary postmodern era art (along with almost everything else) has been thoroughly commodified and that "aesthetic production today has been integrated into commodity production generally."[2]

Despite their offbeat nature and satirical orientation, *Ghost World* and *Art School Confidential* are relatively realistic, slice-of-life works. Meanwhile, the comic that is perhaps the best known for such mundane realism is Harvey Pekar's *American Splendor*, a serial that was collected in two volumes in 1986 and 1987, but republished in a single volume (which has sometimes been considered to be a graphic novel) in 2003 to accompany the release of a film adaptation (directed by Shari Springer Berman and Robert Pulcini) with the same title as the comic. In the film, Paul Giamatti plays Pekar, the lowly file clerk turned comics writer, in an autobiographical tale that also features numerous inserted cameos by the real Pekar. *American Splendor* the comic features artwork by a variety of different artists, including the legendary underground comix artist Robert Crumb, so it has no single distinctive artistic style of its own that might be reflected in the film. Instead, the film merely reflects the distinctive content of the comic, with its focus on the experiences of an ultra-ordinary individual, in a spirit that celebrates without romanticizing the day-to-day struggles of working-class people.

Such examples of graphic novel realism are, however, the exception rather than the rule, and graphic-novel-to-film adaptations have, to a large extent, been dominated by "genre" works that eschew straightforward realism. This limitation, however, is not all that restrictive given that graphic novels have been adapted to film in virtually every genre in which graphic novels themselves have been produced – which is to say, in essentially every literary genre. In some genres – such as science fiction and horror – the use of graphic novels as source material makes obvious sense, both because those genres tend to feature extreme subject matter that is particularly well suited to the graphic novel format, and because (especially in the era of computer-generated images) the visuals of such films are also often over-the-top in ways that resemble the spectacular visuals of graphic novels. Thus, in the realm of horror, while psychological thrillers such as *The Shining* (1980) have tended to be based on conventional novels, violent, action-oriented films such as the ultra-bloody vampire film *30 Days of Night* (2007) have been derived from graphic novels. Such horror adaptations have covered a wide range of material, pushing into unlikely scenarios such as that of *I, Frankenstein* (2014), a 3D effects-driven action film in which Frankenstein's monster, two hundred years later, is drawn into a cataclysmic battle of good versus evil as the armies of the gargoyles (good) and the demons (bad) face off, with the fate of the human race in the balance. The film, developed in concert with a graphic novel concept by Kevin Grevioux, the co-creator of the *Underworld* series of action horror films, is mostly as silly as it sounds. At the other extreme, Alan Moore and Eddie Campbell's graphic novel *From Hell* (collected in 1999 from original serial publication between 1989 and 1996), a fictionalized version of the Jack the Ripper story, has also been adapted to film (in 2001). However, the graphic novel version of this story, which combines crime fiction with horror, is perhaps too subtle for film; it is certainly the case that the film version is somewhat lackluster in comparison with the comic. Other hybrid adaptations include the two films based on Mike Mignola's *Hellboy* comics (directed by Guillermo del Toro in 2004 and 2008), which combine horror with the superhero genre, with elements from numerous other genres thrown in as well. Of course, perhaps the single most notable example of a comics-to-screen adaptation in horror is the *Walking Dead* television program (which has now run on the AMC cable network since 2010). Based on the ongoing serial comic from Robert Kirkman (rather than on a graphic novel), this series illustrates the way in which the narrative form of serial comics is perhaps better suited to long-form television than to film.

In the realm of science fiction, adaptations of original films into comics or graphic novels have generally been more important than the reverse, as in the case of the highly successful comics adaptations of the *Star Wars* novels that appeared from Marvel during the period 1977 to 1987 (and that have since appeared from other publishers as well). Still, graphic novels and comics in general have exerted a notable influence on film at least since 1982, when the seminal visuals of Ridley Scott's *Blade Runner* (1982) were at least partly inspired by the artwork contained in the French science fiction comic magazine *Métal Hurlant* (published in the United States in an English-language version as *Heavy Metal*).

One of the few major examples of comic-to-film science fiction adaptations, John Bruno's *Virus* (1999), is really as much a horror film as a science fiction film, somewhat in the manner of the highly successful sequence of *Alien* films. Based on the Dark Horse comic book series by Chuck Pfarrer (and scripted by Pfarrer with Dennis Feldman), *Virus* has the distinction of having first been written as a film script, but then produced as a comic in the early 1990s before adaptation to film. This adaptation has some of the feel of the *Alien* films as a crew of humans is trapped aboard a claustrophobic ship at sea that has been taken over by a murderous alien invader that appears to regard humans as a sort of viral infestation on the ship, thus the title. *Virus* also goes for some especially horrifying scenes in which the alien entity (made of pure energy, or maybe pure information, it is able to inhabit and control various sorts of machinery) builds weird cyborg zombies, combining mechanical parts with the bodies of its human victims. Unfortunately, these concocted creatures look more ridiculous than frightening, and *Virus* is never able to attain the level of foreboding and suspense that had made the *Alien* films so special. In addition, the ending (in which the two surviving humans, played by Jamie Lee Curtis and William Baldwin, are launched from the ship out of a rocket tube, while the ship explodes behind them, killing the alien) is just plain silly. As a result, the film's negative reviews were perfectly understandable, even if the film isn't quite as bad as some reviewers seemed to feel. *Virus* was also a commercial failure, making back less than half of its US$75 million budget in worldwide gross receipts, an outcome that might explain Hollywood's lack of enthusiasm for further films based on science fiction comics.

On the other hand, *V for Vendetta* (2005), a dark dystopian fantasy based on Moore's graphic novel, was a successful adaptation within a major science fiction subgenre, though its title character is also a superhero of sorts. Also somewhat in the dystopian vein is Bong Joon-ho's English-language South Korean film *Snowpiercer* (2013), a post-apocalyptic political fable based on the 1982 French graphic novel by Jacques Lob and Jean-Mark Rochette, *Le Transperceneige*. Here, attempts to combat global warming have backfired, producing a new ice age so severe that human civilization has been essentially destroyed, surviving only on a single supertrain that continually circles the globe. The train, meanwhile, serves as a sort of allegorical microcosm of capitalist society before the environmental apocalypse, including the fact that the location occupied by the individuals on the train mirrors the hierarchical class structure of capitalist society. In many ways, the scenario of this story is too far-fetched to even qualify as science fiction: it's really more of a fantasy/fable (based on a French comic) that makes absolutely no sense and has no basis in anything scientific. On the other hand, it could be argued that this scenario is so unlikely as to produce a form of cognitive dissonance of the kind that is typically associated with the best science fiction. The allegorical commentary on class inequality may be a bit predictable, though, and it is certainly heavy-handed. Moreover, the system on the train is not very much like capitalism except for the basic class inequality; indeed, it seems more like feudalism, or even like the Roman Empire. Equally problematic is the film's setting in a post-apocalyptic world in which the apocalypse (a disastrous worldwide freeze) was caused not by global warming but by attempts to *combat* global warming, as if everything would have been fine if we had just left it alone. Still, the completely unrealistic nature of the whole scenario, one that might be described as comic-book-like, might be taken to suggest that capitalism itself is not all that rational or realistic if one can just pierce the veil of ideology that surrounds it and presents it as the *only* system that is rational or realistic.

Both the horror and the science fiction genres of graphic novels have profited significantly from the recent emergence of a market for darker and more mature subject matter in comics. Comics of all genres have tended to become darker and grittier with the rising importance of graphic novels, with their largely adult readership, as a marketing category in comics. But the movement toward more adult imagery and subject matter has perhaps been seen most obviously of all in the genre of crime comics, a genre that was at the very center of the controversies over the possible negative impact of comics on younger readers back in the notorious days of the mid-1950s. This resurgence in the subgenre of crime comics has been reflected in film adaptations as well, some of the most effective of which have been in this subgenre.

Indeed, crime fiction has been particularly well represented in graphic novel adaptations, as in the case of *Road to Perdition* (2002), a relatively conventional period gangster film, featuring an A-list cast led by multiple Oscar winner Tom Hanks and Hollywood legend Paul Newman. Designed to attract a large mainstream audience, this beautifully photographed film (shot by famed cinematographer Conrad L. Hall, who won a posthumous

Oscar for Best Cinematography for the film) is significantly more slickly produced than is the violent and brutal graphic novel (by Max Allan Collins) on which it is based. Indeed, it is even more elegant aesthetically than most other gangster films, suggesting a conscious departure from the aesthetics of the graphic novel.

Road to Perdition is an interesting hybrid story based partly on Kazuo Koike's legendary Japanese samurai manga epic *Lone Wolf and Cub* (itself the source of a series of Japanese films) and partly on historical reality from the American 1930s. Of course, that same period was also the birthplace of the modern gangster film, and *Road to Perdition* was influenced by an entire cinematic tradition, including the gangster films from the period in which it is set, which are by now almost inseparable in American cultural memory from the real-world gangsterism of the Depression era. However, the lighting and cinematography of *Road to Perdition* set it apart from the relatively gritty look of the gangster films that were actually made in the early 1930s, such as *Little Caesar* (1931), *The Public Enemy* (1931), and *Scarface* (1932). The film is also much more slickly produced than the noir crime films of the 1940s and early 1950s, which are an important part of the cinematic tradition on which it builds. On the other hand, Collins' original graphic novel employs gritty black-and-white artwork that is closer in style and spirit to early gangster films or to film noir than to its own film adaptation.

Probably due to the desire to attract a broad audience, the film version of *Road to Perdition* also significantly sanitizes the violent and brutal content of the graphic novel. Thus, though it functions quite well on its own as a work of cinematic art, the film adaptation of *Road to Perdition* clearly indicates the way in which mainstream Hollywood film, needing to attract a wide audience to recoup the many millions of dollars spent on production, tends to shy away from the kind of extreme and experimental material which comics, with much lower production costs, can afford to explore.

This particular adaptation thus serves as an unusually clear demonstration of the way in which comics and graphic novels are, more and more, becoming a sort of experimental laboratory for the film industry, trying out new kinds of content and new visual styles on an inexpensive basis before they are put into practice in the higher-stakes world of film, often with significant modifications, given the need to attract wider audiences. This view, which would seem to be supported by events such as Disney's acquisition of Marvel Comics, would make direct adaptations of graphic novels to film a sort of transitional phenomenon, trying out techniques from graphic novels in the medium of film on a limited basis before those techniques are then adapted to the wider world of film as a whole.

A History of Violence (2005) is another example of a crime novel adapted from a graphic novel in which the film version is considerably toned down in comparison with the comics original, even though the film was directed by David Cronenberg, who originally made his reputation as a creator of films featuring graphic images of bodily destruction. On the other hand, *A History of Violence* differs significantly from *Road to Perdition* in that it sanitizes its source material mostly by leaving out some of the most graphic and horrifying content, but does not employ a fancy cinematic style as a means of taking the edges off the gritty source material, even though its style is different from that of the novel.

The original graphic novel was written by John Wagner and drawn by Vince Locke; it employs rough-edged black-and-white art that is appropriate to its grim subject matter and that is reminiscent of film noir, as is its basic plot, in which central character Tom McKenna (named Tom Stall in the film, where he is played by Viggo Mortensen) tries to escape his dark, criminal past and to pursue a life as a respectable Midwestern family man. McKenna/Stall attempts to go straight but finds it difficult to escape the legacy of his violent, criminal past, a narrative that would be very much at home in the world of film noir as well. One thinks, for example, of Jacques Tourneur's suggestively titled *Out of the Past* (1947), in which past criminal associates of a small-town gas station attendant catch up with him, disrupting his new, peaceful life. In addition to film noir, the film also adds elements derived from other film genres, especially the western, creating a postmodern mixture of genres that goes well beyond any genre-mixing that can be found in the graphic novel. For example, the film makes it particularly clear that Stall, as the former violent gangster attempting to go straight and live a quiet life, resembles no figure from American popular culture more than the retired gunslinger who tries to settle down peacefully, only to find that events force him to go back to his guns.

One reason, of course, for the more mainstream look and feel of *A History of Violence* is its US$32 million budget, rather modest by the standards of present-day blockbusters, but well beyond that of Cronenberg's early films. For example, the film that probably did the most to build Cronenberg's reputation was *Videodrome* (1983), which had a meager budget of under US$6 million and still lost money at the box office, though it did do well on home video, where it went on to become a cult favorite. *A History of Violence*, on the other hand, grossed a respectable US$60 million worldwide, propelling Cronenberg into the ranks of mainstream Hollywood filmmakers.

A History of Violence belongs in the ranks of graphic novel adaptations in which the visual aesthetics of the film owe little to those of the original graphic novel. However, 2005 also saw the release of *Sin City*, which was, in many ways a landmark film in the history of graphic-novel-to-film adaptations, precisely because of the unprecedented extent to which it attempts, via computer image processing, to mimic the distinctive, stark visual style of Frank Miller's graphic novel series. Though the film involves live actors, they were shot in front of green screens with almost every other element of the film added by director Robert Rodriguez using relatively inexpensive computer techniques, working closely with Miller. Indeed, Miller was intimately involved with the production of the film, so much so that Rodriguez insisted on listing Miller as a co-director, even though the move brought him into conflict with the Directors Guild.

Miller's original *Sin City* graphic novel series is striking for the way its exaggerated black-and-white artwork captures the expressionistic tendencies of film noir, creating a highly effective atmospheric evocation of the sinfulness and decadence of the title city (which is actually "Basin City"). What is striking about the film is the way it goes all out in its effort to replicate the brutal style of the graphic novels, however extreme, rather than moderating the style (or, for that matter, the content) for a film audience. The film, meanwhile, is notable both for the extent to which it attempts to replicate the aesthetics of the graphic novel series on which it is based and for the success with which it achieves this objective. On the other hand, subsequent attempts to achieve somewhat the same effect have been less impressive. For example, Miller's solo directorial debut in *The Spirit* (2008) was panned by critics and despised by fans of Will Eisner's original comics. Meanwhile, the joint Miller–Rodriguez sequel *Sin City: A Dame to Kill For* (2014) was less disastrous, but failed to add anything to the achievement of the original *Sin City* film – or even to reach the level of that original.

Still, the *Sin City* films are leading examples both of the attempt to replicate the aesthetics of comics on film and of the use of extreme and violent subject matter in both comics and their film adaptations. Of course, the most obvious way to replicate the artistic style of a comic in film is through the use of animation in a similar style. Meanwhile, in certain parts of the world, historical events have been such that the ability of the comics medium to capture the horrors of extreme violence and hardship has made comics ideal for a more realist, even a documentary/journalistic function. This has especially been the case in the Middle East and Northern Africa, where events and conditions have inspired such phenomena as the comics journalism of Joe Sacco, but have also led to the production of several interesting animated films. One of the best known of these, the 2008 Israeli film *Waltz with Bashir*, deals with horrific events in the 1982 Lebanon War, centering on the massacre of perhaps 3,000 refugees, mostly Palestinians, in Beirut's Sabra and Shatila refugee camps, by members of a radical Christian militia. This film was not adapted from a graphic novel, though it was subsequently adapted *to* the graphic novel form. Two other highly effective films dealing with the Middle East and Northern Africa – *Persepolis* (2007) and *The Rabbi's Cat* (2011) – have, however, been based on graphic novels.

Persepolis adapts Marjane Satrapi's much-admired autobiographical graphic novel about growing up in Iran, which was originally published in four installments in France between 2000 and 2003. Co-directed by Satrapi herself (along with French comics artist Vincent Paronnaud), *Persepolis* won the Jury Prize at the 2007 Cannes Film Festival and has received international critical acclaim (including an Academy Award nomination for Best Animated Feature) as a document of life in Iran during the critical historical times of the 1980s in the wake of the 1979 revolution that removed the Shah from power in Iran and including the subsequent Iran–Iraq War (1980–88). The film version deals with the same basic religious, gender, and political issues as the graphic novel, while also mimicking its high-contrast black-and-white visual style, though Satrapi's childhood narrative is presented in the film within a frame narrative that is animated in color. On the other hand, the much less detailed presentation of events in the relatively brief ninety-five-minute film gives these events, if anything, an even more whimsical quality than they have in the graphic novel. Still, what is perhaps most striking about the graphic novel, as Hillary Chute notes, is the presentation of the "ordinariness" of the events of Satrapi's life, despite the seemingly extraordinary historical circumstances in which they occurred.[3] In addition, both the graphic novel and the film indicate that the personal can never be disentangled from the political, or (as Jennifer Brock puts it) that history and memory are closely intertwined.[4] Despite the highly stylized artwork, the novel presents an extremely realistic-seeming account of Satrapi's experiences, putting to rest the old notion that "comic book" representations have to be exaggerated and over-the-top. The film, meanwhile, captures this aspect of the novel quite well, partly because the visual style, which is similar in both the film and the graphic novel, is well suited to conveying that ordinariness, despite the fact that it is far from realistic.

Both the film and the graphic novel of *Persepolis* are remarkable for a number of reasons, including the effective integration of their thematic material and the visual style, which reinforces the entanglement of the personal and the political that lies at the heart of the novel. As a narrative of past events, this entanglement is expressed in *Persepolis* as an exploration of the way in which public history and private memory become interrelated particularly closely in crucial times and places such as 1980s Iran. But *Persepolis* is also a particularly striking intercultural narrative that dramatizes the complexities of the confrontation in this context between the repressive anti-Western Islamicization of post-revolutionary Iran and the continuing influence of Western popular culture, especially on the minds of the young, such as the youthful Satrapi. This cross-cultural aspect of the narrative then takes a new turn midway through the film when the teenage Satrapi moves to Vienna, before returning for a second sojourn in Iran. Finally, with conditions in her home country becoming more and more repressive, Satrapi ends the film by once again leaving Iran, this time for Paris.

The Rabbi's Cat is based on the graphic novel by Joann Sfar, who also co-directed the film, which might explain why it does a particularly good job of capturing the visual spirit of the graphic novel. The details of the plot of the film differ somewhat from those of the graphic novel, largely because the film leaves out two of the five segments of the graphic novel and extends the fifth section to take up the bulk of the runtime film. Still, the total impact (which relies less on plot than on the overall scenario and themes, as reinforced by the art) is pretty much the same. The visual style of the film is also fairly close to that of the book, while drawing on American animated films of the 1930s (especially those from Fleischer Studios) for additional stylistic models. Using the scruffy cat of the title as a sort of picaro figure who views the antics of the film's humans as a bemused outsider, the film gives us an interesting look at the Jewish community of Algiers, with some nods to global Judaism as well. It also suggests the tremendous cultural crossover that has occurred between Algeria's Jewish and Arab Muslim communities, often without the awareness of those communities. All religions tend to look a bit silly when viewed from the perspective of an outsider, and Algerian Judaism is no exception. But that just makes the film more fun. Generally, the narrative is a little disjointed, but that is the kind of tale it is. The longest part of the story involves a trek across North Africa in search of Ethiopia's lost Jewish community, during which the travelers (one of whom is a Chagallesque painter) meet Tintin along the way – indicating the extent to which this film relies on intertextual connections to achieve its effects. Similar connections occur in the graphic novel, which is probably a bit richer overall, including an extended treatment of a trip to Paris that is entirely missing from the film. The film probably does less than the graphic novel to explore topics such as rabbinical authority, though both the film and the graphic novel deliver a gentle plea for cross-cultural understanding between Jews and Muslims.[5] Maybe too gentle, given the violence that has often informed cross-cultural contact between Jews and Muslims in the real world.

Relatively small films such as *Persepolis* and *The Rabbi's Cat* indicate the versatility of graphic novel adaptations as a film form, showing that there is room for more than big-budget, high-action adaptations. Meanwhile, films such as *Sin City* show that increasing advances in computer generated imagery offer significant new possibilities for relatively inexpensive adaptations even in high-action dramas, while films such as *A History of Violence* suggest the extent to which graphic novels can provide source material for mainstream films that are not informed by easily identifiable comic book content or style. Together, such films indicate a rich future for adaptations of graphic novels to film, though the ultimate impact of such adaptations on the graphic novel form itself remains to be seen.

Works Cited

30 Days of Night. Dir. David Slade. Sony Pictures, 2007. Film.

American Splendor. Dirs. Shari Springer Berman and Robert Pulcini. HBO Films, 2003. Film.

Art School Confidential. Dir. Terry Zwigoff. Sony Pictures Classics, 2006. Film.

Booker, M. Keith. *"May Contain Graphic Material": Comic Books, Graphic Novels, and Film*. Westport, CT: Praeger, 2007.

Brock, Jennifer. "'One Should Never Forget': The Tangling of History and Memory in *Persepolis*," in Richard Iadonisi, ed., *Graphic History: Essays on Graphic Novels and/as History*. Newcastle upon Tyne: Cambridge Scholars, 2012, 223–41.

Chute, Hillary L. *Graphic Women: Life Narrative and Contemporary Comics*. New York: Columbia University Press, 2010.

Clowes, Daniel. *The Complete Eightball*. Seattle, WA: Fantagraphics Books, 2015.
    Ghost World. Seattle, WA: Fantagraphics Books, 2001.

Collins, Max Allan, and Richard Piers Rayner. *Road to Perdition*. New York: Pocket Books, 1998.

Eisenstein, Paul. "Imperfect Masters: Rabbinic Authority in Joann Sfar's *The Rabbi's Cat*," in Samantha Baskind and Ranen Omer-Sherman, eds., *The Jewish Graphic Novel: Critical Approaches*. New Brunswick, NJ: Rutgers University Press, 2008, 163–80.

From Hell. Dirs. Albert Hughes and Allen Hughes. Twentieth Century Fox, 2001. Film.

Ghost World. Dir. Terry Zwigoff. United Artists, 2001. Film.

Gordon, Ian, Mark Jancovich, and Matthew P. McAllister, eds. *Film and Comic Books*. Jackson, MS: University Press of Mississippi, 2007.

Hellboy. Dir. Guillermo del Toro. Columbia Pictures, 2004. Film.

Hellboy II: The Golden Army. Dir. Guillermo del Toro. Universal Pictures, 2008. Film.

A History of Violence. Dir. David Cronenberg. New Line Cinema, 2005. Film.

I, Frankenstein. Dir. Stuart Beattie. Lionsgate, 2014. Film.

Jameson, Fredric. *Postmodernism, or, The Cultural Logic of Late Capitalism*. Durham, NC: Duke University Press, 1991.

Lob, Jacques, and Jean-Marc Rochette. *Le Transperceneige*. Tournai, Belgium: Casterman, 1982.

Mignola, Mike. *Hellboy: Seed of Destruction*. Milwaukie, OR: Dark Horse Books, 2004.

Miller, Frank. *Sin City*. 7 vols. Milwaukie, OR: Dark Horse Comics, 1992–2000.

Moore, Alan, and Eddie Campbell. *From Hell*. Marietta, GA: Top Shelf Productions, 2004.

Moore, Alan, Dave Gibbons, et al. *Watchmen*. New York: DC Comics, 1986.

Moore, Alan, and David Lloyd. *V for Vendetta*. New York: Vertigo, 2008.

Niles, Steve, and Ben Templesmith. *30 Days of Night*. San Diego, CA: IDW Publishing, 2007.

Pekar, Harvey, Kevin Brown, et al. *American Splendor and More American Splendor: The Life and Times of Harvey Pekar*. New York: Ballantine Books, 2003.

Persepolis. Dirs. Vincent Paronnaud and Marjane Satrapi. Sony Pictures Classics, 2007. Film.

Pfarrer, Chuck, and Howard Cobb. *Virus*. Milwaukie, OR: Dark Horse Comics, 2005.

The Rabbi's Cat. Dirs. Antoine Delesvaux and Joann Sfar. GKids, 2011. Film.

Road to Perdition. Dir. Sam Mendes. Dreamworks Distribution, 2002. Film.

Satrapi, Marjane. *Persepolis: The Story of a Childhood*. Trans. from vols. 1–2 of the French original. New York: Panthcon Books, 2004.

  Persepolis 2: The Story of a Return. Trans. from vols. 3–4 of the French original. New York: Pantheon Books, 2005.

Sfar, Joann. *The Rabbi's Cat*. Trans. Alexis Siegel and Anjali Singh from books 1–3 of the French original. New York: Pantheon Books, 2007.

  The Rabbi's Cat 2. Trans. Alexis Siegel from books 4–5 of the French original. New York: Pantheon Books, 2008.

Sin City. Dirs. Robert Rodriguez and Frank Miller. Dimension Films, 2005. Film.

Sin City: A Dame to Kill For. Dirs. Frank Miller and Robert Rodriguez. Miramax, 2014. Film.

Snowpiercer. Dir. Bong Joon-ho. The Weinstein Company, 2013. Film.

V for Vendetta. Dir. James McTeigue. Warner Bros., 2005. Film.

Virus. Dir. John Bruno. Universal Pictures, 1999. Film.

Wagner, John, and Vince Locke. *A History of Violence*. New York: Paradox Press, 2004.

Waltz with Bashir. Dir. Ari Folman. Sony Pictures Classics, 2008. Film.

Watchmen. Dir. Zack Snyder. Warner Bros., 2009. Film.

NOTES

1 M. Keith Booker, *"May Contain Graphic Material": Comic Books, Graphic Novels, and Film* (Westport, CT: Praeger, 2007); Ian Gordon, Mark Jancovich, and Matthew P. McAllister, eds., *Film and Comic Books* (Jackson, MS: University Press of Mississippi, 2007).

2 Fredric Jameson, *Postmodernism, or, The Cultural Logic of Late Capitalism* (Durham, NC: Duke University Press, 1991), 4.

3 Hillary L. Chute, *Graphic Women: Life Narrative and Contemporary Comics* (New York: Columbia University Press, 2010), 135.

4 Jennifer Brock, "'One Should Never Forget': The Tangling of History and Memory in *Persepolis*," in Richard Iadonisi, ed., *Graphic History: Essays on Graphic Novels and/as History* (Newcastle upon Tyne: Cambridge Scholars, 2012), 223–41.

5 Paul Eisenstein, "Imperfect Masters: Rabbinic Authority in Joann Sfar's *The Rabbi's Cat*," in Samantha Baskind and Ranen Omer-Sherman, eds., *The Jewish Graphic Novel: Critical Approaches* (New Brunswick, NJ: Rutgers University Press, 2008), 163–80.

II

BART BEATY

Some Classics

In her 2011 article, "What's in a Name? The Academic Study of Comics and the 'Graphic Novel'," Catherine Labio persuasively argues that "scholars who use the term 'graphic novel' to mean an entire genre are running from [the] basic facts."[1] For Labio, the term "graphic novel" (and "graphic narrative," the term preferred by the Modern Language Association) compounds many of the definitional problems that have long plagued comics studies. Centrally, it privileges the literary character of comics over the visual. The term elides too much work produced in the comics form in an effort to "sanitize" comics by positioning the literary as a marker of quality and by treating the visual as subsidiary in any formal analysis. In so doing, comics become subject to the same problematic tendencies in so much scholarship in the humanities, relying heavily on "the distinction between high and low, major and minor; and reinforc[ing] the ongoing ghettoization of works deemed unworthy of critical attention, either because of their inherent nature (as in the case of works of humor) or because of their intended audience (lower, less-literate classes; children; and so on)" (126). Labio's contention here recalls Joseph Witek's observation that the earliest reviews of Art Spiegelman's *Maus* in the non-comics press sought to distance that work from the comics traditions in which it was so clearly rooted ("Art Spiegelman doesn't draw comics," sniffed Lawrence Langer in *The New York Times*).[2] As I have argued elsewhere, too many scholars working within the traditions of comics studies have moved strongly against the study of the popular by focusing on the graphic novel rather than the comic book (or comic strip, which is even less studied).[3] Moreover, even within the confines of the graphic novel, comics scholars have overwhelmingly, but by no means exhaustively, focused on an exceptionally narrow range of texts, consecrating certain works or creators at the expense of the field of comics as a whole. This is not surprising. Indeed, it is homologous with the approach adopted by scholars in a wide range of humanities disciplines from literary studies to art history and, to a lesser degree, film studies. As scholars, it is necessary for us to critique such naive practices of canonization, but it is even more necessary to recall how such practices take place. In this chapter I seek to outline the frameworks that are required for a comics work to be taken up by scholars as an important "graphic novel," and also to outline how the conception of comics as "graphic novels" has distorted the field of comics studies by subsuming those few chosen works under the umbrella of literary studies.

Discussing "Our Aesthetic Categories," Sianne Ngai highlights the ways that the Kantian expression of taste is constituted by the error of confusing subjective judgments with objective fact.[4] Here her observations run close to those of Pierre Bourdieu, whose critique of the Kantian conception of judgment has become widely influential. Bourdieu argues that "absolute judgement" is "the interest, the investment" that drives position taking in the cultural field, and that to judge absolutely, as Kant proposes, is a process of domination.[5] For Bourdieu, the absolute judgment is derived from a conception of beauty that can be seen as an "occupational ideology" among artists and which contributes to the development of a "professorial aesthetic": a lack of attention to historical and sociological processes that conceals social relations in favor of an "illusion of universality."[6] At one time it might have been possible that the study of the graphic novel could have been dominated by approaches derived from mass communication or the sociology of the arts, but a number of historical factors lead to the center of gravity being situated in departments of literature where the professorial aesthetic has manifest itself in a focus on atypical comics work that scholars can position as exceptional – and therefore deserving of the moniker "novel" rather than the lowly "comic." The scholarly operation of investing in certain works rather than others is by no means natural. It is not true that some comic books are self-evidently "better" than others and more worthy of study. These kinds of judgments are always expressions of power and professional ideologies that deserve to be interrogated. The rise of comics scholarship has been largely abetted by the social construction of the "graphic novel" as a discrete category that obscures the commercial origins of comic books and comic strips. The focus on atypical comics – most notably, long form comics – has had the effect of distorting the field of comics studies by reducing the range of texts that are appropriate subjects for study in a desire to align the field with the better-established and more powerful field of literary studies.

The occupational ideology of much of comics scholarship, its "normal science" in the phraseology of T. S. Kuhn, is the focus on the expression of the "self" through processes of interpretation. While this is most clearly seen in the abundant criticism of autobiographical comics (a minor genre within the comics field that is wildly disproportionately represented in the scholarship), one might also note a strong tendency to identify individual "authors" within the contexts of commercial comic book publishing (for example, Carl Barks or Jack Kirby).[7] Self-expression, with its evident connections to ideas of literary greatness, has quickly, and unfortunately, come to dominate the field of comics studies. To this end, comics studies has followed a trajectory exactly parallel to that of film studies as outlined by David Bordwell: "The growth of film studies attests to the powerful role of literature departments in transmitting interpretive values and skills. Academic humanism's omnivorous appetite for interpretation rendered cinema a plausible 'text'."[8] In the remainder of this chapter, I will consider three examples from three different national comics contexts (Lynda Barry's *What It Is*, David B.'s *Epileptic*, and Jiro Taniguchi's *The Walking Man*) in order to suggest some of the ways that the field's emphasis on the interpretation of aesthetic exceptionality have produced blind spots in the understanding of how comics operate and the general position of the graphic novel within the field. In short, I will consider why it is that certain works have been so widely and rapidly taken up by comics scholars, while some other works (equally available for study) have been largely ignored. I will demonstrate how the intersection of a single methodology (close reading) and a limited range of psychoanalytically informed theoretical models rooted in notions of personal/subjective/experiential knowledge and the liberal-individual treatment of marginality as authenticity has abetted comics scholars in the proper identification of what David Bordwell has termed "plausible texts."

Lynda Barry: Postmodern Autobiography as Scholarly Success Story

There can be no doubt that English-language comics scholarship, which locates its pre-history in the immediate post-Second World War period, and which began to consolidate its position only in the 1990s, has now entered into a phase that is preoccupied with expansion through legitimation. During this phase a small number of artists and works have been selected by scholars for what Hillary Chute has unironically termed "today's contemporary canon."[9] A quick search of the *MLA International Bibliography* is enough to reveal that the most frequently written about cartoonist in English-language scholarship is Art Spiegelman, whose autobiographical works *Maus* and *In the Shadow of No Towers* account for the bulk of his two hundred and seven citations. Behind him trail other significant autobiographical cartoonists, including Marjane Satrapi (eighty-five citations, predominantly for *Persepolis*) and Alison Bechdel (fifty-nine, mostly for *Fun Home*). Lynda Barry, while not in the first rank of cartoonists studied, emerges as a major figure in the field, with twenty-three articles and book chapters dedicated to her work. Interestingly, while the sheer volume of work on Barry pales in comparison to the most studied cartoonists, a scholarly monograph exists about her work (Susan Kirtley's *Lynda Barry: Girlhood Through the Looking Glass*), which is not currently the case for the more widely studied Spiegelman, Bechdel, or Satrapi.[10] It is also striking that while Barry began publishing newspaper comics in the 1970s, and her first book collection appeared in 1981, the first scholarly work on her comics was not published until 2004. Despite being published for many years by a major multinational (HarperCollins), Barry was not the subject of scholarly inquiry until after the online publication of the autobiographical graphic novel *One Hundred Demons* (subsequently collected by Sasquatch Books) and her subsequent shift to the prominent Montreal-based alternative comics publishing house, Drawn & Quarterly. The institutional rediscovery of Barry by Drawn & Quarterly has not only facilitated new work by the artist (notably *What It Is*, 2008, *Picture This*, 2010, and *Syllabus*, 2014) and the re-issuing of her earlier works in new formats (*Blabber Blabber Blabber*, 2011, and *The Freddie Stories*, 2013), but authorized a series of scholarly interventions into the meaning of her work. The symbiosis between publisher and scholars in the recuperation of Barry's reputation and the construction of "today's contemporary canon" seems quite evident.

Scholarship on Lynda Barry arose relatively slowly. If one compares, for instance, the gap between the publication of major works and the earliest scholarly studies of those works, it is striking that the earliest peer-refereed work on Marjane Satrapi's *Persepolis* was published in 2005, only two years after the final volume appeared in French and one year after it appeared in English, yet more than two decades passed before scholars turned their eyes to Barry's work.[11] In the case of Satrapi, it seems clear that *Persepolis* was released at a moment (the early 2000s) in which the attacks of September 11, 2001 and the American invasions of Afghanistan and Iraq had placed an emphasis on the representation of Muslim populations. Scholars, particularly feminist scholars, were seeking works that would complicate popular understandings of the veil, and *Persepolis* provided such an opening; although unintentionally, Satrapi's intervention was particularly well timed. No such context originally appeared for the work of Lynda Barry. Although she has been remarkably consistent with her narrative concerns over time, as Kirtley and others have demonstrated, her focus on memory and girlhood failed to find scholarly traction early in her career; her space was occupied by other, more traditional literary works that explored similar themes.

The earliest interventions into Barry's work focused on her importance within a tradition of Filipino writing, although she is much more commonly taken up in terms of the intersection of girlhood and trauma.[12] Indeed, the rise of trauma studies within departments of literature since the turn of the century has provided an important standpoint for investigations of Barry's work. Hillary Chute, writing in her book *Graphic Women*, argues that Barry's comics of the 2000s stress the "ordinariness" of trauma, as well as its hidden dimensions.[13] Theresa Tensuan sees *One Hundred Demons* as "an ongoing critique of the forms of discursive violence that structure and modulate day-to-day life," while Olga Michael, like Chute, deploys the trauma theory of Cathy Caruth, to understand how "the autobiographical subject is performed through what I will describe as the artist's childish artistic revision of the paternal canon, beyond the injury of maternal estrangement and in a state of conflation with the mother."[14] Michael's unpublished dissertation chapter is particularly instructive about the steps taken to carve out a scholarly position for Barry's work: she compares a work like *What It Is* to the art of Caravaggio, William Blake, and the Pattern and Decoration movement of the 1970s (to name but a few).

It is not surprising that within the corpus of scholarship on Barry the vast majority of studies have focused on her explicitly autobiographical works, beginning with *One Hundred Demons* (Kirtley is a strong exception in this regard). Barry's concept of autobiofictionalography to describe her work has led her to the center of ongoing discussions of comics autobiography, itself a dominant area in contemporary comics studies.[15] If, as I have already noted, comics studies is disproportionately interested in the subject of autobiography (with Spiegelman occupying the position of comics' Shakespeare – the most studied and most lauded exemplar in the field), Barry is near to that center. A mapping of her position relative to the most studied figures in the field would suggest a high degree of overlap, as her work is commonly discussed relative to that of the autobiographical masters, Spiegelman, Satrapi, and Bechdel.[16] Barry is central to the widely shared view that autobiographical comics – autographics, to use a term coined by Gillian Whitlock – are essential for understanding the subjective positionality of the comics author.[17] As I have argued elsewhere, autobiography as a genre has been central to the legitimization of comics generally because it has facilitated the ability of cartoonists to assert themselves as authors.[18] Similarly, Chute contends that the concept of handwriting, insofar as it carries a trace of the mark of the comics maker, intimately binds together comics and autobiography even in non-autobiographical works.[19]

In Chute's words, "handwriting underscores the subjective positionality of the author," and in many ways it is the unusual visual stylistics of Barry's handwriting that has made her such an important figure of scholarly interest" (11). Kirtley has described Barry's approach to image-making as "polyscopic" in general, and the book *What It Is* as a "Künstlerroman/writing workbook/philosophy text."[20] Özge Samanci, better than any other critic, has called attention to the formal visual elements deployed by Barry in her work, including the thick contour lines that are the result of her choice of brushes, the absence of formal detail, the presence of flat representations and the eschewing of traditional perspective, and the "aimlessly drawn" cross-hatching.[21] Barry's mixed media approach in *One Hundred Demons* and *What It Is* is particularly noteworthy in the scholarship on her work. Chute argues that *What It Is* offers "an intensification of the themes and formal concerns of *One Hundred Demons*" that is founded on formal instability. Notably, she suggests that "each page...requires slowness and fresh concentration."[22] These traits, slowness and concentration, are, of course, posited here as strengths of the work. To the degree that *What It Is* traffics in what Kirtley refers to as an expansion of "the boundaries of comic art," it participates in an aesthetics of difficulty that is commonly venerated by scholars.[23] Paul Ricoeur notes "the work of thought which consists in deciphering the hidden meaning in the apparent meaning, in unfolding the levels of meaning implied in the literal meaning," suggesting a distinction between manifest and hidden meanings, and David Bordwell has expanded on this observation to suggest that in the logic of the academy the revelation of non-obvious meaning is the dominant framework in which the literary scholar functions.[24] Barry's appeal to comics scholars, then, resides in her convoluted use of mixed media and mixed genres that require, or, at the very least, enable critical interventions. As Chute notes, "Lynda Barry uses the elliptical structure of comics precisely to...suggest the scene of trauma," a scene that may only be fully available to the trauma theorist.[25]

In the field of contemporary comics scholarship, Lynda Barry's hybrid works occupy a position closely tied to a complex aesthetic presentation of the self. Unlike Marjane Satrapi, who is often praised precisely for the directness of her approach to cartooning (allowing scholars to explicate purportedly hidden depths), or Alison Bechdel, who emphasizes strong intertextual connections to the history of literature (in *Fun Home*) and psychoanalysis (in *Are You My Mother?*), Barry is perceived to be referential in a manner that collapses the distinction between high and low cultures. Yaël Schlick describes Barry's work as "highly intertextual," noting an incredible array of references in *What It Is* to Japanese Zen scrolls, Richard Adams' *Watership Down*, Sylvia Plath's *The Bell Jar*, D. W. Winnicott's psychoanalytical writings, and Marcel Proust's *À la Recherche du Temps Perdu*.[26] Similarly, Melinda de Jesus highlights Barry's "bordercrossing between graphic and text, high and popular culture."[27] To the extent that Barry occupies an aesthetics in which "the degraded landscape of schlock and kitsch" are no longer simply quoted but "incorporate[d] into their very substance," to use the phrasing of Fredric Jameson, she is capable of inhabiting a unique space within the consecrated subfield of autobiographical graphic novels, even though her most studied works do not easily align with that category, except in the most expansive sense of the term. In sum, Lynda Barry occupies a central position within the study of the graphic novel because her work is perceived to be highly complex, highly personal, and thoroughly postmodern, even while she has been assigned modernist values of the personal, the subjective, and the authorial that are presumed to carry a self-evident value. It is the questioning of the ideological function of these values within scholarly paradigms that remains silenced even as Barry's work is venerated.

David B.: Autobiography and the Scholarly Near-Miss

In the context of English-language comics scholarship, David B.'s *Epileptic* is a work at a crossroads. Significantly less studied than the works of Lynda Barry, *Epileptic* is, nonetheless, the subject of several scholarly investigations. Widely praised in his home country of France, where he was awarded an Alph-Art prize for the fourth volume of *L'Ascension du Haut Mal* (the original language version of *Epileptic*), and where he was the subject of a critical dossier in the eleventh issue of the influential semi-scholarly journal *9e Art*, David B. remains a somewhat under-studied figure in the anglophone comics community and its scholarly apparatus.[28] Born Pierre-François Beauchard, the artist changed his name to David in his youth, publishing his earliest works under his full name before eventually shortening it to his current nom de plume. In North America, as in France, David B. is best known for his award-winning autobiographical epic, *L'Ascension du Haut Mal*, released between 1996 and 2003 in six volumes by L'Association, a publishing house that he co-founded in 1990. The first half of the English-language version of the book was published in 2002, and the entire work was produced by Pantheon in 2005. The book was widely heralded in the United States, with *Publishers Weekly* terming it "one of the greatest graphic novels ever published."[29] As with Lynda Barry's work, the book was quickly taken up by scholars working in the area of autobiographical comics after its translation. Murray Pratt argued that the work challenged the notion of the "autobiographical pact" as it was explained by Philippe Lejeune, and Stephen E. Tabachnick argued that it problematized William Howarth's typology of autobiographical works by introducing a new category: the autobiography of discovery.[30] Certainly, the work seemed poised for a significant scholarly expansion that has yet to fully materialize.

Scholarly interest in *Epileptic* most frequently hinges around the book's non-literary formal elements. Following the work of Charles Hatfield, Elisabeth El Refaie notes that the book deploys a tension between written and pictorial codes.[31] Scholars have paid particular attention to David B.'s drawing style. His use of chiaroscuro and "nightmarishly cramped" panels with stark black inks is discussed by Adrielle Mitchell, while the particular use of visual symbols and metaphors is also a recurrent thread.[32] Pratt ties David B.'s use of symbolism to the historical use of medieval emblems – a reading that nicely aligns with the book's own fixation with the visual history of France – and suggests that "it is only through David B's discovery and elaboration of an equally involved visual lexicon, an epileptic 'imagetext', that he can cope" with the complex emotions he feels toward his brother.[33] Arguing along similar lines, Susan Squier highlights the importance of reptilian symbolism in the depiction of the epilepsy in the work, and Bruce Dadey provides a nuanced reading of the processes of dependence and destabilization that trouble the visual allegories in the text.[34] For El Refaie, these issues loop back to the way that the artist conveys a strong sense of circularity and entrapment with his page designs, and she argues, following Henri Bergson, that the book is atypical in its attentive construction of a subjective sense of time.[35] All of these formal elements conspire, as Mitchell notes, to create a palimpsestic image of the artist as a young man that is generated in an accretive process.[36] From this standpoint, it is clear that scholars who have approached *Epileptic* have identified within it a wide range of formal operations, in particular, the highly subjective use of personal symbolism and elaborate visual metaphor that can be central to certain forms of comics storytelling. So, then, why is the book so relatively under-studied?

One of the reasons may be the way that *Epileptic* has been "deflected" into a subfield of comics studies, namely its intersection with the nascent area of disability studies. As Susan Squier notes in one of her two essays about the book, comics studies and disability studies are both emerging areas of research that provide sites of potential mutual advantage.[37] For Squier, *Epileptic*, through its canny use of the comics form, has the significant advantage of being able to show how disability feels. To this end, David B. is able to provide a "thick representation," in the sense defined by Clifford Geertz, of a medicalized condition.[38] The focus for Squier is on the ability of the graphic novel to represent things "that can't be said."[39] Similar insights are provided by Dadey, who considers the work in the context of other graphic novels about disease, and Courtney Donovan who emphasizes the geographic concepts in graphic novels about illness and disease.[40] Perhaps it is not surprising that fully half of the scholarly commentary on *Epileptic* would be found not in journals devoted to the study of comics (though Mitchell and El Refaie have both written about the work in one such context), but in publications with titles like *Literature and Medicine* and the *Journal of Medical Humanities*. In this way we can begin to discern the positioning of *Epileptic* as a special-case graphic novel that is open to scholars with three particular interests: the study of autobiography and self-representation; the study of formal elements within comics, including page design and visual metaphor; and the study of the representation of disease and disability.

Of these three constituencies writing about *Epileptic*, the one that is most central to the project of comics studies are those scholars working in the area of autobiography. Yet despite the fact that it is a critically acclaimed auto-biographical graphic novel, David B.'s work seems under-represented in the scholarship when compared to other, similar works published at the same time to similar levels of critical approbation (notably Bechdel's *Fun Home* and Satrapi's *Persepolis* – also published by L'Association and translated and published in English at approximately the same time and by the same American publisher). It may be impossible to theorize an absence in the scholarship but several possibilities immediately arise. First, it should be noted that the work is particularly French in its presentation and viewpoints. Not only is the work rooted in a Franco-Belgian cartooning idiom, but the narrative elements that it depicts – particularly the presentation of national politics and the social movements dotting France in the 1970s – may seem quite alien to many readers, but not in a particularly exotic manner. *L'Ascension du Haut Mal* draws on antiquated French concepts (as in its very name, which proved impossible for publishers to translate into English but would be literally read as "The Ascension of High Illness"), and in French criticism is situated in relation to other comics that are absent from so much English-language scholarship. For instance, despite the fact that David B. explicitly ties the work to his first major graphic novel, *Le Cheval Blême* (1992), few Anglophone scholars have teased out these connections, perhaps because that important early work remains untranslated.

Second, the book raises a particular ethical issue to the degree that the disease it depicts is, importantly, not the disease of the cartoonist, but of his brother. Unlike works like David Small's *Stitches* or *Our Cancer Year* by Harvey Pekar, Joyce Brabner, and Frank Stack that present first-person testimony about illness, *Epileptic* can be read as invasive. Indeed, this is an interpretation that the book itself invites in its paratext. While it is true that the second-hand depiction of trauma did not bring Spiegelman's *Maus* less scholarly attention, it is notable that Spiegelman has been routinely criticized for the appropriation of his father's narrative and voice in much of the work about that book. *Epileptic*, perhaps, suffers a similar fate, and, consequently, loses the battle against graphic novels that evince no such ethical issues. Similarly, the work does not employ a classical political orientation – it is not easily presented as aligned within contemporary Anglo-American debates about identity politics because of its focus on the trauma of a cis-gendered, able-bodied French white male. This last might inform Chute's passing dismissal of the book in a footnote during her discussion of Satrapi. Chute, whose focus is on a feminist politics in the graphic novel that would exclude the work of David B., argues that *Epileptic* should not be read as a strong influence on Satrapi despite the close personal connection that existed between the authors at the time the works were created.[41] Where she seems to imply a form of anti-feminism rooted in jealousy on the part of David B., I would want to stress that the two works are differentially aligned with the normal science of scholarly production on graphic novels and that David B.'s work simply does not fit with the arbitrary criteria of Anglo-American comics scholarship and its determination to define a canon that is co-existent with predetermined expectations of both form and ideology. To the degree that B.'s work is too French, too steeped in literary and historical traditions that are untranslatable to anglophone scholars, and therefore cannot meet the narrow and arbitrary criteria for canonization in the ways his contemporaries can, is a theory tested further in the examination of Japanese comics artist Jiro Taniguchi.

Jiro Taniguchi: The Ignored Graphic Novelist

Prior to his death in 2017, Jiro Taniguchi was the most acclaimed Japanese comics artist in France. He twice won the Alph-Art prize at the Angoulême International Comics Festival, had two major museum retrospectives of his extensive career, and, in 2011, he was awarded the Chevalier de l'Ordre des Arts et des Lettres. In the English-speaking world, he is considerably less well known, although his comics have been extensively translated and are widely available. Within scholarly circles, however, he is a virtual non-entity, and his name rarely appears in peer-refereed journals (not even in *Mechademia*, the pre-eminent English-language journal for the study of manga and anime). Strongly influenced by Franco-Belgian comics traditions in the 1970s, Taniguchi's work is broadly transnational, bridging, as it does, Japanese *seinen* manga and *gekiga* manga traditions with the Belgian *ligne claire* visual tradition. In addition to being widely translated into French and English, Taniguchi has published original French-language *bande dessinée* albums in collaboration with Moebius and Jean-David Morvan. His stand-alone, 140-page graphic novel *L'Homme qui Marche* (1992) was one of the foundational texts in the manga invasion of France in the early 1990s, and he has remained a key figure in transnational comics production for more than two decades. He was one of the twenty-six named nominees for the 2016 presidency of the Angoulême Festival, the most prestigious award in global comics. And yet aside from a book-length interview/appreciation by Benoît Peeters and a few short articles in German, his work is virtually unstudied. How can this be?

The Walking Man, originally published in Japan between 1980 and 1982, in French in 1992 and in English in 2007 (where it was nominated for an Eisner Award) can help illuminate why Taniguchi remains so unstudied. Strongly influenced by the filmmaking of Yasujiro Ozu, the nearly wordless book collects a series of related short stories featuring a middle-aged salaryman who walks around his neighborhood. Eschewing narrative high and low points, the book is contemplative and lyrical in its pacing, and relies upon a visual strategy that emphasizes the harmony and interconnectedness of people and nature, themes that are routinely developed in Taniguchi's other, longer, graphic novels. From the perspective of comics scholarship, Taniguchi does not fit into any of the usual categories and does not respond to the types of questions that are most often posed within the field. His work is not closely aligned with the manga modes that are most frequently studied in the United States (science fiction, post-humanism, gender-swapping) and does not typify manga practices as they are studied in the English-speaking world. At the same time, his work also does not fall into traditional political categories. It does have a decidedly ecological point of view, although eco-criticism itself is not, at present, a strong thread in contemporary comics studies. The transnational nature of the work puts it at odds with current writing on postcoloniality. It is possibly too Western for many scholars of manga, but too Eastern for scholars of comics. The work, it seems, falls between many of the established paradigms in which comics scholarship most often functions.

When *The Walking Man* is discussed passingly in comics scholarship, close attention is being paid to the importance of drawing. In her essay on *Epileptic* in *Studies in Comics*, for example, Adrielle Mitchell suddenly, and perhaps unexpectedly, detours into a discussion of Taniguchi's rendering style. Taking issue with Scott McCloud's contention that highly detailed backgrounds in manga are a form of realism, Mitchell argues, following Taniguchi, that the comics background can carry affective weight.[42] Mitchell's diversion here confounds the traditions of the discipline to the extent that she reads *The Walking Man* through an art-historical rather than literary lens. Strikingly, her analysis focuses on the explicit meaning of the backgrounds in *The Walking Man*, rather than implicit or symptomatic readings. Indeed, as Bordwell argues in *Making Meaning*, the primary driver of humanities scholarship – and, I would argue, comics scholarship – is the revelation of implicit, or hidden, meanings. This is the primary way in which discussions of the work of Lynda Barry and, to a lesser degree, David B. are organized. *The*

Walking Man, with its deliberate appeal to the explicit – it is literally as the title suggests, a depiction of a man walking – seems to counter so much of the Anglo-American comics scholarship project by rejecting tradition-ally constructed notions of "depth" so that there is little for the scholarly interlocutor to explicate. It is possible, certainly, to imagine a symptomatic reading of the text that persuasively contends that the work is not really as simple as it seems, but even that would require a greater commitment to a formalist visual analysis than is typically the norm in comics studies. Returning to Labio's objection, raised at the opening of this essay, the very term "graphic novel" treats the adjective as a mere qualifier of the noun in privileging the normal science of literary studies. It is clear that a volume like *The Walking Man*, celebrated as it might be, cannot be easily recon-ciled within traditional literary approaches. If one's scholarly focus is on the "novel," it is often difficult to conceptualize a fulsome way to discuss the "graphic." Anglo-American comics scholarship's privileging of the liter-ary may be able to welcome certain transnational texts into its purview, but only if they can be translatable into the terms most valued – yet decidedly unquestioned – by the field. In subsuming comics to the dictates of liter-ary studies, the unique formal properties of comics, its transnational con-texts, and its multiple levels of legibility and narratological sense-making, is suppressed.

Conclusion

A considerable challenge in briefly summarizing scholarly approaches to the study of the graphic novel is the fact that the term is so incredibly elastic. Indeed, in this chapter I have addressed three works that are not "novels" in any conventional sense of that term: Barry's work is a com-bination of memoir and art instruction manual; David B. has produced a classic non-fiction memoir; Taniguchi's book is a collection of short stories. Nonetheless, this definitional question is not the key issue affecting the field. Rather, the historically narrow scope of works that have been studied as graphic novels has distorted the field. Operating as a sort of confirmation bias, comics scholars have all too commonly relied on paradigms derived from elsewhere – in particular the study of literature, into which it has been rapidly subsumed. Works are selected for scholarly study because they are perceived not only to have veiled meanings that can be revealed through close reading, but because they fit within established critical paradigms that fit within psychoanalytic and identity politics approaches. Comics scholarship operates, therefore, in a dominated position relative to better-established scholarly areas, and it borrows from areas that are more legitimated than it is. As a result, the methodological, theoretical, and political potential of comics studies is blunted. Rather than offer original and provocative insights into the study of culture, comics studies simply seems to be trying to add itself into an already well-established (perhaps even calcifying) set of scholarly traditions. As Bordwell notes, due to the foundational and dominant position of close reading for literary criticism, "These assumptions shape the arrangement of specialties in the field, the nature of departments, the patterns of academic conferences, the sorts of books and journals that are published, the way people find jobs and get grants and promotions."[43] These assumptions dictate, in sum, the way that the emergent field of comics studies is set to operate, by building a system of "winners" and "losers" that erects in miniature a canon of graphic novels in parallel to the traditions of literature. The necessary first step on this path has been the reduction of comics to a more narrowly defined "graphic novel." The maintenance of that category, therefore, ensures comics' marginalized "little brother" status within the academy, not as an area that will provide new and invigorating forms of scholarship that transcend artificial distinctions between visual/literary, high/low, national/transnational, but as one that only meekly waits its turn at the big table.

Works Cited

9e Art 11 (Oct. 2004).
Barry, Lynda. *Blabber Blabber Blabber: Everything.* Vol. 1. Montreal: Drawn & Quarterly, 2011.
  The Freddie Stories. Montreal: Drawn & Quarterly, 2013.
  Picture This. Montreal: Drawn & Quarterly, 2010.
  Syllabus. Montreal: Drawn & Quarterly, 2014.
  What It Is. Montreal: Drawn & Quarterly, 2008.
Beaty, Bart. *Comics Versus Art.* University of Toronto Press, 2012.
  Twelve-Cent Archie. New Brunswick, NJ: Rutgers University Press, 2015.
  Unpopular Culture: Transforming the European Comic Book in the 1990s. University of Toronto Press, 2007.
B.[eauchard], David. *Epileptic.* Trans. Kim Thompson. New York: Pantheon Books, 2005.
Bordwell, David. *Making Meaning: Inference and Rhetoric in the Interpretation of Cinema.* Cambridge, MA: Harvard University Press, 1989.
Bourdieu, Pierre. *Distinction: A Social Critique of the Judgement of Taste.* Cambridge, MA: Harvard University Press, 1984
  The Field of Cultural Production. New York: Columbia University Press, 1984.
Chaney, Michael. *Graphic Subjects: Critical Essays on Autobiography and Graphic Novels.* Madison, WI: University of Wisconsin Press, 2011.

Chute, Hillary L. *Graphic Women: Life Narrative and Contemporary Comics*. New York: Columbia University Press, 2010.

Chute, Hillary L., and Marianne DeKoven, eds. Special issue on "Graphic Narrative." *Modern Fiction Studies* 52, no. 4 (2006).

Dadey, Bruce. "Breaking Quarantine: Image, Text, and Disease in *Black Hole, Epileptic*, and *Our Cancer Year*." *ImageText* 7, no. 2 (2011). Web.

De Jesus, Melinda. "Liminality and Mestiza Consciousness in Lynda Barry's 'One Hundred Demons'." *MELUS* 29, no. 1 (2004): 219–52.

Donovan, Courtney. "Epileptic." *Publishers Weekly* (2005). www.publishersweekly.com/978-0-375-42318-5.

"Graphic Pathogeographies." *Journal of Medical Humanities* 35, no. 3 (2014): 273–99.

El Refaie, Elisabeth. *Autobiographical Comics: Life Writing in Pictures*. Jackson, MS: University Press of Mississippi, 2012.

"Subjective Time in David B.'s Graphic Memoir *Epileptic*." *Studies in Comics* 1, no. 2 (2010): 281–99.

Jameson, Fredric. *Postmodernism, or, The Cultural Logic of Late Capitalism*. Durham, NC: Duke University Press, 1991.

Kirtley, Susan. *Lynda Barry: Girlhood Through the Looking Glass*. Jackson, MS: University Press of Mississippi, 2012.

Labio, Catherine. "What's in a Name?: The Academic Study of Comics and the 'Graphic Novel'." *Cinema Journal* 50, no. 3 (2011): 123–26.

Langer, Lawrence. "A Fable of the Holocaust." *The New York Times Book Review*, Nov. 3, 1991, 1.

Michael, Olga. "Pastiche and Family Strife in Contemporary American Women's Graphic Memoirs: Phoebe Gloeckner, Lynda Barry, and Alison Bechdel." Unpublished dissertation, University of Manchester, 2013.

Mitchell, Adrielle. "Distributed Identity: Networking Image Fragments in Graphic Memoirs." *Studies in Comics* 1, no. 2 (2010): 257–79.

Naghibi, Nima, and Andrew O'Malley. "Estranging the Familiar: 'East' and 'West' in Satrapi's *Persepolis*." *ESC: English Studies in Canada* 31, nos. 2–3 (2005): 223–47.

Ngai, Sianne. "Our Aesthetic Categories." *PMLA* 125, no. 4 (2010): 948–58.

Pratt, Murray. "Dramatizing the Self and the Brother: Auto/biography in David B's *L'Ascension du Haut Mal*." *Australian Journal of French Studies* 44, no. 2 (2007): 132–52.

Ricoeur, Paul. "Existence and Hermeneutics," in Josef Bleicher, ed., *Contemporary Hermeneutics: Hermeneutics as Method, Philosophy and Critique*. London: Routledge and Kegan Paul, 1980.

Samanci, Özge. "Lynda Barry's Humor: At the Juncture of Private and Public, Invitation and Dissemination, Childish and Professional." *International Journal of Comic Art* 8, no. 2 (2006): 181–99.

Schlick, Yaël. "What is an Experience? Selves and Texts in the Comic Autobiographies of Alison Bechdel and Lynda Barry," in Jane Tolmie, ed., *Drawing From Life: Memory and Subjectivity in Comic Art*. Jackson, MS: University Press of Mississippi, 2013.

Squier, Susan. "Literature and Medicine, Future Tense: Making it Graphic." *Literature and Medicine* 27, no. 2 (2008): 124–52.

"So Long as They Grow Out of It: Comics, the Discourse of Developmental Normalcy, and Disability." *Journal of Medical Humanities* 29 (2008): 71–88.

Tabachnick, Stephen E. "Autobiography as Discovery in *Epileptic*," in Michael Chaney, ed., *Graphic Subjects: Critical Essays on Autobiography and Graphic Novels*. Madison, WI: University of Wisconsin Press, 2011, 101–16.

Taniguchi, Jiro. *The Walking Man (L'Homme qui Marche/Aruku Hito)* (1990–92). Trans. Shizuka Shimoyama and Elizabeth Tierman. Wisbech, Suffolk, UK: Fanfare/Ponent Mon, 2004.

Tensuan, Theresa. "Comic Visions and Revisions in the Work of Lynda Barry and Marjane Satrapi." *Modern Fiction Studies* 52, no. 4 (2006): 947–64.

Whitlock, Gillian. "Autographics: The Seeing 'I' of the Comics." *Modern Fiction Studies* 52, no. 4 (2006): 965–79

Witek, Joseph. "Imagetext, or, Why Art Spiegelman Doesn't Draw Comics." *ImageText: Interdisciplinary Comics Studies* 1, no. 1 (2002). www.english.ufl.edu/imagetext/archives/v1_1/witek/

NOTES

1 Catherine Labio, "What's in a Name? The Academic Study of Comics and the 'Graphic Novel'," *Cinema Journal* 50, no. 3 (2011): 124.

2 Joseph Witekk, "Imagetext, or, Why Art Spiegelman Doesn't Draw Comics," *ImageText: Interdisciplinary Comics Studies* 1, no. 1 (2002), www.english.ufl.edu/imagetext/archives/v1_1/witek/; Lawrence Langer, "A Fable of the Holocaust," *The New York Times Book Review*, Nov. 3, 1991, 1.

3 See Bart Beaty's *Unpopular Culture: Transforming the European Comic Book in the 1990s* (University of Toronto Press, 2007); *Comics Versus Art* (University of Toronto Press, 2012); and *Twelve-Cent Archive* (New Brunswick, NJ: Rutgers University Press, 2015).

4 Sianne Ngai, "Our Aesthetic Categories," *PMLA* 125, no. 4 (2010): 948–58.

5 Pierre Bourdieu, *The Field of Cultural Production* (New York: Columbia University Press, 1984).

6 Pierre Bourdieu, *Distinction: A Social Critique of the Judgement of Taste* (Cambridge, MA: Harvard University Press, 1984), 493.

7 See Beatty, *Comics Versus Art*.

8 David Bordwell, *Making Meaning: Inference and Rhetoric in the Interpretation of Cinema* (Cambridge, MA: Harvard University Press, 1989), 17.

9 Hillary L. Chute, *Graphic Women: Life Narrative and Contemporary Comics* (New York: Columbia University Press, 2010), 14.

10 Susan Kirtley, *Lynda Barry: Girlhood Through the Looking Glass* (Jackson, MS: University Press of Mississippi, 2012).

11 Nima Naghibi and Andrew O'Malley, "Estranging the Familiar: 'East' and 'West' in Satrapi's *Persepolis*," *ESC: English Studies in Canada* 31, nos. 2–3 (2005): 223–47.

12 Melinda de Jesus, "Liminality and Mestiza Consciousness in Lynda Barry's 'One Hundred Demons'," *MELUS* 29, no. 1 (2004): 219–52.

13 Chute, *Graphic Women*, 108, 114.

14 Theresa Tensuan, "Comic Visions and Revisions in the Work of Lynda Barry and Marjane Satrapi," *Modern Fiction Studies* 52, no. 4 (2006): 948–49; Olga

Michael, "Pastiche and Family Strife in Contemporary American Women's Graphic Memoirs: Phoebe Gloeckner, Lynda Barry, and Alison Bechdel," unpublished dissertation (University of Manchester, 2013), 21.

15 Chute, *Graphic Women*; Michael Chaney, *Graphic Subjects: Critical Essays on Autobiography and Graphic Novels* (Madison, WI: University of Wisconsin Press, 2011); and Elisabeth El Refaie, *Autobiographical Comics: Life Writing in Pictures* (Jackson, MS: University Press of Mississippi, 2012), all provide some sense of the scope of current interest in this field.

16 See, for example, Tensuan, "Comic Visions," for an analysis of Barry and Satrapi; Yaël Schlick, "What is an Experience? Selves and Texts in the Comic Autobiographies of Alison Bechdel and Lynda Barry," in Jane Tolmie, ed., *Drawing from Life: Memory and Subjectivity in Comic Art* (Jackson, MS: University Press of Mississippi, 2013) for Barry and Bechdel; and the special issue on "Graphic Narrative" of *Modern Fiction Studies* 52, no. 4 (2006), edited by Hillary Chute and Marianne DeKoven, for more on Spiegelman in relation to these cartoonists.

17 Gillian Whitlock, "Autographics: The Seeing 'I' of the Comics," *Modern Fiction Studies* 52, no. 4 (2006): 965–79.

18 Beaty, *Unpopular Culture*.

19 Chute, *Graphic Women*, 10.

20 Kirtley, *Lynda Barry*, xi, 179.

21 Özge Samanci, "Lynda Barry's Humor: At the Juncture of Private and Public, Invitation and Dissemination, Childish and Professional," *International Journal of Comic Art* 8, no. 2 (2006): 187.

22 Chute, *Graphic Women*, 127.

23 Kirtley, *Lynda Barry*, 186.

24 Paul Ricoeur, "Existence and Hermeneutics," in Josef Bleicher, ed., *Contemporary Hermeneutics: Hermeneutics as Method, Philosophy and Critique* (London: Routledge and Kegan Paul, 1980).

25 Chute, *Graphic Women*, 13; Bordwell, *Making Meaning*.

26 Schlick, "What is an Experience?," 27, 34.

27 De Jesus, "Liminality and Mestiza Consciousness," 27.

28 *9e Art* 11 (Oct. 2004).

29 Courtney Donovan, "Epileptic," *Publishers Weekly* (2005), www.publishersweekly.com/978–0–375–42318–5.

30 Murray Pratt, "Dramatizing the Self and the Brother: Auto/biography in David B's *L'Ascension du Haut Mal*," *Australian Journal of French Studies* 44, no. 2 (2007): 132–52; Stephen E. Tabachnick, "Autobiography as Discovery in *Epileptic*," in Michael Chaney, ed., *Graphic Subjects: Critical Essays on Autobiography and Graphic Novels* (Madison, WI: University of Wisconsin Press, 2011), 101–16.

31 El Rafaie, *Autobiographical Comics*, 287.

32 Adrielle Mitchell, "Distributed Identity: Networking Image Fragments in Graphic Memoirs," *Studies in Comics* 1, no. 2 (2010): 277.

33 Pratt, "Dramatizing the Self," 148.

34 Susan Squier, "Literature and Medicine, Future Tense: Making it Graphic," *Literature and Medicine* 27, no. 2 (2008): 136; Bruce Dadey, "Breaking Quarantine: Image, Text, and Disease in *Black Hole*, *Epileptic*, and *Our Cancer Year*," *ImageText* 7, no. 2 (2011): 26.

35 Elisabeth El Refaie, "Subjective Time in David B.'s Graphic Memoir *Epileptic*," *Studies in Comics* 1, no. 2 (2010): 281–99.

36 Mitchell, "Distributed Identity," 261.

37 Susan Squier, "So Long as They Grow Out of It: Comics, the Discourse of Developmental Normalcy, and Disability," *Journal of Medical Humanities* 29 (2008): 72.

38 Ibid., 74, 82.

39 Squier, "Literature and Medicine," 131.

40 Dadey, "Breaking Quarantine"; Conrad Donovan, "Graphic Pathogeographies," *Journal of Medical Humanities* 35, no. 3 (2014): 273–99.

41 Chute, *Graphic Women*, 242–43.

42 Mitchell, "Distributed Identity," 275.

43 Bordwell, *Making Meaning*, 23.

12

JAMES BUCKY CARTER

Learning from the Graphic Novel

By the time this chapter has been published, I will have celebrated a decade since teaching my first all-graphic novels course, a variable topics junior-level English class generally entitled "Trends and Issues in Contemporary Literature" offered at the University of Southern Mississippi. Since my days in Hattiesburg, MS, I have integrated graphic novels into a host of different university courses. Some focused specifically on graphic novels; others incorporated them to help me teach other concepts. Indeed, the major affordances from graphic novels in my classes usually fall into one of two categories: Teaching *about* comics or teaching *with/through* comics. As an English Education professor, I confess connections to literacy and pedagogy are inherent in both, usually.

Herein are lessons learned from ten years of sequential art narrative integration across a host of college-level courses. Hemingway's quotation "We are all apprentices in a craft where no one ever becomes a master" weighs heavy. I am not sure one can hone his or her teaching skills to perfection, and, certainly, as texts on studying and teaching graphic novels continue to be published and brilliant exemplars of the medium multiply, instructors have their proverbial hands full when considering the teaching of graphic novels. With humility grounded in imperfect experience and imperfect personhood, though, I present criteria and techniques for constructing comics-centric classes and for teaching graphic novels in post-secondary settings. I start with advice for course construction, then move to early deep-reading strategies designed to key in students on the demands of comics reading. Next I offer an amalgam of three critical lenses which I suggest constitute a "PIM pedagogy" (page/panel analysis, imagetext, and multimodality) for teaching graphic novels which reinforces earlier lessons. I suggest a means for guiding reading incorporating PIM but allowing for professors to explore their own thematic and critical preferences, and I suggest students should engage in the act of creating comics in one way or another in comics-centric classes because creation is the ultimate higher-order thinking skill. Finally, via a link, I share two full syllabi from graphic novel-heavy courses I have been honored to teach.

First off, advice for initial construction of any course utilizing graphic novels via the concept of backward design: backward design is among the most important constructs to consider when crafting any curriculum, but given the variance of approaches and agendas inherent in teaching comics – so numerous some contend there can be no such construct as "comic studies" as a discipline[1] – employing backward design can help an educator focus a course. Popularized among teacher educators by Wiggins and McTighe in *Understanding by Design*, backward design is a three-pronged approach to developing curriculum:

1. Identify desired results.
2. Determine assessment evidence.
3. Plan learning experiences and instruction.[2]

Essentially, when planning a course on graphic novels, it helps to start where one wants to end, or wants the students to end. What does an instructor want them to have learned – and how will a professor know they've learned it well – by the end of the course? When one has an inchoate sense of what these things are, actually articulating them helps give shape to the course. Most likely one needs to include a goals or objective section in one's syllabus, anyway. Backward design can help with that.

Using specific language when stating goals or objectives is essential, but a work in progress and joyfully prone to revision. Often a teacher will complete a course and find conversations yielded new avenues for learning. In my earliest syllabi, I did not articulate what I hoped would be the learning outcomes, but I grew to see the value in stating my goals. Now, I construct my goals via the formula "Students will _X_ via/by/through _Y_" wherein X is an action and Y is the means or product that will meet that action, showing evidence the X was accomplished.

The syllabus for the second iteration of my "Contemporary Trends and Issues in the Graphic Novel" ("CTI") course, offered in the spring of 2007, states:

> Graphic novels combine words and images to create texts with unique reading properties. This course offers students a thorough understanding of how to read and study this emerging literary form and critically examines themes and issues in graphic novels of the last twenty years via primary materials and critical works. Themes include "Pop" Art/The Post-Modern Family; Social Issues from Comics?; and American Identities.

Major assignments included:

> Reflections: For each day's class, please prepare a type-written reflection of your reading. In your reflection, discuss questions or items that interested you in the reading. Assume that these reflections will be turned in at the beginning of each class, for every class. They will be used to help us craft daily discussion, attendance checking, and to help you do well in your participation grade. Each reflection should be at least a half page in length.

> Essay 1: Independent Graphic Novel Reading (3–5 pages): You will read an additional graphic novel that is not on the class reading list and offer an explication of it in this essay. You may analyze the work for similar or conflicting themes, interpretations, etc. you have noticed in class or go your own route. You will prepare and deliver an informal presentation on the work and your thoughts on it.

> Essay 2: Midterm Essay: Comic Book Scholarship (5–7 pages): You will read one book on comic book/graphic novel scholarship (or one on general visual narrative theory) and write an analysis of the work. Your essay should summarize the main arguments of the text, critique the text, and offer your reflections on how the article has expanded your ideas on comics scholarship/visual narrative and how it can do so for other members of the class. As well, you should prepare a brief informal presentation on the work to share with the class. Be prepared to have your book picked out prior to the due date to help make sure we have no overlap.

> Essay 3: Final Paper (7–10 pages): You will craft an essay on any aspect of comics/graphic novels of your interest. The essay may be a deep explication or critique of themes in a single work or across various works. The use of outside sources is highly encouraged. Papers that make use of research tend to score better than those that do not.

Were I to teach an updated version of this course, I might construct backward design objectives such as the following, which no doubt would help me as I taught the class and help students see why they were asked to engage in specific tasks.

Students will:

- Note the unique reading properties of graphic novels via reading, lectures, and assignments.
- Develop a thorough understanding of how to read and study graphic novels through multiple encounters with literary and scholarly texts.
- Analyze graphic novels through multiple themes via class discussion and independent scholarship.

- Offer evidence of meeting these objectives via daily reflections and longer-form scholarly writing.

"CTI" is a course in which learning about the medium was important. In contrast, the graduate-level "Literature for Youth" variable topics course I taught at the University of Texas at El Paso in 2012 used exemplars of the format to help teach about social aspects of secondary schools and the experience of being an adolescent.

The objectives for "Literature for Youth" signify teaching *through* literary comics and differed from those in "CTI," a course *about* them. In the syllabus, I state:

> This course will mine the intersections of adolescence, secondary education, and literary analysis through the intense study of and reflection on works of scholarly merit in the domains of the humanities and the social sciences and will provide literary texts through which various lenses, critical approaches, and concepts from that literature may be applied or explored. This section of the course focuses on the graphic novel as primary literary text.

As such, the course goals looked like this:
Students will:

- Mine the intersections of adolescence, secondary education, and literary analysis through the intense study of and reflection on works of scholarly merit in the domains of the humanities and the social sciences.
- Examine literary texts with an aim toward connecting them to various lenses, critical approaches, and concepts from that scholarship.
- Engage in extensive reading, writing, reflecting, and research to assist in meeting the above objectives.
- Create scholarship and research to indicate their growing knowledge of the stated intersections and objectives.
- Build community and constructivist knowledge in the pursuit of the above objectives via sharing responses and critiques online and in class.

It is incumbent upon those teaching comics courses to accept backward design in construction, publication, and discussion of comics courses and syllabi. My advice as a seasoned teacher-educator and teacher of graphic novel courses is that professors use backward design while in the nascent stage of course planning and show evidence of having done so by publishing course goals on the syllabus.

Having offered advice on how to create a course on graphic novels or studying other concepts through them, I offer means to help students know how to read a work of comics art deeply and effectively enough to contribute to a developing academic discourse on graphic novels in one's classes.

There may be those who think teachers needn't offer any background priming on the comics form when they first ask students to read them. This "immersion" technique can facilitate a situation in which the students and teacher can draw on the experiences and expertise of one another and the organic nature of exploration. While a teacher may feel that she or he loses some control via this means of introducing the form, the emergent "messy work" may yield information one might otherwise have taken an entire semester to learn about the students' intellect, creativity, and so on. Further, this "immersion" approach may help students invest personally in the course, as the course began investing in them. One could use this approach by asking broad-based discussion questions early in the course, even on day one, questions such as "What makes graphic novels graphic novels?" and "How do we read a graphic novel?" or "What elements or aspects of the medium should we attend to for a fluent reading?" Correctness is not the paramount concern in the earliest conversations. Rather, the goal is to get students invested in sharing what they think they know and talking intelligently about what they'd like to know, and about which they do not know very much at all.

Others feel that not providing some more formal background knowledge may be irresponsible, especially if the class contains many first-time comics readers. Sean Connors, for example, suggests a focus on "shapes, perspective, and left-right visual structures."[3] Indeed, knowing the associated vocabulary of comics – page, panels, gutters, emanata, balloons, and so on – is important if one is going to ask students to analyze and create comics (both of which I suggest). Many may claim students must understand the vocabulary of comics before they can critique the form. Furthermore, examining the form's component parts may help students who are familiar with comics to share their knowledge and take on the role of experts, breaking down traditional classroom dynamics. So, one needn't worry about an approach which is either completely immersive in a student-centered sense or one that is immersive in an outside-in approach. Either method implies the importance of starting with thought about formal elements of the structure/language of comics.

To that end, I recommend moving to panel analysis, as I have done many times with solid success, once one has implemented a form of introductory session with the above in mind. Versaci talks about using panel analysis as a means of getting students to move beyond basic understanding of comics and into deep reading. For example, using a nine-panel grid from Jaime Hernandez's "Flies on the Ceiling," Versaci helps students see that comics reading needn't always be linear, helping them to know to seek multiple entry points into a story just in case the left-to-right, top-to-bottom formula popular in many comics doesn't hold up – or in case the action leads to a revisioning of the story.[4]

Even focusing on a single panel can help students prepare for the intellectual skill and stamina required in reading comics. For example, I'll often lead with a single panel from Art Spiegelman's *Maus* (fig. 12.1).

I ask students to brainstorm what this panel represents narratively, historically, and stylistically. If no one knows the setting and basic plot of *Maus*, I'll offer that information. However, I prefer to let a knowledgeable student leader offer it. Guiding questions/discussion prompts for this panel analysis have included iterations of the following (again, I offer basic information on plot, setting, and themes if no one is familiar with the text, a phenomenon more and more unlikely as *Maus* enjoys a fairly strong presence in high school and university curricula):

- Does anyone recognize the graphic novel from which this scene is taken?
- Can anyone explain the overall plot of *Maus*?
- What is the specific setting and situation of this scene?
- How do the narrative language and the word balloons form multiple senses of time and setting?
- What visual signifiers do we have that help explicate the situation?
- Are there signifiers in one character that suggest differences in power or safety in comparison with the other character?

Eventually, we note the signifiers of spoken language via balloons and narration and past tense via the bottom text. We note that even in one panel, comics offer a simultaneity we may observe again. Keen students note the masks, and those who have read the book before are able to explain that the masks mark the Jewish mice passing for Polish non-Jews. Yes, part of appropriate scaffolding of comics reading/teaching is helping students see comics as a self-scaffolding medium, one which offers comprehension assistance to those who read deeply enough to see the assistance offered and accept comics as a clever, playful, deliberate art and literature. Whether I teach *Maus* in a given course is inconsequential; analysis of a panel as loaded as this one helps students know to dig deep not only between panels, but within them. Often, students are excited and impressed at exactly how much literary and artistic information there can be in a single cell from a strong graphic novel.

I have had success priming students' awareness of the need for attentive, analytical readings of graphic novels using images from the first page of the third chapter of Alan Moore and Dave Gibbons' *Watchmen* as well (fig. 12.2). Sometimes I use the entire page – helping us move from panel

Fig. 12.1 Page 136 of Volume 1 of *Maus* affords a panel rich with text complexity, a strong scaffold for readers, some who may not know to look for such depth from comics.

Fig. 12.2 This page from Alan Moore and Dave Gibbons' *Watchmen* offers many clues for understanding textual elements, especially for a deep reader willing to hypothesize from visual elements. © DC Comics.

analysis to page analysis – while sometimes I just use the largest panel. I suggest herein that using this entire page can act as a good extension of the work one does on single-panel analysis with the *Maus* excerpt, and a logical extension from the *Watchmen* page analysis could be found in using Versaci's work with the nine-panel page from "Flies on the Ceiling."

In leading students through analysis of this page from *Watchmen*, I have asked versions of the following questions:

- What is the setting of this scene, and how do you know?
- Does the city look like a nice place to be? Why or why not?
- What do the magazines suggest to us about the culture and politics of the setting?
- What can we make of the different types of narrative communication in the panels?
- What is the relationship between the young man and the older man in panel three? What evidence supports your answer?

Again, if students know nothing about *Watchmen*, offering a short summary is beneficial. Also, if there are students who have read the text, help them to become class leaders and exemplars in the discussion. Eventually, my students come to learn that the page is loaded, especially the fourth panel. Indeed, virtually all plot lines from the text intersect with it. The apple and "NY" signify New York as a setting; the trash and water suggest a dankness; the backdrop of nuclear war looms large in tone and tenor; even the conversation between the two people in panel four seems disconnected and disinterested. Malaise dominates, but subtle textual clues via posters, magazines, and newspapers suggest something big is coming. The different kinds of direct communication, namely the traditional word balloons for spoken language and the crinkly narrator blocks help us get a sense of the multiple narratives and multiple temporalities the medium affords readers. Indeed, after completing a reading of *Watchmen*, students can come to see this one page as the intricate masterpiece it is – if a professor helps them revisit it.

Now that one has pointers on how to organize a syllabus with graphic novels as key texts and means of helping students get in the mindset of reading conscientiously and analytically, I share several perspectives from which to teach once instructors are into the meat of the course. Regardless of overall theme, utilizing these lenses will help a teacher reinforce the need to read comics as complex, multilayered works.

As we saw with the verbal and visual interplays in the *Maus* and *Watchmen* excerpts, panel and page analyses are inherently connected to the concept of multimodality. An understanding of the multimodal is essential for teaching comics effectively. Rooted in the work of Cope and Kalantzis and the New London Group, a multimodal lens seeks to examine texts through a series of interconnected modes, or designs, and asks readers to consider what "affordances" a medium offers – what it can and can't do or allows us to do.[5] Indeed, the work Versaci does with his students via Hernandez's "Flies on the Ceiling" and that I've done with *Maus* are basically activities in noting comics' affordances. New London Group scholars identify five modes, or designs, worthy of attention: the auditory, spatial (including ecosystems and architecture, important distinctions if we are to give attention to comics formal elements), gestural, visual, and linguistic. Adding the language of modes of design to panel and page analysis can create and boost students' metacognitive awareness of what they are studying, giving them added terminology and frames to help them note their own critical thought processes. Further, doing so may help them see that in graphic novel study, one must always attend to the myriad frames and framing devices, from the smallest cell within the smallest panel, to the page, to the chapter, the book, the reader, and the world.

Thankfully, scholars and educators are catching on to the power of the multimodal lens for examining comics. Dale Jacobs' work is exceptionally important in this regard. Wolfe and Kleijwegt write about how the multimodal lens helps them teach comics versions of Shakespeare. Katie Monnin pulls from New London Group writer Gunther Kress as the basis for much of her comics-and-literacy work. Leber-Cook and Cook suggest the multimodal lens deepened their appreciation of comics as teachers and scholars and afforded their adult ESL students learning opportunities. Connors finds fluent comics readers pull from available designs or modes inherently, suggesting educators might do well to embrace multimodal analysis in formal instruction and in informal reading.

I suggest, as does Jacobs, that building students' skills in multimodal analysis pairs well with work from McCloud, whose *Understanding Comics* and *Making Comics* are pivotal in many comics courses but should be braided with the work of others.[6] (As Horrocks suggests, McCloud's definition of comics and system of studying them needn't be the official definition.[7] Others exist). Braiding New London Group-informed multimodal analysis with McCloud's six types of panel progressions and rudimentary imagetext theory fully frontloads/scaffolds comics courses. McCloud suggests comics advance via either moment-to-moment, action-to-action, subject-to-subject, scene-to-scene, aspect-to-aspect, or non-sequitur progressions between and among panels. Mitchell illuminates two basic image-text distinctions: imagetext, in which pictorial and alphabetic language work in consonance as logical co-scaffolds, and image/text, in which the imagistic and the alphabetic seem to cleave from one another, working in dissonance to suggest rupture or discord.

I have asked audiences of both practicing teachers (who hadn't read the texts) and pre-service teachers (who had) to apply these lenses simultaneously to the images from Vera Brosgol's *Anya's Ghost*. I provided the plot for the teachers, who were based in Michigan and interacting with me at a Michigan Reading Association panel, given their cold reading of the images. The pre-service teachers read the comic in one of my "Young Adult Literature" courses at Washington State Pullman in 2013. Generally, both audiences suggested engaging in this tripartite strategy helped them know how to read a comic deeply, revealed new insights into the text or prompted prediction-making/investment in the comics, and deepened their appreciation for the rigor inherent in comics-reading and comics-making.

For example, in promotional material for *Anya's Ghost*, teen Anya is seen smoking and ensconced in the spectral cloud of ghostly teen Emily.[8] Some noted that the gestural and spatial dynamics suggested a dissonant relationship. Anya seems irked while Emily seems happy; Emily's arms seem to grab for Anya; Anya is encircled, possibly as if trapped. Is the smoke of Emily bad for Anya, as is the smoke of the tobacco? The imagetext dynamics suggest a narrative with multiple perspectives and possibilities, where what is beneficial to one party may not always be beneficial to the other.

The imagetext in the initial well scene (roughly pages 12–17), in which Anya falls into a well and has a foreshadowing of future problems, is more consonant in that the texts and images offer less ambiguity, and the multiple panels afford readers the ability to note how Brosgol uses formal elements of comics construction, how she utilizes various modes, how the panels progress, and how all those things work together to form meaning. Overlapping panels on page 13 reveal how the spatial/architectural mode blends naturally with the gestural, for example. Jagged lines reveal Anya's emotional turmoil and inattention to her surroundings. The modes combine poignantly on page 17 when Anya calls for help frantically, the length of the panel, the shape of the balloon, and the weakening of her voice contributing to her growing hopelessness of getting out of the well into which she has distractedly fallen. Using McCloud's panel principles, multimodal awareness, and imagetext theory basics throughout a course assure that there is always a means to examine, always something intellectual to say, about even the seemingly most insignificant aspects of a visual narrative.

To summarize, adequate attention to course goals and outcomes and to comics structure are essential to building students' appreciation and understanding of the form. Introducing well-engrained, widely applicable terminology about form, function, and fluidity in early classes or experiences with comics facilitates students' learning. Guided or communal panel and page analysis, when excerpts are chosen carefully, offers opportunities for illustrating the potential complexity inherent in comics' central frame.

As an important side note: some readers may point to abstract comics as potential scuttles to this approach.[9] However, I assert that abstract comics' potency comes largely from their essential challenge to engrained notions of comics narrative normativity, so these approaches do remain strong places from which to start, as challenging assumptions from earlier in a course should be part of work carried out later in a course. Initially, panel and page analysis may focus on keying students in on the level of work it takes to read comics well, but may or may not include direct interaction with formalist critical approaches. However, braiding basics from McCloud's panel progression theory, Mitchell's imagetext, and multimodal theory may strengthen discourse and analysis initially and throughout a course, as they offer students structural, formal, and theoretical vocabulary. These "PIM" (panel/page analysis + imagetext + McCloud/multimodal) strategies have focused on planning and starting a comics course.

Below, I offer a model for evolving instruction, discussion, and activities through classes once heavy reading begins.

Milner and Milner suggest four stages of reading literature. Each stage builds on the work of the preceding stage and prepares the next. The four-step model is neither "linear nor circular" but recursive as needed.[10] This model may offer a bridge between reading comics and reading other types of literature while also offering a means of addressing the unique qualities of comics to which readers can attend and which may have been introduced via the suggested earlier strategies.

The stages are Reader Response, Interpretive Community, Formal Analysis, and Critical Synthesis. Reader Response and Interpretive Community attend to basic understanding, text-to-self relationships, and general comprehension. In other words, at this level of questioning or interaction, work to establish students' personal reactions to the graphic novels read and focus on basic elements like plot, characters, and setting. Work in the Interpretive Community and Formal Analysis modes transition from basic comprehension to applying text-to-text formal analysis. Once the basics are known to the class, move toward getting students to see how a given text compares and contrasts with other texts – those read in class and even in other classes. In Formal Analysis and Critical Synthesis, continue to integrate text-to-text connections as well as text-to-world notions of analysis and critique and creation. Text-to-world connections should help instructors and students think about the work at the macro level: in relation to social issues, critical lenses, current events, and the given graphic novel's own historicity.

A progression through these modes of thinking and learning – through guided questioning, written responses, Socratic discussion, or group activities – may properly scaffold a reading of any graphic novel once students know to attend to formal elements via their work with panel and page analysis. Further, students can build and hone their budding knowledge of comics formalism/structuralism throughout the model. One can argue the braiding of panel progression, imagetext, and multimodal (PIM) theories already moves students into formal analysis and critical synthesis, of course. Remember, one *can* implement the Milner and Milner model one stage after the other, but one *needn't*. Indeed, if students seem to jump in and out of one stage – or the professor prompts them to do so during a particularly enthusiastic aside or moment in a lecture portion of a class – all the better.

Also, just as critical theory often builds historically from formalist to post-structuralist, applying this four-pronged loose progression affords opportunities to integrate new critical concepts with students who have a foundation. Again, it should be noted strategies based in this development needn't be stringent. Individuals and specific classes will find their way to these stages with adequate leadership. However, as one plans daily readings and goals per meeting, this model may facilitate both a whole course evolution and learning per session.

I have articulated means through which to create, begin, and evolve a course on comics and graphic novels. Two goals remain: considering the later part of courses and braiding together the principles and constructs explored thus far.

First, a rather obvious but easily ignored component from which I feel virtually every graphic novel course and every student in it can benefit. Bitz's longitudinal research finds students engaged in comics-making develop skills, strength, and understandings even their traditional academic preparation may not have developed or revealed.[11] Having experience teaching comics to a range of students spanning from middle school to graduate school, I find tasking students to create comics essential to their understanding of the complexity of the form, and I've asked even graduate students to do so. In action research in which I examined journal entries from college students in which they reflected on their growing understanding and appreciation of comics as a thoughtful craft and a labor- and intellectually intensive narrative medium, I found asking students to create their own comics was an activity which helped them respect the form and challenge lingering preconceived notions of worth and rigor. Stated simply, comics-making is hard work.[12]

Given the second-class status afforded the image in literary studies, asking students to make their own comics in those courses may be even more imperative. Consider asking students to produce short comics to illustrate mastery of certain concepts, like those from PIM, throughout the course. To note their understanding of new critical elements of comics or the critical theories they present (Lacanian notions of othering, for example, in X-Men comics or Freudian concepts at play in Chris Ware's *Jimmy Corrigan*) as students move through Formal Analysis and Critical Synthesis stages, an instructor might ask students to create their own brief narratives. Or, some type of comics-making could be factored in to the end-of-course summative assignments. While that option may require a professor to check in periodically with students to note their plans and progress, leaving room for a major comics product toward the end of a course allows adequate time for the labor-intensive comics production process and allows students to pull from as much structural and critical knowledge of the form gleaned from the semester as possible, and may allow for a purer, gradual-release approach.

To reiterate: comics-making is an essential part of any and every comics course. I abide by the principle that creation is the utmost iteration of understanding and critique. Asserted simply: creating is a higher order of thinking. A key goal of multimodal pedagogy is facilitating students' design knowledge. Meaning making – and evidence thereof, for professors seeking to illustrate how learning objectives were met – comes from noting available designs and their affordances; engaging in the work of designing/creating; and examining and articulating the affordances of the redesigned. Through design work/creating, students illustrate understandings of current trends, issues, and thought ("situated practice," as per the parlance), critically engage with those conditions, and demonstrate "transformed practice" through a product which illustrates their understanding while offering something new to facilitate the understandings of others. For some multimodal scholars – especially those concerned with representations and power dynamics in popular media – creation/recreation, designing through redesigning, and newly situating practice via transforming practice, the most powerful form of creation and communication is parody.

Revisiting abstract comics' potential to "go rogue," we may view the work of abstract comics makers as seeking to move us into transformed practice and to make us aware of redesigns within comics narratology. Abstract comics parody sourced norms via elucidating a tremendous understanding and critique of them. Either through parody or design (or, to reconcile the constructs, via seeing all designing within a form as parody, regardless of connotative utterances of the word), students can illustrate formal and critical proficiency as well as earn an appreciation for the craft via the making process. Some comics-creation assignments should be part of any comics or graphic novel course, and offer means to elucidate the complexity and dexterity inherent in thinking about and producing comics. What's more, pedagogically speaking, creating is seen as paramount evidence of actual learning in various models of teaching and across educational theories.

In ending our time together, I reiterate that herein I have offered advice for crafting a college-level course on or through graphic novels via backward design. I have suggested panel and page analysis as an excellent early activity to assist students acclimatizing to the reality that comics panels and pages can be and, in literary graphic novels, are often loaded with layers of signification requiring thoughtful, attentive, and curious inspection. Via examples from *Maus* and *Watchmen*, and with a nod to Jaime Hernandez from Versaci, I have offered specific means by which to help students unpack panels and pages. To support teaching once these basics have been covered, I have presented in-progress approaches to apply to the reading, studying, and discoursing about graphic novels. Teaching formal elements and vocabulary of comics and design and panel/page analysis (PIM) get them started; offering myriad opportunities to explore the form – as a form, and connected to other texts in meaningful ways (such as through critical lenses, guided big questions, history, or thematic foci), can carry much of the meat of a course. Presenting opportunities for students to consider, critique, *and create* comics informed by multiple theories or lenses can facilitate professors' efforts to offer students highly organized, goals- and student- oriented organic comics courses in any discipline and with any focus, while retaining an organic quality to the course. My hope is that current and future teachers, instructors, and professors of graphic-novel-inclusive courses have found this helpful. At the very least, I thank readers for bearing in mind the raspy winds of this hoary, whispering trace who knows while he has a decade under his belt, he still has much to learn about teaching with and through graphic novels. As well, I ask readers to enjoy the two full syllabi offered as an appendix, which provides specific graphic novel titles – captured in the historical moments of the syllabi's creation, of course – I have had the pleasure of enjoying with students.[13]

Works Cited

Beaty, Bart. *Comics Versus Art*. University of Toronto Press, 2012.

Bitz, Michael. *Manga High: Literacy, Identity, and Coming of Age in an Urban High School*. Cambridge, MA: Harvard Education Press, 2009.

    When Commas Meet Kryptonite: Classroom Lessons from the Comic Book Project. New York: Teachers College Press, 2010.

Brosgol, Vera. *Anya's Ghost*. New York: First Second, 2011.

Carter, James Bucky. "'What The–?': Pre-service Teachers Meet and Grapple Over Graphic Novels in the Classroom," in Carrye Kay Selma and Robert G. Weiner, eds., *Graphic Novels and Comics in the Classroom*. Jefferson, NC: McFarland, 2013, 58–72.

"Comics," in Roger Levesque, ed., *Encyclopedia of Adolescence*. New York: Springer, 2012, 460–68.

Connors, Sean P. "Toward a Shared Vocabulary for Visual Analysis: An Analytic Toolkit for Deconstructing the Visual Design of Graphic Novels." *Journal of Visual Literacy* 31, no. 1 (2011): 71–91.

"Weaving Multimodal Meaning in a Graphic Novel Reading Group." *Visual Communication* 12, no. 1 (2013): 27–53.

Cope, Bill, and Mary Kalantzis, eds. *Multiliteracies: Literacy Learning and the Design of Social Futures*. New York: Routledge, 2000.

Hatfield, Charles. "Indiscipline or, The Condition of Comics Studies." *Transatlantica* 1 (2010), Jan. 20, 2015. http://transatlantica.revues.org/4933.

Hemingway, Ernest. *New York Journal-American*, July 11, 1961.

Hernandez, Jaime. *Complete Love and Rockets*, Vol. 9: *Flies on the Ceiling*. Seattle, WA: Fantagraphics Books, 1991), 1–15.

Horrocks, Dylan. "Inventing Comics: Scott McCloud's Definition of Comics." *The Comics Journal* 234 (June 2001). Jan. 21, 2015. www.hicksville.co.nz/Inventing%20Comics.htm.

Jacobs, Dale. *Graphic Encounters: Comics and the Sponsorship of Multimodal Literacy*. New York: Bloomsbury Academic, 2013.

"Marveling at 'The Man Called Nova': Comics as Sponsors of Multimodal Literacy." *College Composition and Communication* 59, no. 2 (2007): 180–205.

"More Than Words: Comics as a Means of Teaching Multiple Literacies." *English Journal* 96, no. 3 (2007): 19–25.

"'There are no rules. And here they are': Scott McCloud's *Making Comics* as a Multimodal Rhetoric." *Journal of Teaching Writing* 29, no. 1 (2014): 1–20.

"Webcomics, Multimodality, and Information Literacy." *ImageText* 7, no. 3 (2014): n. pag. Dept of English, University of Florida. Jan. 21, 2015.

Kress, Gunther. *Literacy in the New Media Age*. New York: Routledge, 2003.

Leber-Cook, Alice, and Roy T. Cook. "Stigmatization, Multimodality, and Metaphor: Comics in the Adult English as a Second Language Classroom," in Carrye Kay Selma and Robert G. Weiner, eds., *Graphic Novels and Comics in the Classroom*. Jefferson, NC: McFarland, 2013, 23–34.

Marzano, Robert J., and John S. Kendall, eds. *The New Taxonomy of Educational Objectives*. 2nd ed. Thousand Oaks, CA: Corwin Press, 2007.

McCloud, Scott. *Making Comics*. New York: William Morrow Paperbacks, 2006.

Understanding Comics: The Invisible Art. New York: Harper Perennial, 1993.

McTighe, Jay, and Grant Wiggins. *Understanding by Design Framework*. Alexandria, VA: Association for Supervision and Curriculum Development, 2012. Jan. 20, 2015. www.ascd.org/ASCD/pdf/siteASCD/publications/UbD_WhitePaper0312.pdf.

Milner, Joseph O'Bierne, and Lucy Floyd Morcock Milner. *Bridging English*. 3rd ed. Upper Saddle River, NJ: Merrill Prentice Hall, 2003.

Mitchell, W. J. T. *Iconology: Image, Text, Ideology*. University of Chicago Press, 1986.

Picture Theory. University of Chicago Press, 1994.

Molotiu, Andrei, ed. *Abstract Comics: The Anthology*. Seattle, WA: Fantagraphics Books, 2009.

Monnin, Katie. *Teaching Graphic Novels*. Gainesville, FL: Maupin House/Capstone, 2010.

Teaching Reading Comprehension with Graphic Texts. North Mankato, MN: Capstone, 2013.

Moore, Alan, and Dave Gibbons. *Watchmen*. New York: DC Comics, 1986.

Spiegelman, Art. *Maus*. Vol. 1. New York: Pantheon Books, 1986.

Tilley, Carol. "Comics: A Once-Missed Opportunity." *The Journal of Research on Libraries and Young Adults*. May 5, 2014. Jan. 21, 2015. www.yalsa.ala.org/jrlya/2014/05/comics-a-once-missed-opportunity/.

"Seducing the Innocent: Fredric Wertham and the Falsifications that Helped Condemn Comics." *Information & Culture: A Journal of History* 47, no. 4 (2012): 383–413.

"Superman Says, 'Read!': National Comics and Reading Promotion." *Children's Literature in Education* 44, no. 3 (2013): 251–63.

"Using Comics to Teach the Language Arts in the 1940s and 1950s," in Carrye Kay Selma and Robert G. Weiner, eds., *Graphic Novels and Comics in the Classroom*. Jefferson, NC: McFarland, 2013, 12–22.

Ware, Chris. *Jimmy Corrigan: The Smartest Kid on Earth*. New York: Pantheon Books, 2003.

Wiggins, Grant P., and Jay McTighe. *Understanding by Design*. 2nd ed. Alexandria, VA: Association for Supervision and Curriculum Development, 2005.

Wolfe, Paula, and Danielle Kleijwegt. "Interpreting Graphic Versions of Shakespearean Plays." *English Journal* 101, no. 5 (2012): 30–36.

Versaci, Rocco. *This Book Contains Graphic Language: Comics as Literature*. New York: Continuum, 2007.

NOTES

1 See Charles Hatfield, "Indiscipline or, The Condition of Comics Studies," *Transatlantica* 1 (2010), Jan. 20, 2015: http://transatlantica.revues.org/4933.

2 Grant P. Wiggins, and Jay McTighe, *Understanding by Design*, 2nd ed. (Alexandria, VA: Association for Supervision and Curriculum development, 2005).

3 Sean P. Connors, "Toward a Shared Vocabulary for Visual Analysis: An Analytic Toolkit for Deconstructing the Visual Design of Graphic Novels," *Journal of Visual Literacy* 31, no. 1 (2012), 73.

4 Rocco Versaci, *This Book Contains Graphic Language: Comics as Literature* (New York: Continuum, 2007).

5 Bill Cope and Mary Kalantzis, eds., *Multiliteracies: Literacy Learning and the Design of Social Futures* (New York: Routledge), 2000.

6 Scott McCloud, *Understanding Comics: The Invisible Art* (New York: Harper Perennial, 1993), and *Making Comics* (New York: William Morrow Paperbacks, 2006).

7 Dylan Horrocks, "Inventing Comics: Scott McCloud's Definition of Comics," *The Comics Journal* 234 (June 2001), www.hicksville.co.nz/Inventing%20Comics.htm.

8 Available at http://apeonthemoon.com/wp-content/uploads/2010/10/ft7.jpg.

9   See Andrei Molotiu, ed., *Abstract Comics: The Anthology* (Seattle, WA: Fanta-graphics Books, 2009), and Bart Beaty, *Comics Versus Art* (University of Toronto Press, 2012).

10 Joseph O'Bierne Milner and Lucy Floyd Morcock Milner, *Bridging English*, 3rd ed. (Upper Saddle River, NJ: Merrill Prentice Hall, 2003), 104.

11 See Michael Bitz, *Manga High: Literacy, Identity, and Coming of Age in an Urban High School* (Cambridge, MA: Harvard Education Press, 2009), and *When Commas Meet Kryptonite: Classroom Lessons from the Comic book Project* (New York: Teachers College Press, 2010).

12 James Bucky Carter, "'What the–?': Pre-service Teachers Meet and Grapple Over Graphic Novels in the Classroom," in Carrye Kay Selma and Robert G. Weiner, eds., *Graphic Novels and Comics in the Classroom* (Jefferson, NC: McFarland, 2013), 58–72.

13 http://tinyurl.com/oj5dusa

FURTHER READING

Books

Andelman, Bob. *Will Eisner: A Spirited Life*. Milwaukie, OR: M Press, 2005.

Baetens, Jan, and Hugo Frey. *The Graphic Novel: An Introduction*. Cambridge University Press, 2014.

Baetens, Jan, and Ari J. Blatt, eds. *Writing and the Image Today*. New Haven, CT: Yale University Press, 2008.

Ball, David, and Martha Kuhlman, eds. *The Comics of Chris Ware: Drawing is a Way of Thinking*. Jackson, MS: University Press of Mississippi.

Barker, Martin. *Comics: Ideology, Power and the Critics*. Manchester University Press, 1989.

Baskind, Samantha, and Ranen Omer-Sherman, eds. *The Jewish Graphic Novel: Critical Approaches*. New Brunswick, NJ: Rutgers University Press, 2008.

Beaty, Bart. *Fredric Wertham and the Critique of Mass Culture*. Jackson, MS: University Press of Mississippi, 2005.

   Unpopular Culture: Transforming the European Comic Book in the 1990s. University of Toronto Press, 2007.

Beaty, Bart, and Stephen Weiner, eds. *Critical Survey of Graphic Novels*. 3 vols. Ipswich, MA: Salem Press, 2012.

Beauchamp, Monte, ed. *The Life and Times of R. Crumb: Comments from Contemporaries*. New York: St. Martin's Press, 1998.

Bell, Roanne, and Mark Sinclair. *Pictures and Words: New Comic Art and Narrative Illustration*. New Haven, CT: Yale University Press, 2005.

Berlatsky, Eric L., ed. *Alan Moore: Conversations*. Jackson, MS: University Press of Mississippi, 2011.

Bongco, Mila. *Reading Comics: Language, Culture, and the Concept of the Superhero in Comic Books*. New York: Garland, 2000.

Booker, M. Keith. *"May Contain Graphic Material": Comic Books, Graphic Novels, and Film*. Westport, CT: Praeger, 2007.

Brown, Jeffrey A. *Black Superheroes, Milestone Comics, and Their Fans*. Jackson, MS: University Press of Mississippi, 2001.

Buhle, Paul, ed. *Jews and American Comics: An Illustrated History of an American Art Form*. New York: New Press, 2008.

Carrier, David. *The Aesthetics of Comics*. University Park, PA: Penn State University Press, 2001.

Carter, James Bucky, ed. *Building Literary Connections with Graphic Novels: Page by Page, Panel by Panel*. Urbana, IL: NCTE, 2007.

Chute, Hillary L. *Graphic Women: Life Narrative and Contemporary Comics*. New York: Columbia University Press, 2010.

Cohn, Neil. *The Visual Language of Comics: Introduction to the Structure and Cognition of Sequential Images*. London and New York: Bloomsbury, 2014.

Duncan, Randy, and Matthew J. Smith. *The Power of Comics: History, Form and Culture*. New York: Continuum, 2009.

Eisner, Will. *Comics and Sequential Art*. Tamarac, FL: Poorhouse, 1985.

Graphic Storytelling and Visual Narrative: Principles and Practices from the Legendary Cartoonist. New York: W. W. Norton, 2008.

Feiffer, Jules. *The Great Comic Book Heroes*. Seattle, WA: Fantagraphics Books, 2003.

Gardner, Jared. *Projections: Comics and the History of Twenty-First-Century Storytelling*. Palo Alto, CA: Stanford University Press, 2011.

Geis, Deborah, ed. *Considering Maus: Approaches to Art Spiegelman's "Survivor's Tale" of the Holocaust*. Tuscaloosa, AL: University of Alabama Press, 2003.

Gordan, Ian, Mark Jancovich, and Matthew McAllister, eds. *Film and Comic Books*. Jackson, MS: University Press of Mississippi, 2007.

Gravett, Paul. *Graphic Novels: Everything You Need to Know*. New York: Harper-Collins, 2005.

Green, Matthew J. A., ed. *Alan Moore and the Gothic Tradition*. Manchester University Press, 2009.

Groensteen, Thierry. *The System of Comics*. Trans. Bart Beaty and Nick Nguyen. Jackson, MS: University Press of Mississippi, 2007.

Groth, Gary, and Robert Fiore, eds. *The New Comics*. New York: Berkeley Books, 1988.

Harris, Michael D. *Colored Pictures: Race and Visual Representation*. Chapel Hill, NC: University of North Carolina Press, 2003.

Hatfield, Charles. *Alternative Comics: An Emerging Literature*. Jackson, MS: University Press of Mississippi, 2005.

Heer, Jeet, and Kent Worcester, eds. *Arguing Comics: Literary Masters on a Popular Medium*. Jackson, MS: University Press of Mississippi, 2004.

A Comics Studies Reader. Jackson, MS: University Press of Mississippi, 2009.

Inge, Thomas. *Comics as Culture*. Jackson, MS: University Press of Mississippi, 1990.

Jones, William B. *Classics Illustrated: A Cultural History, with Illustrations*. Jefferson, NC: McFarland, 2011.

Kaplan, Arie. *From Krakow to Krypton: Jews and Comic Books*. Philadelphia, PA: Jewish Publication Society, 2003.

Keller, James R. *V for Vendetta as Cultural Pastiche: A Critical Study of the Graphic Novel and Film*. Jefferson, NC: McFarland, 2008.

Kick, Russ, ed. *The Graphic Canon: The World's Great Literature as Comics and Visuals*. 3 vols. New York: Seven Stories Press, 2012–13.

Knowles, Christopher. *Our Gods Wear Spandex: The Secret History of Comic Book Heroes*. San Francisco, CA: Weiser Books, 2007.

Lent, John A., ed. *Illustrating Asia: Comics, Humor Magazines, and Picture Books*. Richmond, UK: Curzon, 2001.

Mazur, Dan, and Alexander Danner. *Comics: A Global History, 1968 to the Present.* London: Thames and Hudson, 2014.

McCloud, Scott. *Understanding Comics: The Invisible Art.* Northampton, MA: Tundra, 1993.

McLaughlin, Jeff, ed. *Comics as Philosophy.* Jackson, MS: University Press of Mississippi, 2005.

Millidge, Gary Spencer, ed. *Alan Moore: Portrait of an Extraordinary Gentleman.* Leigh-on-Sea, UK: Abiogenesis Press, 2003.

Nyberg, Amy Kiste. *Seal of Approval: The History of the Comics Code.* Jackson, MS: University Press of Mississippi, 1998.

Reidelbach, Maria. *Completely Mad: A History of the Comic Book and Magazine.* Boston, MA: Little, Brown and Company, 1991.

Robbins, Trina. *From Girls to Grrrlz: A History of Women's Comics from Teens to Zines.* San Francisco, CA: Chronicle Books, 1999.

Rosenkranz, Patrick. *Rebel Visions: The Underground Comics Revolution, 1963–1975.* Seattle, WA: Fantagraphics Books, 2002.

Sabin, Roger. *Adult Comics: An Introduction.* London and New York: Routledge, 1993.

   Comics, Comix, and Graphic Novels: A History of Comic Art. London: Phaidon, 1996.

Schodt, Frederik L. *Dreamland Japan: Writings on Modern Manga.* Berkeley, CA: Stone Bridge Press, 1996.

Skinn, Dez. *Comix: The Underground Revolution.* New York: Thunder's Mouth Press, 2004.

Spiegelman, Art. *MetaMaus.* New York: Pantheon Books, 2011.

Stein, Daniel, and Jan-Noël Thon, eds. *From Comic Strips to Graphic Novels: Contributions to the Theory and History of Graphic Narrative.* Boston, MA: De Gruyter, 2013.

Strömberg, Fredrik. *Black Images in the Comics: A Visual History.* Seattle, WA: Fantagraphics Books, 2003.

Tabachnick, Stephen E. *The Quest for Jewish Belief and Identity in the Graphic Novel.* Tuscaloosa, AL: University of Alabama Press, 2014.

Tabachnick, Stephen E., ed. *Teaching the Graphic Novel.* New York: Modern Language Association of America, 2009.

Tabachnick, Stephen E., and Esther Bendit Saltzman, eds. *Drawn from the Classics: Essays on Graphic Adaptations of Literary Works.* Jefferson, NC: McFarland, 2015.

Varnum, Robin, and Christina T. Gibbons, eds. *The Language of Comics: Word and Image.* Jackson, MS: University Press of Mississippi, 2002.

Versaci, Rocco. *This Book Contains Graphic Language: Comics as Literature.* New York: Continuum, 2007.

Weiner, Stephen. *Faster Than a Speeding Bullet: The Rise of the Graphic Novel.* New York: NBM, 2004.

   100 Graphic Novels for Public Libraries. Northampton, MA: Kitchen Sink Press, 1996.

White, Mark D., and Robert Arp, eds. *Batman and Philosophy: The Dark Knight of the Soul.* Hoboken, NJ: Wiley, 2008.

Willett, Perry. *The Silent Shout: Frans Masereel, Lynd Ward, and the Novel in Woodcuts*. Bloomington, IN: Indiana University Libraries, 1997.

Witek, Joseph, ed. *Art Spiegelman: Conversations*. Jackson, MS: University Press of Mississippi, 2007.

   Comic Books as History: The Narrative Art of Jack Jackson, Art Spiegelman, and Harvey Pekar. Jackson, MS: University Press of Mississippi, 1990.

Wolk, Douglas. *Reading Comics: How Graphic Novels Work and What They Mean*. Cambridge, MA: Da Capo Press, 2007.

Websites

www.comicon.com
www.comicsresearch.org
www.english.ufl.edu/comics/scholars
www.english.ufl.edu/imagetext
www.hicksville.co.nz
www.lib.msu.edu/comics/
www.teachingcomics.org

INDEX

Italicized page numbers refer to illustrations.

Cambridge Companions to...

AUTHORS

Edward Albee edited by Stephen J. Bottoms

Margaret Atwood edited by Coral Ann Howells

W. H. Auden edited by Stan Smith

Jane Austen edited by Edward Copeland and Juliet McMaster (second edition)

Beckett edited by John Pilling

Bede edited by Scott DeGregorio

Aphra Behn edited by Derek Hughes and Janet Todd

Walter Benjamin edited by David S. Ferris

William Blake edited by Morris Eaves

Boccaccio edited by Guyda Armstrong, Rhiannon Daniels, and Stephen J. Milner

Jorge Luis Borges edited by Edwin Williamson

Brecht edited by Peter Thomson and Glendyr Sacks (second edition)

The Brontës edited by Heather Glen

Bunyan edited by Anne Dunan-Page

Frances Burney edited by Peter Sabor

Byron edited by Drummond Bone

Albert Camus edited by Edward J. Hughes

Willa Cather edited by Marilee Lindemann

Cervantes edited by Anthony J. Cascardi

Chaucer edited by Piero Boitani and Jill Mann (second edition)

Chekhov edited by Vera Gottlieb and Paul Allain

Kate Chopin edited by Janet Beer

Caryl Churchill edited by Elaine Aston and Elin Diamond

Cicero edited by Catherine Steel

Coleridge edited by Lucy Newlyn

Wilkie Collins edited by Jenny Bourne Taylor

Joseph Conrad edited by J. H. Stape

H. D. edited by Nephie J. Christodoulides and Polina Mackay

Dante edited by Rachel Jacoff (second edition)

Daniel Defoe edited by John Richetti

Don DeLillo edited by John N. Duvall

Charles Dickens edited by John O. Jordan

Emily Dickinson edited by Wendy Martin

John Donne edited by Achsah Guibbory

Dostoevskii edited by W. J. Leatherbarrow

Theodore Dreiser edited by Leonard Cassuto and Claire Virginia Eby

John Dryden edited by Steven N. Zwicker

W. E. B. Du Bois edited by Shamoon Zamir

George Eliot edited by George Levine

T. S. Eliot edited by A. David Moody

Ralph Ellison edited by Ross Posnock

Ralph Waldo Emerson edited by Joel Porte and Saundra Morris

William Faulkner edited by Philip M. Weinstein

Henry Fielding edited by Claude Rawson

F. Scott Fitzgerald edited by Ruth Prigozy

Flaubert edited by Timothy Unwin

E. M. Forster edited by David Bradshaw

Benjamin Franklin edited by Carla Mulford

Brian Friel edited by Anthony Roche

Robert Frost edited by Robert Faggen

Gabriel García Márquez edited by Philip Swanson

Elizabeth Gaskell edited by Jill L. Matus

Goethe edited by Lesley Sharpe

Günter Grass edited by Stuart Taberner

Thomas Hardy edited by Dale Kramer

David Hare edited by Richard Boon

Nathaniel Hawthorne edited by Richard Millington

Seamus Heaney edited by Bernard O'Donoghue

Ernest Hemingway edited by Scott Donaldson

Homer edited by Robert Fowler

Horace edited by Stephen Harrison

Ted Hughes edited by Terry Gifford

Ibsen edited by James McFarlane

Henry James edited by Jonathan Freedman

Samuel Johnson edited by Greg Clingham

Ben Jonson edited by Richard Harp and Stanley Stewart

James Joyce edited by Derek Attridge (second edition)

Kafka edited by Julian Preece

Keats edited by Susan J. Wolfson

Rudyard Kipling edited by Howard J. Booth

Lacan edited by Jean-Michel Rabaté

D. H. Lawrence edited by Anne Fernihough

Primo Levi edited by Robert Gordon

Lucretius edited by Stuart Gillespie and Philip Hardie

Machiavelli edited by John M. Najemy

David Mamet edited by Christopher Bigsby

Thomas Mann edited by Ritchie Robertson

Christopher Marlowe edited by Patrick Cheney

Andrew Marvell edited by Derek Hirst and Steven N. Zwicker

Herman Melville edited by Robert S. Levine

Arthur Miller edited by Christopher Bigsby (second edition)

Milton edited by Dennis Danielson (second edition)

Molière edited by David Bradby and Andrew Calder

Toni Morrison edited by Justine Tally

Alice Munro edited by David Staines

Nabokov edited by Julian W. Connolly

Eugene O'Neill edited by Michael Manheim

George Orwell edited by John Rodden

Ovid edited by Philip Hardie

Petrarch edited by Albert Russell Ascoli and Unn Falkeid

Harold Pinter edited by Peter Raby (second edition)

Sylvia Plath edited by Jo Gill

Edgar Allan Poe edited by Kevin J. Hayes

Alexander Pope edited by Pat Rogers

Ezra Pound edited by Ira B. Nadel

Proust edited by Richard Bales

Pushkin edited by Andrew Kahn

Rabelais edited by John O'Brien

Rilke edited by Karen Leeder and Robert Vilain

Philip Roth edited by Timothy Parrish

Salman Rushdie edited by Abdulrazak Gurnah

John Ruskin edited by Francis O'Gorman

Shakespeare edited by Margareta de Grazia and Stanley Wells (second edition)

Shakespearean Comedy edited by Alexander Leggatt

Shakespeare and Contemporary Dramatists edited by Ton Hoenselaars

Shakespeare and Popular Culture edited by Robert Shaughnessy

Shakespearean Tragedy edited by Claire McEachern (second edition)

Shakespeare on Film edited by Russell Jackson (second edition)

Shakespeare on Stage edited by Stanley Wells and Sarah Stanton

Shakespeare's History Plays edited by Michael Hattaway

Shakespeare's Last Plays edited by Catherine M. S. Alexander

Shakespeare's Poetry edited by Patrick Cheney

George Bernard Shaw edited by Christopher Innes

Shelley edited by Timothy Morton

Mary Shelley edited by Esther Schor

Sam Shepard edited by Matthew C. Roudané

Spenser edited by Andrew Hadfield

Laurence Sterne edited by Thomas Keymer

Wallace Stevens edited by John N. Serio

Tom Stoppard edited by Katherine E. Kelly

Harriet Beecher Stowe edited by Cindy Weinstein

August Strindberg edited by Michael Robinson

Jonathan Swift edited by Christopher Fox

J. M. Synge edited by P. J. Mathews

Tacitus edited by A. J. Woodman

Henry David Thoreau edited by Joel Myerson

Tolstoy edited by Donna Tussing Orwin

Anthony Trollope edited by Carolyn Dever and Lisa Niles

Mark Twain edited by Forrest G. Robinson

John Updike edited by Stacey Olster

Mario Vargas Llosa edited by Efrain Kristal and John King

Virgil edited by Charles Martindale

Voltaire edited by Nicholas Cronk

Edith Wharton edited by Millicent Bell

Walt Whitman edited by Ezra Greenspan

Oscar Wilde edited by Peter Raby

Tennessee Williams edited by Matthew C. Roudané

August Wilson edited by Christopher Bigsby

Mary Wollstonecraft edited by Claudia L. Johnson

Virginia Woolf edited by Susan Sellers (second edition)

Wordsworth edited by Stephen Gill

W. B. Yeats edited by Marjorie Howes and John Kelly

Xenophon edited by Michael A. Flower

Zola edited by Brian Nelson

TOPICS

The Actress edited by Maggie B. Gale and John Stokes

The African American Novel edited by Maryemma Graham

The African American Slave Narrative edited by Audrey A. Fisch

Theatre History by David Wiles and Christine Dymkowski

African American Theatre by Harvey Young

Allegory edited by Rita Copeland and Peter Struck

American Crime Fiction edited by Catherine Ross Nickerson

American Modernism edited by Walter Kalaidjian

American Poetry Since 1945 edited by Jennifer Ashton

American Realism and Naturalism edited by Donald Pizer

American Travel Writing edited by Alfred Bendixen and Judith Hamera

American Women Playwrights edited by Brenda Murphy

Ancient Rhetoric edited by Erik Gunderson

Arthurian Legend edited by Elizabeth Archibald and Ad Putter

Australian Literature edited by Elizabeth Webby

British Literature of the French Revolution edited by Pamela Clemit

British Romanticism edited by Stuart Curran (second edition)

British Romantic Poetry edited by James Chandler and Maureen N. McLane

British Theatre, 1730–1830 edited by Jane Moody and Daniel O'Quinn

Canadian Literature edited by Eva-Marie Kröller

Children's Literature edited by M. O. Grenby and Andrea Immel

The Classic Russian Novel edited by Malcolm V. Jones and Robin Feuer Miller

Contemporary Irish Poetry edited by Matthew Campbell

Creative Writing edited by David Morley and Philip Neilsen

Crime Fiction edited by Martin Priestman

Early Modern Women's Writing edited by Laura Lunger Knoppers

The Eighteenth-Century Novel edited by John Richetti

Eighteenth-Century Poetry edited by John Sitter

Emma edited by Peter Sabor

English Literature, 1500–1600 edited by Arthur F. Kinney

English Literature, 1650–1740 edited by Steven N. Zwicker

English Literature, 1740–1830 edited by Thomas Keymer and Jon Mee

English Literature, 1830–1914 edited by Joanne Shattock

English Novelists edited by Adrian Poole

English Poetry, Donne to Marvell edited by Thomas N. Corns

English Poets edited by Claude Rawson

English Renaissance Drama edited by A. R. Braunmuller and Michael Hattaway (second edition)

English Renaissance Tragedy edited by Emma Smith and Garrett A. Sullivan Jr.

English Restoration Theatre edited by Deborah C. Payne Fisk

The Epic edited by Catherine Bates

European Modernism edited by Pericles Lewis

European Novelists edited by Michael Bell

Fairy Tales edited by Maria Tatar

Fantasy Literature edited by Edward James and Farah Mendlesohn

Feminist Literary Theory edited by Ellen Rooney

Fiction in the Romantic Period edited by Richard Maxwell and Katie Trumpener

The Fin de Siècle edited by Gail Marshall

The French Enlightenment edited by Daniel Brewer

French Literature edited by John D. Lyons

The French Novel: From 1800 to the Present edited by Timothy Unwin

Gay and Lesbian Writing edited by Hugh Stevens

German Romanticism edited by Nicholas Saul

Gothic Fiction edited by Jerrold E. Hogle

The Graphic Novel edited by Stephen E. Tabachnick

The Greek and Roman Novel edited by Tim Whitmarsh

Greek and Roman Theatre edited by Marianne McDonald and J. Michael Walton

Greek Comedy edited by Martin Revermann

Greek Lyric edited by Felix Budelmann

Greek Mythology edited by Roger D. Woodard

Greek Tragedy edited by P. E. Easterling

The Harlem Renaissance edited by George Hutchinson

The History of the Book edited by Leslie Howsam

The Irish Novel edited by John Wilson Foster

The Italian Novel edited by Peter Bondanella and Andrea Ciccarelli

The Italian Renaissance edited by Michael Wyatt

Jewish American Literature edited by Hana Wirth-Nesher and Michael P. Kramer

The Latin American Novel edited by Efraín Kristal

The Literature of the First World War edited by Vincent Sherry

The Literature of London edited by Lawrence Manley

The Literature of Los Angeles edited by Kevin R. McNamara

The Literature of New York edited by Cyrus Patell and Bryan Waterman

The Literature of Paris edited by Anna-Louise Milne

The Literature of World War II edited by Marina MacKay

Literature on Screen edited by Deborah Cartmell and Imelda Whelehan

Medieval English Culture edited by Andrew Galloway

Medieval English Literature edited by Larry Scanlon

Medieval English Mysticism edited by Samuel Fanous and Vincent Gillespie

Medieval English Theatre edited by Richard Beadle and Alan J. Fletcher (second edition)

Medieval French Literature edited by Simon Gaunt and Sarah Kay

Medieval Romance edited by Roberta L. Krueger

Medieval Women's Writing edited by Carolyn Dinshaw and David Wallace

Modern American Culture edited by Christopher Bigsby

Modern British Women Playwrights edited by Elaine Aston and Janelle Reinelt

Modern French Culture edited by Nicholas Hewitt

Modern German Culture edited by Eva Kolinsky and Wilfried van der Will

The Modern German Novel edited by Graham Bartram

The Modern Gothic edited by Jerrold E. Hogle

Modern Irish Culture edited by Joe Cleary and Claire Connolly

Modern Italian Culture edited by Zygmunt G. Baranski and Rebecca J. West

Modern Latin American Culture edited by John King

Modern Russian Culture edited by Nicholas Rzhevsky

Modern Spanish Culture edited by David T. Gies

Modernism edited by Michael Levenson (second edition)

The Modernist Novel edited by Morag Shiach

Modernist Poetry edited by Alex Davis and Lee M. Jenkins

Modernist Women Writers edited by Maren Tova Linett

Narrative edited by David Herman

Native American Literature edited by Joy Porter and Kenneth M. Roemer

Nineteenth-Century American Women's Writing edited by Dale M. Bauer and Philip Gould

Old English Literature edited by Malcolm Godden and Michael Lapidge (second edition)

Performance Studies edited by Tracy C. Davis

Piers Plowman by Andrew Cole and Andrew Galloway

Popular Fiction edited by David Glover and Scott McCracken

Postcolonial Literary Studies edited by Neil Lazarus

Postmodern American Fiction edited by Paula Geyh

Postmodernism edited by Steven Connor

The Pre-Raphaelites edited by Elizabeth Prettejohn

Pride and Prejudice edited by Janet Todd

Renaissance Humanism edited by Jill Kraye

The Roman Historians edited by Andrew Feldherr

Roman Satire edited by Kirk Freudenburg

Science Fiction edited by Edward James and Farah Mendlesohn

Scottish Literature edited by Gerald Carruthers and Liam McIlvanney

Sensation Fiction edited by Andrew Mangham

The Sonnet edited by A. D. Cousins and Peter Howarth

The Spanish Novel: From 1600 to the Present edited by Harriet Turner and Adelaida López de Martínez

Textual Scholarship edited by Neil Fraistat and Julia Flanders

Travel Writing edited by Peter Hulme and Tim Youngs

Twentieth-Century British and Irish Women's Poetry edited by Jane Dowson

The Twentieth-Century English Novel edited by Robert L. Caserio

Twentieth-Century English Poetry edited by Neil Corcoran

Twentieth-Century Irish Drama edited by Shaun Richards

Twentieth-Century Russian Literature edited by Marina Balina and Evgeny Dobrenko

Utopian Literature edited by Gregory Claeys

Victorian and Edwardian Theatre edited by Kerry Powell

The Victorian Novel edited by Deirdre David (second edition)

Victorian Poetry edited by Joseph Bristow

Victorian Women's Writing edited by Linda H. Peterson

War Writing edited by Kate McLoughlin

Women's Writing in Britain, 1660–1789 edited by Catherine Ingrassia

Women's Writing in the Romantic Period edited by Devoney Looser

Writing of the English Revolution edited by N. H. Keeble